P9-DOG-543

Facilitator's Guide to Participatory Decision-Making

Sam Kaner
with
**Lenny Lind, Catherine Toldi,
Sarah Fisk, and Duane Berger**

Foreword by Michael Doyle

NEW SOCIETY PUBLISHERS

Published in cooperation with COMMUNITY AT WORK

Copyright © 1996 by Sam Kaner. All rights reserved.

Sixth printing, October 1998

Inquiries regarding requests to reprint all or part of *Facilitator's Guide to Participatory Decision-Making* should be addressed to New Society Publishers.

ISBN Paperback   USA 0-86571-347-2   CAN 1-55092-255-6

Cover art by Karen Kerney. Cover by Parallel Design. Book design by Lenny Lind/CoVision and Sam Kaner. Printed on partially-recycled paper using soy-based ink by Capital City Press of Montpelier, Vermont.

To order directly from the publisher, add $4.00 to the price for the first copy, and add $1.00 for each additional copy (add GST in Canada). Send check or money order to:

New Society Publishers/Canada
P.O. Box 189
Gabriola Island, BC V0R 1X0
(800) 567-6772
(604) 247-7471 fax
email: info@newsociety.com

CONTENTS

Foreword by Michael Doyle   *vii*
Introduction   *xiii*

Part I: Grounding Principles

1   The Dynamics of Group Decision-Making 3
2   Participatory Values 23
3   Introduction to the Role of Facilitator 31

Part II: Facilitator Fundamentals

4   Facilitative Listening Skills 41
5   Facilitating Open Discussion 55
6   Alternatives to Open Discussion 69
7   ChartWriting Technique 85
8   Brainstorming 97
9   Tools for Managing Long Lists 103
10   Dealing with Difficult Dynamics 113
11   Designing Realistic Agendas 123

Part III: Building Sustainable Agreements

12   Principles for Building Sustainable Agreements 139
13   Gathering Diverse Points of View 151
14   Building a Shared Framework of Understanding 169
15   Developing Inclusive Solutions 183
16   Striving for Unanimity 209
17   Reaching Closure 221
18   Facilitating Sustainable Agreements 237

Photocopying Policy 247
Bibliography 249
About the Authors 251

DEDICATION

This book is dedicated to Michael Doyle and David Straus

who found the language, the distinctions and the methods to bring inclusive, participatory values into the mainstream of American management practices

and who, through their own continuing efforts and those of their students and grandstudents and great-grandstudents, may yet inspire humanity to use collaborative technology for finding sustainable, nonviolent solutions to the world's toughest problems.

ACKNOWLEDGEMENTS

The ideas contained in this book are the result of contributions from many people whose names do not appear on the cover.

The first and most important acknowledgement goes to our editor, Barbara Hirshkowitz, whose vision and commitment to this project is the reason this book exists. In early 1988 Barbara took Sam and Duane on a retreat and convinced us to write a serious theoretical book on participatory decision-making. Over the next four years, with help from an ever-changing team of co-thinkers, we wrote countless drafts and felt dissatisfied with them all. Barbara patiently encouraged us to keep going. In late 1993, Barbara saw that we had produced about a hundred pages of facilitation tools, and she persuaded us to publish the book you are now reading. So Barbara shepherded us through two years more of revising and adding and re-organizing and ambivalating . . . And finally, thanks to Barbara's unwavering faith and persistence, you have in hand the results of her labor.

Next we want to strongly thank and acknowledge two people who, from their hearts, each made enormous contributions over several years time: Herman Gyr, Ph.D. and Eileen Palmer. Herman Gyr, founder and Principal of CoDevelopment International, is surely among the most thoughtful, sophisticated Organization Development consultants in the San Francisco Bay Area. Herman's involvement and support from 1977 to 1986 was crucial in all regards – theoretical, practical and technical. Without Herman, there would have been nothing to show Barbara Hirshkowitz in the first place. Eileen Palmer, founder of the Center For Group Learning, is one of the Bay Area's leading figures in the movement to develop intelligent, integrated models of workgroup dynamics. From 1988 to 1991 Eileen played a major role in the creation of this book. She helped consolidate the material that had previously been written, and she drew on her considerable practical experience with workgroups and communities to help us define and clarify the underlying values and identify the basic skills and tools for putting those values into practice. To both Eileen and Herman, thank you very much for your many, many gifts.

We would also like to thank the following contributors. Marianne Laruffa, who assisted with the sifting and sorting and editing of the preliminary drafts, gave her wholehearted support and encouragement to this project in its earliest forms, from 1988–1990. Rick Peterson helped refine the logic and organization of many of our models circa 1990–91. Pat Morris in 1990–91 co-authored the entire second draft of our collection of structured thinking activities. David Barkan in 1990 was the first "road-tester" of the decision-making procedures described in the chapter, *Reaching Closure*. Marianne Bush, who since 1992 has given us countless hours of perceptive editorial advice, also provided the insightful critique which led us to the discovery of the Groan Zone. Jim MacQueen in 1992 co-authored the early drafts of the chapters on *Reaching Closure*. David Kirkpatrick in 1993 co-authored early drafts of two structured thinking activities. Amaran Tarnoff in 1993 co-authored early drafts of many pages appearing in the chapter, *Alternatives To Open Discussion*. Nancy Feinstein in 1995 wrote a draft of the introduction to the same chapter. Julie King in 1995 copyedited a draft of the entire manuscript. Ritch Davidson in 1995 co-authored every draft of two structured thinking activities. Michael Tertes in 1995 co-authored many drafts of the six case studies in *Finding Inclusive Solutions*. Michael also co-authored early drafts of four structured thinking activities. Evi Kahle in 1995-96 edited every draft of the chapter *Facilitating Open Discussion*. Evi also contributed to the description of the theory presented in Chapters 13, 14, 15 and 18. Melanie Burnett, Mitch Glanz, Rob Lawrence, Ritch Davidson and Nancy Feinstein read all or parts of the final manuscript. From 1994 to the date of publication, Sam Fisk was the behind-the-scenes maestro whose clerical support kept everything running smoothly. And for the last year of the project, it was Evi's warmth, enthusiasm and boundless dedication that inspired and sustained our final efforts.

We want to extend our appreciation to the proprietors of the coffee houses where much of this book was actually written. In San Francisco, thanks to *Farley's, Cup O' Blues, The Daily Scoop, Thinker's Cafe, La Boheme, Radio Valencia,* and *Sally's*. In Aptos, thanks to the *Red Apple Cafe*.

Lastly, our deep appreciation goes to Marianne Bush and Monika Steger, who opened their homes to us, who loaned us their partners even when it meant a personal sacrifice, and who share our success as their own.

I see group facilitation as a whole constellation of ingredients: a deep belief in the wisdom and creativity of people; a search for synergy and overlapping goals; the ability to listen openly and actively; a working knowledge of group dynamics; a deep belief in the inherent power of groups and teams; a respect for individuals and their points of view; patience and a high tolerance for ambiguity to let a decision evolve and gel; strong interpersonal and collaborative problem-solving skills; an understanding of thinking processes; and a flexible versus a lock-step approach to resolving issues and making decisions.

Facilitative behaviors and skills are essential for anyone who wants to work collaboratively in groups and organizations today. Facilitative skills honor, enhance and focus the wisdom and knowledge that lay dormant in most groups. These skills are essential to healthy organizations, esprit de corps, fair and lasting agreements, and to easily implement actions and plans.

Sam Kaner and the team from Community At Work have been developing and articulating these tools to further democratic action and to enable people from all walks of life to work together in more constructive and productive ways. The *Facilitator's Guide to Participatory Decision-Making* will give readers additional tools and insights to enable effective, participatory action and the potential to achieve strong principled results and positive social change. Anyone wanting to increase their understanding of group dynamics and improve their skill at making groups work more effectively will benefit from this valuable book.

The Purpose of Group Facilitation

Those who work with and lead organizations today have learned two lasting lessons in the last twenty-five years of concerted action research in this field of organization development and change. Lesson one: if people don't participate in and "own" the solution to the problems or agree to the decision, implementation will be half-hearted at best, probably misunderstood, and more likely than not, fail.

The second lesson is that the key differentiating factor in the success of an organization is not just the products and services, not just its technology or market share, but the organization's ability to elicit, harness, and focus the vast intellectual capital and goodwill resident in their members, employees and stakeholders. When that intellectual capital and goodwill get energized and focused, the organization becomes a powerful force for positive change in today's business and societal environments. Applying these two lessons has become a key element of what we have begun to think of as *the learning organization.*

How do leaders and their organizations apply these two lessons? By creating psychologically safe and involving group environments where people can identify and solve problems, plan together, make collaborative decisions, resolve their own conflicts, trouble-shoot and self-manage as responsible adults. Facilitation enables the organization's teams, groups and meetings to be much more productive. And the side benefits of facilitated or self-facilitated groups are terrific: a sense of empowerment, a deepening of personal commitment to decisions and plans, increased organizational loyalty, and the building of esprit de corps.

Nowhere are these two lessons put more into practice than in groups. The world meets a lot. The statistics are staggering. There are over 25 million meetings every day in the United States and over 85 million worldwide. Making both our work groups and civic groups work much more effectively is a lifelong challenge as rich as the personalities that people them. Thus, what I call "group literacy" – an awareness of and strong skills in group dynamics, meeting facilitation and consensus building tools like the ones in this book – is essential to increasing the effectiveness of group meetings. They enable groups to work smarter, harder, deeper, and faster. These tools help build healthier groups, organizations and communities.

Facilitative mind sets, behaviors and tools are some of the essential ingredients of high commitment/high performance organizations. They are critical to making real what we've come to think of as *the learning organization.* These skills and behaviors are aligned with people's higher selves. People naturally want to learn them in order to increase their own personal effectiveness in groups and in their families as well as to increase the effectiveness of groups themselves.

A Partial History of Group Facilitation

The concept of facilitation and facilitators is as old as the tribes. Alaskan natives report of this kind of role in ancient times. As a society we're starting to come full circle – from the circle of the tribe around the fire, to the pyramidal structures of the last 3,000 years, back to the ecology of the circle, flat pyramids and networks of today's organizations. The philosophy, mind set and skills of facilitation have much in common with the approaches used by Quakers, Gandhi, Martin Luther King, Jr. and people in nonviolence movements over the centuries. More recently these include the civil rights movement, women's consciousness raising groups, some parts of the environmental movement and citizen involvement groups that started in the 1960s and 1970s.

Meeting facilitation started to appear as a formal process in the late 1960s and early 1970s and had become widespread by the late 1980s. Its proponents advocated it as a tool to assist people to become the architects of their own future. It evolved from the role of *learning facilitators* that emerged in the early 1960s. In learning or encounter groups, the facilitator's focus was on building awareness and enabling learning. These *learning/ awareness facilitators* played key roles in the nascent human potential movement and the women's consciousness raising movement and continue to do so in today's version of lifelong learning situations where learning is seen as a dialogue rather than a rote process. Its pragmatic roots also include cognitive science, information processing theory, sociology, psychology, community organizing, arbitration and mediation principles and experience.

Task oriented group facilitation evolved out of the societal milieu of the last thirty years, especially in industrial and information rich societies where time is a key factor. We needed to find methods for people to work together more effectively. Quality circle groups, cross functional task forces and civic groups were the early big users and advocates of this methodology. Facilitation was an informal, flexible alternative to the constricting format of parliamentary procedure and *Robert's Rules of Order.* Group facilitation was also an approach that was proactive, solving conflicts before they arose, as well as one that could handle multiple constituencies. It was a viable alternative to mediation style approaches. Once participants in a learning group or consciousness raising group raised their awareness, they wanted to take action. There was an expressed need to put their new insights and knowledge to work – to take actions, solve problems, plan, and make group decisions. Thus the role of the task oriented facilitator evolved to serve these needs as well as the new approaches to organizational change and renewal that were developing in the early 1970s.

As two of the co-founders of meeting facilitation, David Straus and I were interested in giving people tools to architect their own more powerful futures. That meant giving them frameworks and tools to make the groups they worked and lived with much more effective, powerful and productive. We saw group facilitation as both a social contract and a new, content neutral role – a more formalized third party role in groups. We articulated the difference and power between "content" and "process" neutrality. Content neutrality means not taking a position on the issues at hand; not having a position or a stake in the outcome. Process neutrality means not advocating for certain kinds of processes such as brainstorming. We found that the power in the role of the facilitator was in becoming content neutral and a process advocate – advocating for fair, inclusive and open processes that would balance participation and improve productivity while establishing a safe psychological space in which all group members could fully participate.

The role of the facilitator was designed to help minimize wheel spinning and dysfunctional dynamics and to enable groups to work together much more effectively. Other key pioneers of facilitation in the 1970s were Geoff Ball and David Sibbet with their seminal work in graphic recording and graphic facilitation. The core concepts and tools of group facilitation seemed to grow out of the tight-knit organization development and training community in the San Francisco Bay Area in the 1970s and '80s. It is great to see Sam Kaner and his colleagues continuing this rich legacy of theory and skill building.

Researchers at the Institute for the Future postulate that it takes about thirty years for social inventions to become widespread. Group facilitation is one such social invention. Over these last twenty-five years, facilitation skills have spread widely in the United States and are being spread around the world. And now, in the mid-90s, organizations are coming full circle to where facilitators once again are being utilized in *learning organizations* to facilitate dialogue processes that surface deep assumptions and mental models about how we view our world. These existing mental models are often the underlying sources of our conflict and dysfunction. By surfacing, examining and changing them, we are able to work together in new ways to build new systems thinking models that assist groups in articulating their core values and beliefs. These new mental models serve as the foundation for organizations as they evolve, grow and transform themselves to meet the challenges of the next century.

Expanding Definitions of Facilitation

These skills have become so useful in organizations that they have spread beyond the role of facilitator: to facilitative leaders; to self-facilitative groups and teams; to facilitative individuals and even facilitative, user friendly procedures. Facilitation has become part of our everyday language. The Latin root of facilitate means "to enable, to make easy." Facilitation has evolved to have a number of meanings today.

A facilitative individual is an individual who is easy to work with, a team player, a person aware of individual and group dynamics. He or she assists colleagues to work together more effectively. A facilitative individual is a person who is skilled and knowledgeable in the interpersonal skills of communication, collaborative problem solving and planning, consensus building, and conflict resolution.

A facilitator is an individual who enables groups and organizations to work more effectively; to collaborate and achieve synergy. She or he is a "content neutral" party who by not taking sides or expressing or advocating a point of view during the meeting, can advocate for fair, open, and inclusive procedures to accomplish the group's work. A facilitator can also be a learning or a dialogue guide to assist a group in thinking deeply about its assumptions, beliefs and values and about its systemic processes and context.

A facilitative leader is a leader who is aware of group and organizational dynamics; a leader who creates organization-wide involvement processes which enable members of the organization to more fully utilize their potential and gifts in order to help the organization articulate and achieve its vision and goals, while at the same time actualizing its spoken values.

Facilitative leaders often understand the inherent dynamics between facilitating and leading and frequently utilize facilitators in their organizations.

A facilitative group (team, task force, committee, or board) is one in which facilitative mind sets and behaviors are widely distributed among the members; a group that is minimally dysfunctional and works very well together; a group that is easy to join and works well with other groups and individuals.

I think you, the reader, will find this book very useful for your work in groups whether you are a leader, a group member or a facilitator. I especially recommend to you the insightful chapters on understanding group dynamics, facilitative listening, and the importance of values. Where this book also makes a real contribution is in the chapters on reaching closure and the gradients of an agreement. I enjoyed the learnings and insights I received from this book and I am sure you will too.

Michael Doyle
San Francisco, California
March 1996

INTRODUCTION

The benefits of group decision-making have been widely publicized: better thinking, better "buy-in," better decisions all around. Yet the promise often fails to materialize. Many decisions made in groups are neither thoughtful nor inclusive; they are unimaginative, watered-down mediocrities.

Why is this so?

To a large degree, the answer is deeply rooted in prevailing cultural values that make it difficult for people to actually think in groups. Without even realizing it, many people make value judgments that inhibit spontaneity and deter others from saying what is really on their minds. For example, ideas that are expressed in clumsy ways, or in tentative terms, are often treated as if they were decidedly inferior to ideas that are presented with eloquent rhetorical flourish. Efforts at exploring complexities are discouraged, in favor of pithy judgments and firm-sounding conclusions. Making action plans – no matter how unrealistic they might be – is called "getting something done," while analyzing the underlying causes of a problem is called "going off on a tangent." Mixed messages abound: speak your mind but don't ask too many questions; be passionate but don't show your feelings; be productive but hurry up – and get it right the first time. All in all, conventional values do not promote effective thinking in groups.

Yet group decision-making remains the best hope for solving difficult problems. There is no substitute for the wisdom that results from a successful integration of divergent points of view. Successful group decision-making requires a group to take advantage of the full range of experience and skills that reside in its membership. This means encouraging people to speak up. It means *inviting* difference, not fearing it. It means struggling to understand one another, *especially* in the face of the pressures and contradictions that typically drive group members to shut down. In short, it means operating from *participatory* values.

Participatory and conventional approaches to group decision-making yield entirely different group norms. Some of the differences are presented in the table on the next page.

PARTICIPATORY GROUPS	CONVENTIONAL GROUPS
Everyone participates, not just the vocal few.	The fastest thinkers and most articulate speakers get more air time.
People give each other room to think and get their thoughts all the way out.	People interrupt each other on a regular basis.
Opposing viewpoints are allowed to co-exist in the room.	Differences of opinion are treated as *conflict* that must either be stifled or "solved."
People draw each other out with supportive questions. "Is *this* what you mean?"	Questions are often perceived as challenges, as if the person being questioned has done something wrong.
Each member makes the effort to pay attention to the person speaking.	Unless the speaker *captivates* their attention, people space out, doodle or check the clock.
People are able to listen to each other's ideas because they know *their own ideas will also be heard.*	People have difficulty listening to each other's ideas because they're busy rehearsing what *they* want to say.
Each member speaks up on matters of controversy. Everyone knows where everyone stands.	Some members remain quiet on controversial matters. No no one really knows where everyone stands.
Members can accurately represent each other's points of view – even when they don't agree with them.	People rarely give accurate representations of the opinions and reasoning of those whose opinions are at odds with their own.
People refrain from talking behind each other's backs.	Because they don't feel permission to be direct *during* the meeting, people talk behind each other's backs outside the meeting.
Even in the face of opposition from the person-in-charge, people are encouraged to stand up for their beliefs.	People with discordant, minority perspectives are commonly discouraged from speaking out.
A problem is not considered solved until everyone who will be affected by the solution understands the reasoning.	A problem is considered solved as soon as the fastest thinkers have reached an answer. Everyone else is then expected to "get on board" regardless of whether s/he understands the logic of the decision.
When people make an agreement, it is assumed that the decision still reflects a wide range of perspectives.	When people make an agreement, it is assumed that they are all thinking the exact same thing.

As the table implies, a shift from conventional values to participatory values is not a simple matter of saying, "Let's become a thinking team." It requires a change of mindset – a committed effort from a group to swim against the tide of prevailing values and assumptions.

When a group undertakes this challenge, its participants often benefit from the services a competent facilitator can provide for them. Left to their own devices, many groups would slip back into conventional habits. A facilitator, however, has the skills to help a group outgrow their old familiar patterns. Specifically, the facilitator encourages full participation, s/he promotes mutual understanding, s/he fosters inclusive solutions and s/he teaches the group new thinking skills. These four functions (discussed in depth in chapter 3) are derived from the core values of participatory decision-making.

Putting Participatory Values Into Practice

The facilitator is the keeper of the flame, the carrier of the vision of what Michael Doyle described, in his foreword, as "a fair, inclusive and open process." This is why many facilitators help their groups to understand the dynamics and values of group decision-making. They recognize that it is empowering for participants to acquire common language and shared points of reference about their decision-making processes.

When a facilitator helps group members acquire process skills, s/he is acting in congruence with one of the core values of participatory decision-making: shared responsibility. The entire book is designed to support this value. It was written as a series of stand-alone pages that facilitators can photocopy and distribute to the members of their groups. For example, newly forming groups often benefit from reading and discussing chapters 1 and 2. These pages take less than fifteen minutes to read; they are entertaining; and they provide the basis for meaningful conversations about the dynamics and values of participatory decision-making. Within the guidelines of the policy statement on photocopying (see page 247), feel free to reproduce any part of this book that will strengthen your group's capacity for reaching sustainable agreements.

Facilitating Sustainable Agreements

The process of building a sustainable agreement has four stages: gathering diverse points of view; building a shared framework of understanding; developing inclusive solutions; and reaching closure. A competent facilitator knows how to move a group from start to finish through those stages. To do so, s/he needs a conceptual understanding of the dynamics and values of participatory decision-making (as provided in Part I of this book). S/he also needs a standard set of process management skills (as provided in Part II). And s/he needs a repetoire of sophisticated thinking tools that enable him/her to propose and conduct stage-specific interventions (as provided in Part III).

Fulfilling The Promise of Group Decision-Making

Those who practice participatory methods often come to see that facilitating a meeting is more than merely an occasion for solving a problem or creating a plan. It is also an opportunity to support profound personal learning, and it is an opportunity to strengthen the capacity and effectiveness of the group as a whole. These opportunites are only realizable – the promise of group decision-making can only be fulfilled – through the struggle and the satisfaction of putting participatory values into practice.

Part One

GROUNDING PRINCIPLES

1

THE DYNAMICS OF GROUP DECISION-MAKING

IDEALIZED AND REALISTIC MODELS OF COLLABORATION IN GROUPS

- ▶ Misunderstandings about the Process of Group Decision-Making

- ▶ The Struggle to Integrate Diverse Perspectives

- ▶ The Diamond of Participatory Decision-Making

DYNAMICS OF GROUP DECISION-MAKING

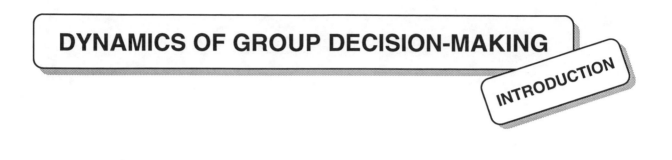

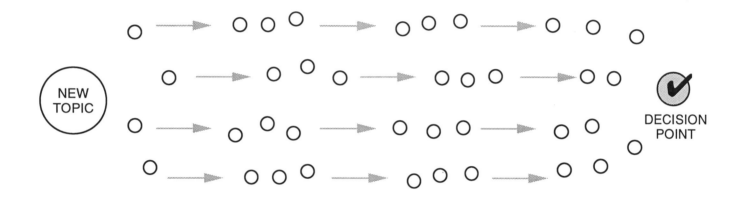

This picture portrays a hypothetical problem-solving discussion.

Each circle – O – represents one idea. Each line of circles-and-arrows represents one person's line of thought as it develops during the discussion.

As diagrammed, everyone appears to be tracking each others' ideas, everyone goes at the same pace, and everyone stays on board every step of the way.

A depressingly large percentage of people who work in groups believe this stuff. They think it realistically portrays a healthy, flowing, decision-making process. And when their actual experience doesn't match up with this model, *they think it's because their own group is defective.*

If people actually behaved as the diagram suggests, group decision-making would be much less frustrating. Unfortunately, real-life groups don't operate this way.

DYNAMICS OF GROUP DECISION-MAKING

SAD BUT TRUE

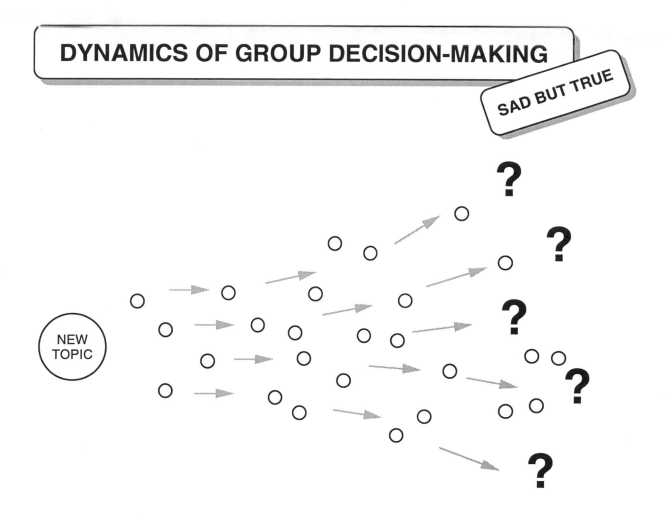

Group members are humans. We *do* go on tangents. We *do* lose track of the central themes of a discussion. We *do* get attached to our ideas. Even when we're all making our best effort to "keep focused" and "stay on track," *we can't change the fact that we are individuals with diverging points of view.*

When confusions like these arise during a discussion, many people see them as indicators that the process is heading out of control. Yet this is not necessarily what's really going on. Sometimes what appears to be chaos is actually a prelude to creativity.

But how can we tell which is which? How do we recognize the difference between a degenerative, spinning-our-wheels version of group confusion and the dynamic, diversity-stretches-our-imagination version of group confusion?

To make the distinction we need an understanding of the dynamics of group decision-making.

DYNAMICS OF GROUP DECISION-MAKING

CLOSER TO REALITY

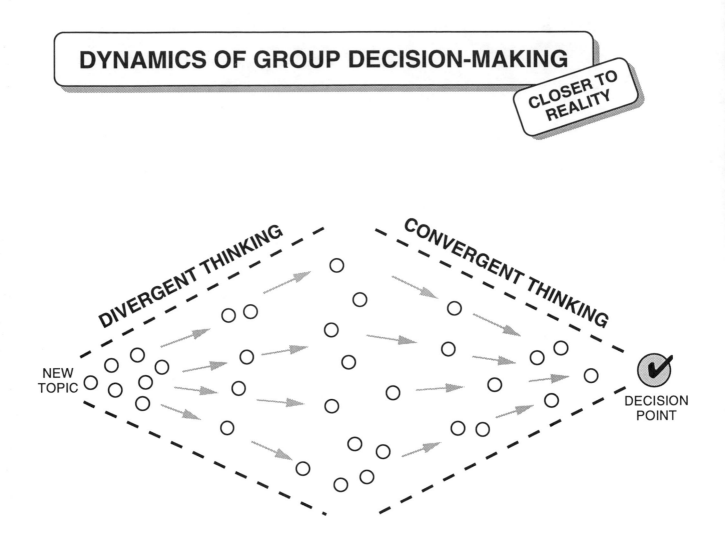

At times the individual members of a group need to express their own points of view. At other times, the same people want to narrow their differences and aim the discussion toward closure. In the following pages, these two sets of processes will be referred to as "divergent thinking" and "convergent thinking."

Here are four examples of the differences between the two thinking processes.

DIVERGENT THINKING		CONVERGENT THINKING
Generating alternatives	vs.	Evaluating alternatives
Free-for-all open discussion	vs.	Summarizing key points
Gathering diverse points of view	vs.	Sorting ideas into categories
Unpacking the logic of a problem	vs.	Arriving at a general conclusion

DYNAMICS OF GROUP DECISION-MAKING

UNANSWERED QUESTIONS

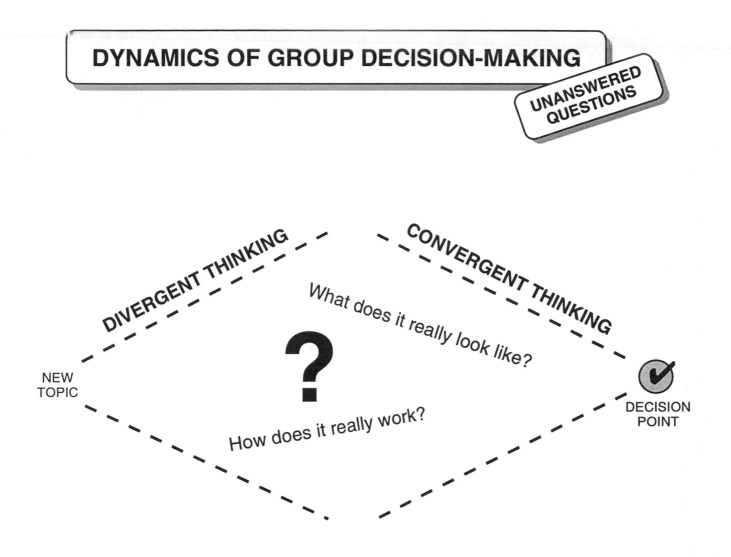

In the early 1980s, a large well known computer manufacturer developed a problem-solving model that was based on the principles of divergent thinking and convergent thinking. It was used by managers throughout the company. But it didn't always work so well. One project manager told us that it took their group *two years* to revise the travel expense-reimbursement forms.

Why would that happen? How does group decision-making *really* work?

To explore these questions in greater depth, the following pages present a series of stop-action snapshots of the process of group decision-making.

DYNAMICS OF GROUP DECISION-MAKING

DISCUSSION BEGINS

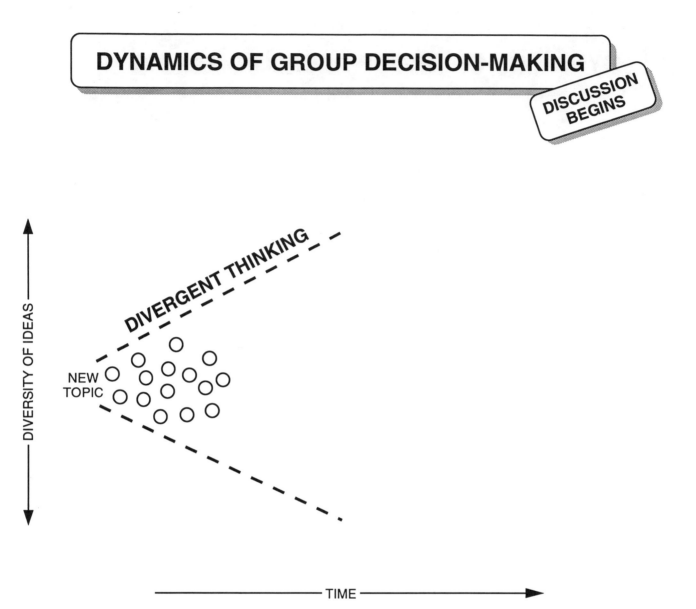

The early rounds of a discussion cover safe, familiar territory. People take positions that reflect conventional wisdom, they rehash well-worn disagreements, and they make proposals for obvious solutions. This is natural – the first ideas we express are the ones we've already thought about.

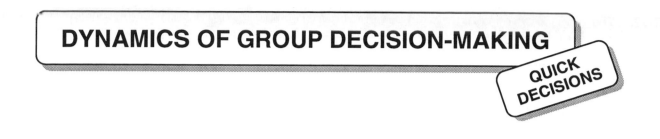

DYNAMICS OF GROUP DECISION-MAKING

QUICK DECISIONS

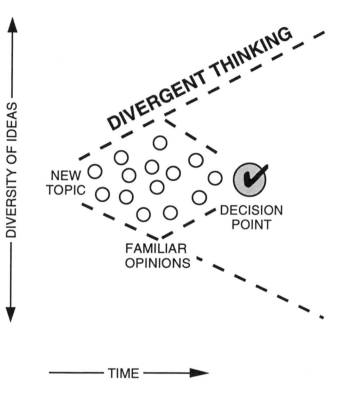

When a problem has an obvious solution, *it makes sense* to close the discussion quickly. Why waste time?

There's only one little problem. Most groups try to bring *every* discussion to closure this quickly.

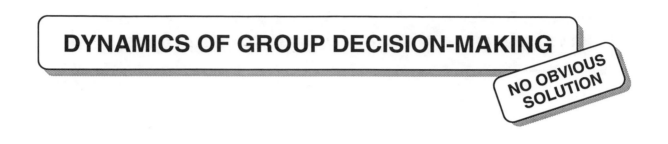

DYNAMICS OF GROUP DECISION-MAKING

NO OBVIOUS SOLUTION

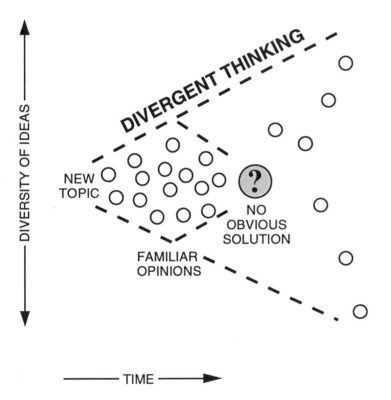

Some problems have *no* easy solutions. For example, how does an inner-city public school prevent campus violence? How much should a business do to support the needs of an increasingly diverse workforce? Cases like these require a lot of thought; the issues are too complex to be solved with familiar opinions and conventional wisdom.

When a group of decision-makers has to wrestle with a difficult problem, they will not succeed in solving it until they *break out of the narrow band of familiar opinions* and explore a wider range of possibilities.

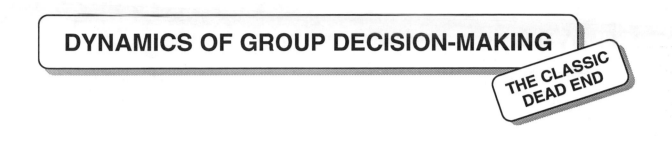

DYNAMICS OF GROUP DECISION-MAKING

THE CLASSIC
DEAD END

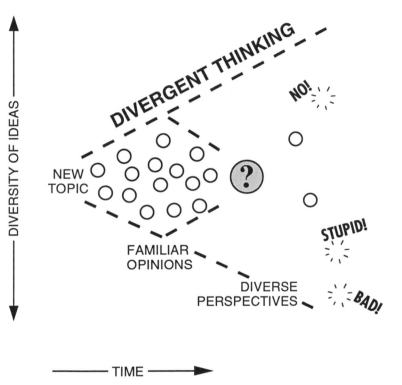

Unfortunately, most groups aren't very good at cultivating unfamiliar or unpopular opinions.

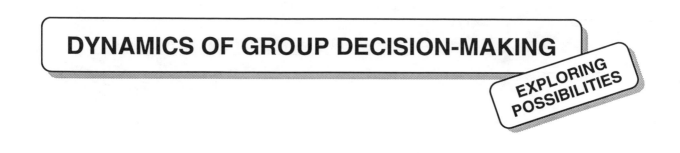

DYNAMICS OF GROUP DECISION-MAKING

EXPLORING POSSIBILITIES

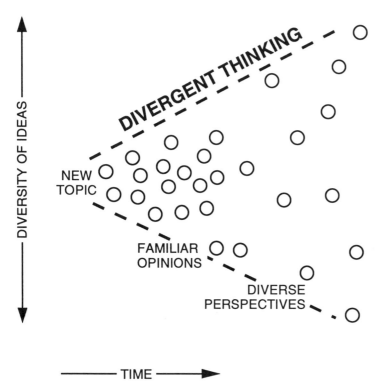

Now and then, if the stakes are sufficiently high and the stars are in proper alignment, a group can manage to overcome the tendency to criticize and inhibit its members. On such occasions, people tentatively begin to consider new perspectives. Some participants might take a risk and express controversial opinions. Others might offer ideas that aren't fully developed.

Since the goal is to find a new way of thinking about the problem, variety is obviously desirable . . . but the spread of opinions can become cumbersome and difficult to manage. Then what?

DYNAMICS OF GROUP DECISION-MAKING

IDEALIZED
PROCESS

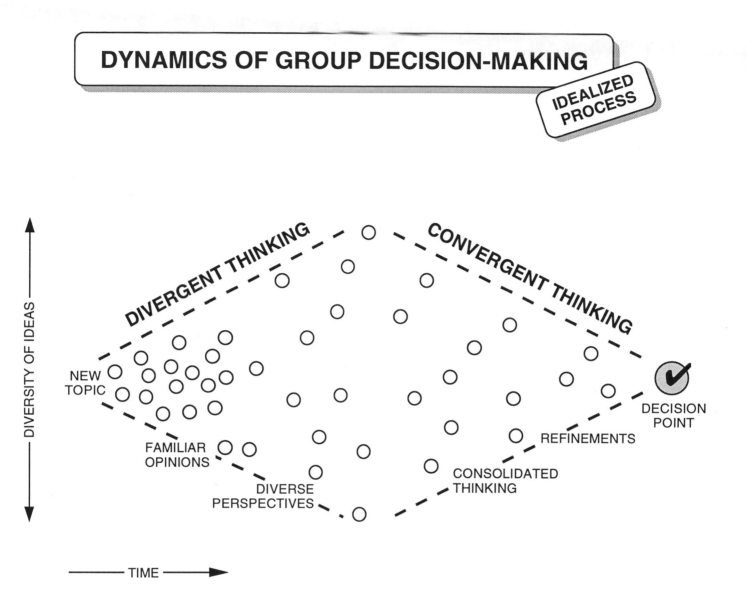

In theory, a group that has committed itself to thinking through a difficult problem would move forward in orderly, thoughtful steps. First, the group would generate and explore a diverse set of ideas. Next, they would consolidate the best thinking into a proposal. Then, they'd refine the proposal until they arrived at a final decision that nicely incorporated the breadth of their thinking.

Ah yes . . . if only *real life* worked that way.

DYNAMICS OF GROUP DECISION-MAKING

TYPICAL PROCESS

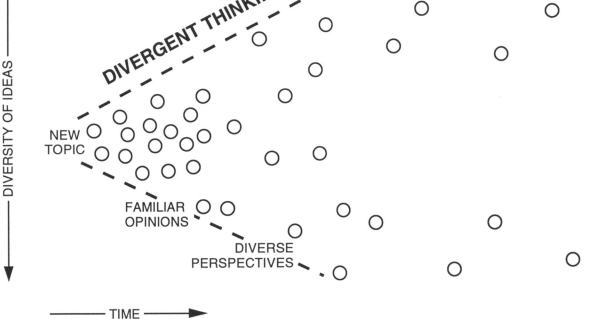

In practice, it's difficult to make the shift from expressing our own opinions to understanding a wide diversity of other people's perspectives. Many people get overloaded, or disoriented, or annoyed, or impatient. (Or all of the above.) Some people feel misunderstood and keep repeating themselves. Others push for closure. Sometimes several subconversations develop, each one occupying the attention of two or three people, and seemingly tangential or irrelevant to everyone else. And so on. Even the most sincere attempts to solve difficult problems often dissipate into confusion.

DYNAMICS OF GROUP DECISION-MAKING

ATTEMPTED STEP-BACKS

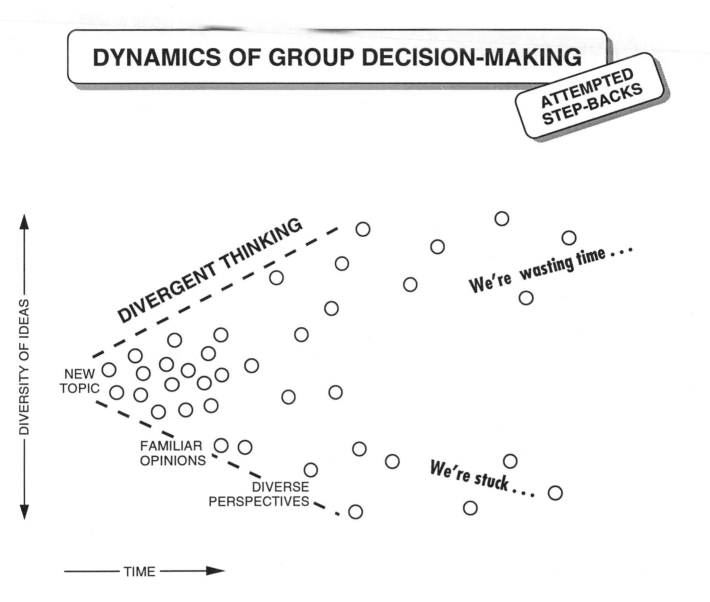

Sometimes one or more participants will attempt to step back from the content of the discussion and talk about the process. They might say things like, "I thought we all agreed to stick to the topic," or "We need better ground rules," or "Does anyone understand what's going on here?" But rarely does a whole group respond intelligently to this line of thought. Typically, a process comment becomes merely one more voice in the wilderness – yet another poorly understood perspective that gets absorbed into the general confusion.

DYNAMICS OF GROUP DECISION-MAKING

POOR TIMING

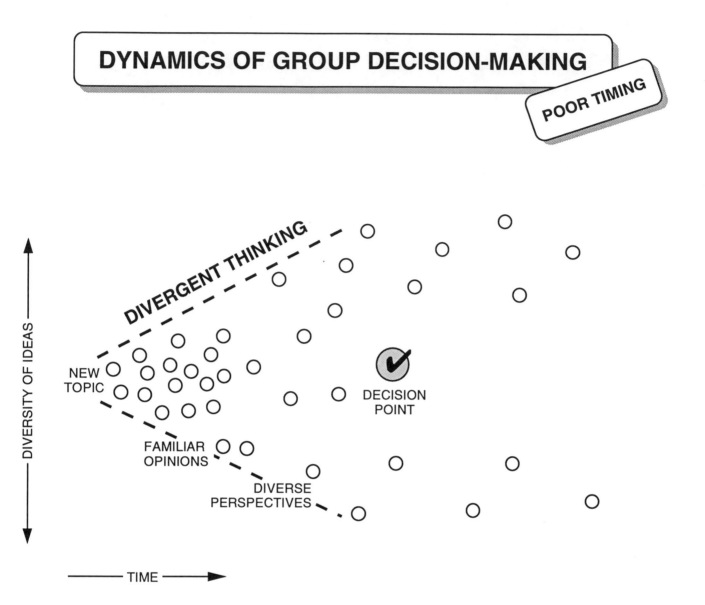

At this stage in a process, the person in charge of a meeting can make the problem worse if s/he tries to resolve the confusion by announcing that s/he has made a decision. This is a common mistake.

The person-in-charge may believe that s/he has found a perfectly logical answer to the problem at hand, but this doesn't mean that everyone else will telepathically grasp the reasoning behind the decision. Some people may still be thinking along entirely different lines.

Furthermore, this is the exact situation in which the person-in-charge *appears* to have made the decision before the meeting began. This leads many people to feel deep distrust. *"Why did s/he tell me I'd have a say in this decision, when s/he already knew what the outcome would be?"*

DYNAMICS OF GROUP DECISION-MAKING

WHAT'S MISSING?

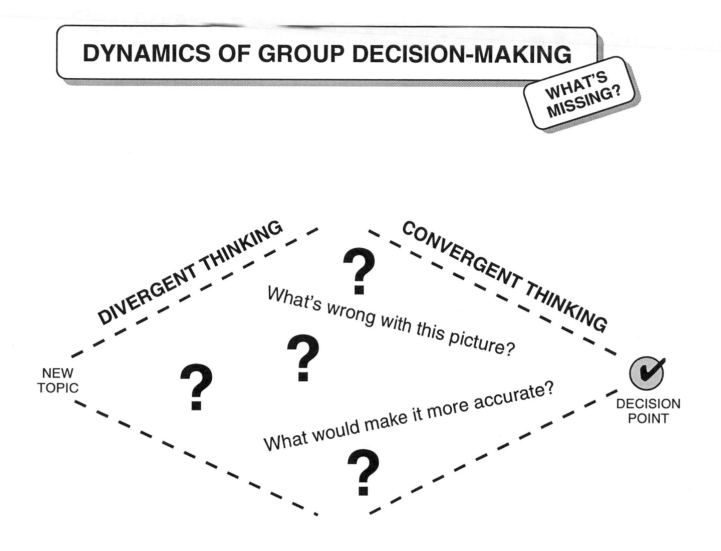

Obviously, there's something wrong with the idealized model. Convergent thinking simply does not follow automatically from a divergent thinking process. What's missing?

DYNAMICS OF GROUP DECISION-MAKING

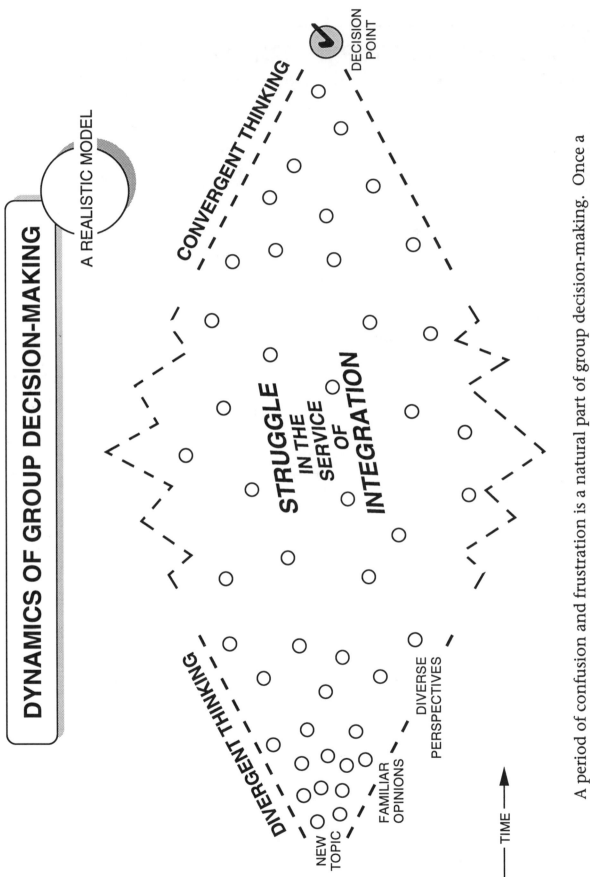

A REALISTIC MODEL

DECISION POINT

CONVERGENT THINKING

STRUGGLE
IN THE
SERVICE
OF
INTEGRATION

DIVERGENT THINKING

NEW TOPIC

FAMILIAR OPINIONS

DIVERSE PERSPECTIVES

TIME

A period of confusion and frustration is a natural part of group decision-making. Once a group crosses the line from airing familiar opinions to exploring diverse perspectives, *group members will have to struggle in order to integrate new and different ways of thinking with their own.*

COMMUNITY AT WORK © 1996

18

DYNAMICS OF GROUP DECISION-MAKING

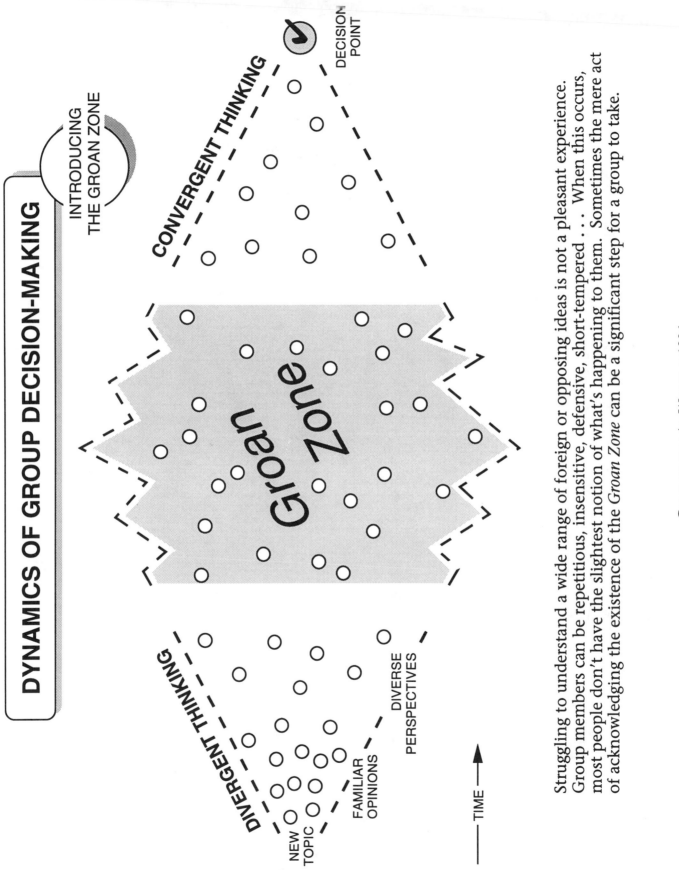

INTRODUCING THE GROAN ZONE

CONVERGENT THINKING

DECISION POINT

Groan Zone

DIVERGENT THINKING

NEW TOPIC

FAMILIAR OPINIONS

DIVERSE PERSPECTIVES

TIME →

Struggling to understand a wide range of foreign or opposing ideas is not a pleasant experience. Group members can be repetitious, insensitive, defensive, short-tempered . . . When this occurs, most people don't have the slightest notion of what's happening to them. Sometimes the mere act of acknowledging the existence of the *Groan Zone* can be a significant step for a group to take.

COMMUNITY AT WORK © 1996

19

DYNAMICS OF GROUP DECISION-MAKING

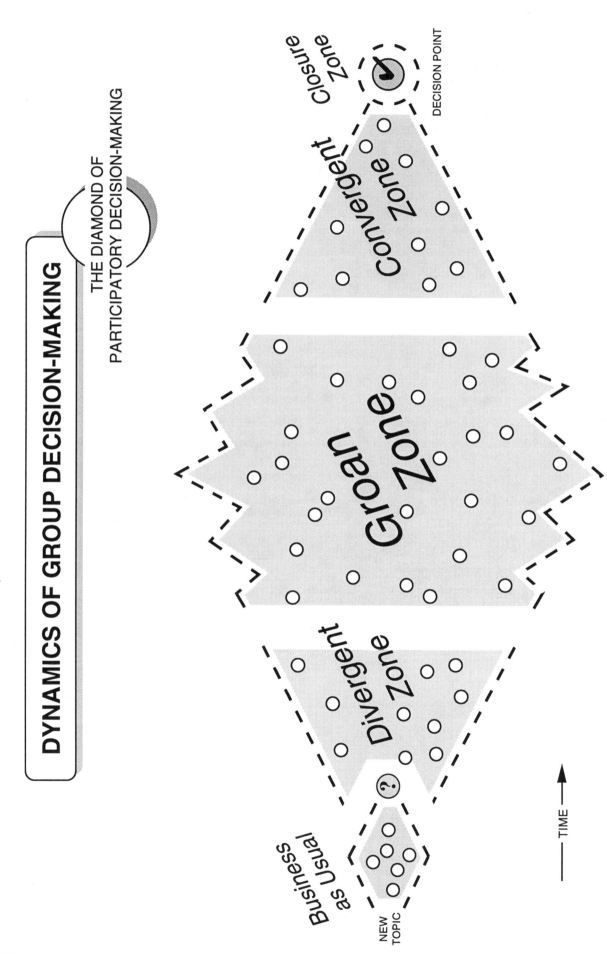

THE DIAMOND OF
PARTICIPATORY DECISION-MAKING

Business
as Usual

NEW
TOPIC

Divergent
Zone

Groan
Zone

Convergent
Zone

Closure
Zone

DECISION POINT

TIME

This is the *Diamond of Participatory Decision-Making.*

The *Diamond* describes the process a group goes through to solve a difficult problem. The process is neither smooth nor sequential. It is characterised by confusion and misunderstanding. Most people find it hard to tolerate the ambiguity and the conflict that are inherent when people don't have shared frames of reference. Yet a group's most significant breakthroughs are often preceded by a period of struggle.

By legitimizing the awkward, uncomfortable, yet entirely normal dynamics of diversity, the *Diamond of Participatory Decision-Making* helps facilitators give their groups more meaningful support during difficult times. This in turn enables all parties to tap the enormous potential of group decision-making.

2

PARTICIPATORY VALUES

HOW FULL PARTICIPATION STRENGTHENS
INDIVIDUALS, DEVELOPS GROUPS AND
FOSTERS SUSTAINABLE AGREEMENTS

- ▶ The Four Participatory Values

- ▶ Full Participation

- ▶ Mutual Understanding

- ▶ Inclusive Solutions

- ▶ Shared Responsibility

- ▶ How Participatory Values Affect
  People and Their Work

- ▶ Benefits of Participatory Values

PARTICIPATORY DECISION-MAKING CORE VALUES

In a participatory group, all member are encouraged to speak up and say what's on their minds. This strengthens a group in several ways. Members become more courageous in raising difficult issues. They learn how to share their "first-draft" ideas. And they become more adept at discovering and acknowledging the diversity of opinions and backgrounds inherent in their group.

In order for a group to reach a sustainable agreement, the members need to understand and accept the legitimacy of one another's needs and goals. This basic sense of acceptance and understanding is what allows people to develop innovative ideas that incorporate everyone's point of view.

Inclusive solutions are wise solutions. Their wisdom emerges from the integration of everybody's perspectives and needs. These are solutions whose range and vision is expanded to take advantage of the truth held not only by the quick, the articulate, the most powerful and influential, but also of the truth held by the slower thinkers, the shy, the disenfranchised and the weak. As the Quakers say, "Everybody has a piece of the truth."

In participatory groups, members feel a strong sense of responsibility for creating and developing sustainable agreements. They recognize that they must be willing and able to implement the proposals they endorse, so they make every effort to give and receive input before final decisions are made. This contrasts sharply with the conventional assumption that everyone will be held accountable for the consequences of decisions made by a few key people.

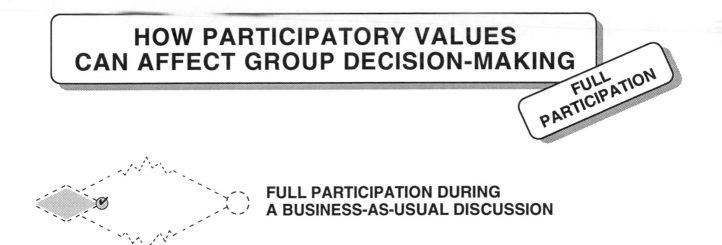

HOW PARTICIPATORY VALUES CAN AFFECT GROUP DECISION-MAKING

FULL PARTICIPATION

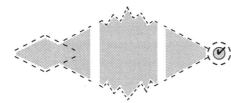

FULL PARTICIPATION DURING A BUSINESS-AS-USUAL DISCUSSION

In a typical business-as-usual discussion, self-expression is highly constrained. People tend to keep risky opinions to themselves. The most highly-regarded comments are those which are the clearest, the smartest, the most well-polished. In business-as-usual discussions, thinking out loud is treated with impatience; people get annoyed if the speaker's remarks are vague or poorly stated. This induces self-censorship, and reduces the quantity and quality of participation overall. A few people end up doing almost all the talking – and in many groups, those few people just keep repeating themselves and repeating themselves.

FULL PARTICIPATION DURING A PARTICIPATORY DECISION-MAKING PROCESS

Participatory decision-making groups go through a business-as-usual phase, too. If familiar opinions lead to a workable solution, then the group can reach a decision quickly. But when a business-as-usual discussion does *not* produce a workable solution, a participatory group will open up the process and encourage more divergent thinking. What does this look like in action? It looks like people making off-the-wall suggestions that stimulate their peers to think new thoughts. It looks like people permitting themselves to state half-formed thoughts that express unconventional – but perhaps valuable – perspectives. It looks like people taking risks to surface controversial issues. And it also looks like a roomful of people encouraging each other to *do* all these things.

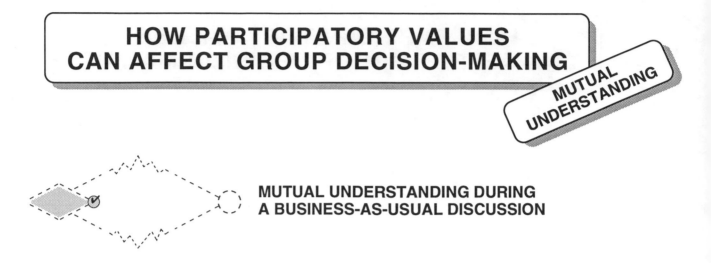

HOW PARTICIPATORY VALUES CAN AFFECT GROUP DECISION-MAKING

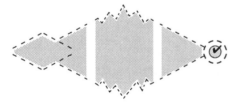

MUTUAL UNDERSTANDING DURING A BUSINESS-AS-USUAL DISCUSSION

In a business-as-usual discussion, persuasion is much more common than mutual understanding. The views of the "other side" are dissected point by point for the purpose of refuting them. Little effort, if any, is put into discovering the deeper reasons people believe what they do. Even when it appears unlikely that persuasion will change anyone's mind, participants continue to press home their points – making it appear as though the pleasures of rhetoric were the true purpose of continuing the discussion. Most participants tend to stop listening to each other, except to prepare for a rebuttal.

MUTUAL UNDERSTANDING DURING A PARTICIPATORY DECISION-MAKING PROCESS

Building a shared framework of understanding means taking the time to understand everyone's perspective in order to find the best idea. To build that framework, participants spend time and effort questioning each other, getting to know one another, learning from each other. They put themselves in each other's shoes. The process is laced with intermittent discomfort: some periods are tense, some are stifling. But participants keep plugging away. Over time, many people gain insight into their own positions. They may discover that their own thinking is out-of-date or misinformed or driven by inaccurate stereotypes. And, by struggling to acquire such insights, members may discover something else about one another: that they truly do care about achieving a mutual goal.

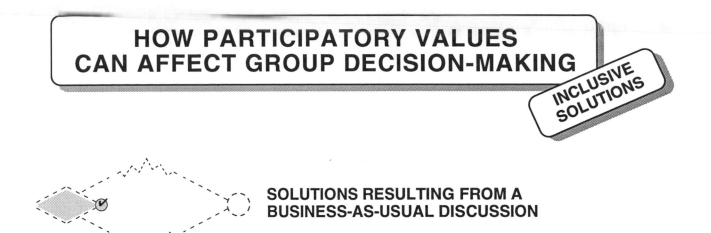

HOW PARTICIPATORY VALUES CAN AFFECT GROUP DECISION-MAKING

INCLUSIVE SOLUTIONS

SOLUTIONS RESULTING FROM A BUSINESS-AS-USUAL DISCUSSION

Business-as-usual discussions seldom result in inclusive solutions. More commonly, people quickly form opinions and take sides. Everyone expects that one side will get what they want and the other side won't. Disagreements, they assume, will be resolved by the person who has the most authority. Some groups settle their differences by majority vote, but the effect is just the same. In either case, the final decision often excludes the views, needs and goals of the minority.

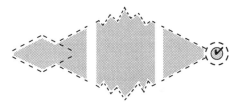

SOLUTIONS RESULTING FROM A PARTICIPATORY DECISION-MAKING PROCESS

Inclusive solutions are not compromises; they work for everyone who holds a stake in the outcome. Typically, an inclusive solution involves the discovery of an entirely new option. For instance, an unexpected partnership might be forged between former competitors. Or a group may invent a nontraditional alternative to a procedure that had previously "always been done that way." Several real-life case examples of inclusive solutions are presented in chapter 15. Inclusive solutions are usually not obvious – they *emerge* in the course of the group's persistence. As participants learn more about each other's perspectives, they become progressively more able to integrate their own goals and needs with those of the other participants. This leads to innovative, original thinking.

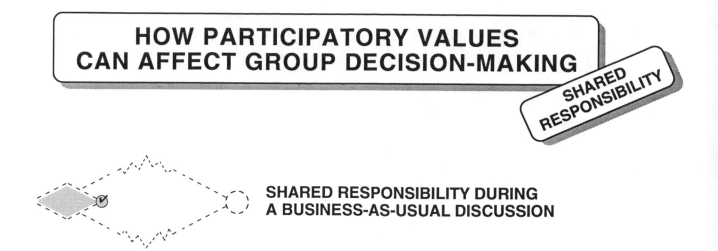

HOW PARTICIPATORY VALUES CAN AFFECT GROUP DECISION-MAKING

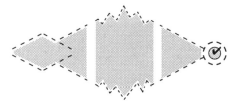

SHARED RESPONSIBILITY DURING A BUSINESS-AS-USUAL DISCUSSION

The operational value in a business-as-usual discussion is dependency on leadership, not shared responsibility. The person-in-charge is expected to run the meeting, monitor the progress of each topic, referee disputes, set ground rules, enforce time boundaries, and generally take full responsibility for all aspects of process management. To bring a discussion to closure, someone puts forward a proposal and says, "Is this okay with everyone?" or "Does anyone have any serious objections?" After a silence of about three seconds, the person-in-charge says, "Okay, it's decided." In this context, shared responsibility means being a (so-called) team-player. In other words, everyone is now expected to put aside their questions or doubts, and pull together to implement the decision.

SHARED RESPONSIBILITY DURING A PARTICIPATORY DECISION-MAKING PROCESS

In order for an agreement to be sustainable, it needs everyone's support. Understanding this principle leads everyone to take personal responsibility for making sure they are satisfied with the proposed course of action. Every member of the group, in other words, recognizes that s/he is an owner of the outcome. Thus, members voice objections even when doing so will delay the group from reaching a decision. Moreover, the commitment to share responsibility is evident throughout the process: in the design of the agenda, in the willingness to discuss and co-create the procedures they will follow and in the overall expectation that everyone will accept and take responsibility for making their meetings work.

THE BENEFITS OF PARTICIPATORY VALUES

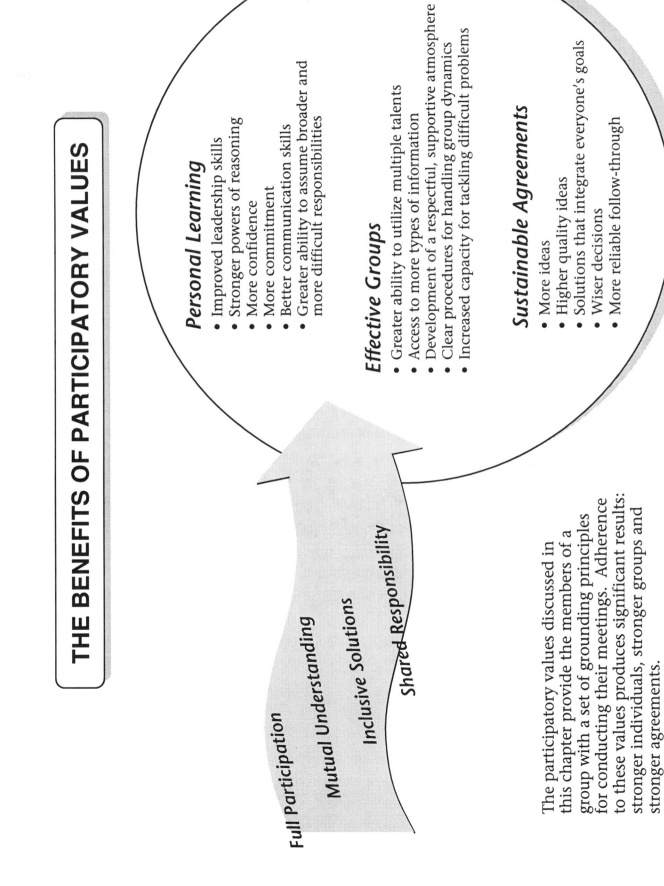

Personal Learning

- Improved leadership skills
- Stronger powers of reasoning
- More confidence
- More commitment
- Better communication skills
- Greater ability to assume broader and more difficult responsibilities

Effective Groups

- Greater ability to utilize multiple talents
- Access to more types of information
- Development of a respectful, supportive atmosphere
- Clear procedures for handling group dynamics
- Increased capacity for tackling difficult problems

Sustainable Agreements

- More ideas
- Higher quality ideas
- Solutions that integrate everyone's goals
- Wiser decisions
- More reliable follow-through

Full Participation

Mutual Understanding

Inclusive Solutions

Shared Responsibility

The participatory values discussed in this chapter provide the members of a group with a set of grounding principles for conducting their meetings. Adherence to these values produces significant results: stronger individuals, stronger groups and stronger agreements.

COMMUNITY AT WORK ©1996

3

INTRODUCTION TO THE ROLE OF FACILITATOR

THE EXPERTISE THAT SUPPORTS A GROUP TO DO ITS BEST THINKING

▶ When is a Facilitator Needed?

▶ First Function:
Encourage Full Participation

▶ Second Function:
Promote Mutual Understanding

▶ Third Function:
Foster Inclusive Solutions

▶ Fourth Function:
Teach New Thinking Skills

THE ROLE OF FACILITATOR

WHAT IS A FACILITATOR AND WHY HAVE ONE?

The facilitator's job is to *support everyone to do their best thinking.* To do this, the facilitator encourages full participation, promotes mutual understanding and cultivates shared responsibility. By supporting everyone to do their best thinking, a facilitator enables group members to search for inclusive solutions and build sustainable agreements.

How much value does this have to a group? The answer depends on the group's goals. Suppose a group holds meetings specifically for the purpose of trading information through announcements and reports. Do the members of that group need much help to do their best thinking? Not really. Likewise, suppose another group has monthly business-as-usual meetings to make routine decisions about standard problems, like task assignments or scheduling. Those kinds of issues could be handled for years without any facilitation whatsoever.

But what about more difficult challenges? For example, suppose a group's goal is to reduce violence on a high school campus. The participants are parents, teachers, administrators, church leaders and union officials. This group will quickly find out how difficult it is to conduct a sustained, thoughtful discussion. Despite a common goal, their frames of reference are very different. What seems to a parent like an obvious solution may seem simple-minded to an administrator. What seems reasonable to an administrator may seem cowardly to a teacher. What seems responsible to a teacher may place too many demands on a parent. What is the chance that this group will survive the Groan Zone?

Groups face difficult challenges all the time. Long-term planning is hard for an organization to do well. So is restructuring or reengineering. Here are some other tough issues groups face: clarifying roles and responsibilities for projects that have not been done before, resolving high-stakes conflicts or introducing new technology into a workplace. In situations like these, a group is likely to make wiser, more lasting decisions if they join forces with someone who knows how to support them to do their best thinking.

Most groups *do not know how* to solve tough problems on their own. They do not know how to build a shared framework of understanding – they seldom even recognize its significance. They dread conflict and discomfort and they try hard to avoid it. Yet, by avoiding the struggle to integrate one another's perspectives, the members of such a group greatly diminish their own potential to be effective. They *need* a facilitator.

THE FACILITATOR ENCOURAGES FULL PARTICIPATION

A Fundamental Problem: Self-Censorship

Inherent in group decision-making is the basic problem that people don't say what they are really thinking. It's hard to take risks, and it's particularly hard to do so when the group's response is likely to be hostile or dismissive. Yet in so many groups, the norms are oppressive. Consider these comments:

- "Haven't we already covered that point?"
- "Let's keep it simple, please."
- "Hurry up – we're running out of time."
- "What does *that* have to do with anything?"
- "Impossible. Won't work. No way."

Statements like these are injunctions against thinking out loud in a group. They discourage people from saying what they're thinking. The message is: if you want to speak, be simple and polished, and be able to say something familiar enough or entertaining enough for the group to accept.

The injunctions against thinking in public run like an underground stream below the surface of a group's discussion. Without realizing it, most people constantly edit their thinking before they speak. Who wants his/her ideas criticised before they are fully formed? Who wants to be told, "We've already answered that question." Who wants to make an effort to express a complex thought while others in the room are doodling or whispering? This type of treatment leaves many people feeling embarrassed or inadequate. *To protect themselves, people censor themselves.*

The Facilitator's Contribution

Imagine now that someone in the group understands this inherent difficulty, and that s/he has taken responsibility for helping people overcome it. Imagine that this person has the skills and the temperament to draw people out and help everyone feel heard. Imagine s/he knows how to make room for quiet members; how to reduce the incidence of premature criticism; how to support everyone to keep thinking instead of shutting down. If such a person is actually permitted to perform this role in a group, the quality of the group's participation will vastly improve.

THE FACILITATOR PROMOTES MUTUAL UNDERSTANDING

A Fundamental Problem: Fixed Positions

A group cannot do its best thinking if the members don't understand one another. But most people find it quite difficult to detach from their fixed positions. Instead, they get caught up in amplifying and defending their own perspectives.

Here's an example. A group of friends began exploring the possibility of forming a new business together. When the topic of money came up, biases emerged. One person wanted the profits divided equally. Another thought everyone should be paid on the basis of how much revenue they would generate. A third person believed the two visionaries should be paid more, to make sure they would not leave. And so on. None of them could change their minds easily. Nor would it have been realistic to expect them to do so – their opinions had been forming and developing for years.

And it gets worse! When people try to discuss their differences, they often misunderstand one another. Each person's life experiences are so individual, so singular; everyone has remarkably different views of the world. What people expect, what they assume, how they use language and how they behave – all these are likely sources of mutual misunderstanding. What's more, when people attempt to clear up a misunderstanding, they usually want their *own* ideas understood *first*. They may not say so directly, but their behavior indicates, "I can't really focus on what you are saying until I feel that you have understood *my* point of view." This easily becomes a vicious cycle. No wonder it's hard for people to let go of fixed positions!

The Facilitator's Contribution

A facilitator helps the group realize that sustainable agreements are built on a foundation of mutual understanding. S/he helps members see that thinking from each other's points of view is invaluable.

Moreover, the facilitator accepts the *inevitability of misunderstanding*. S/he recognizes that misunderstandings are stressful for everyone involved. The facilitator knows that people in distress need support; they need to be treated respectfully. S/he knows it is essential to stay impartial, to honor all points of view and to keep listening, so that each and every group member has confidence that *someone* understands them.

THE ROLE OF FACILITATOR

THIRD FUNCTION

THE FACILITATOR FOSTERS INCLUSIVE SOLUTIONS

A Fundamental Problem: The Win/Lose Mentality

It's hard for most people to imagine that stakeholders with apparently irreconcilable differences might actually reach an agreement that benefits all parties. Most people are entrenched in a conventional mindset for solving problems and resolving conflicts – namely: "It's either my way or your way." As a result, most problem-solving discussions degenerate into critiques, rationalizations and sales jobs, as participants remain attached to their fixed positions and work to defend their own interests.

The Facilitator's Contribution

An experienced facilitator knows how to help a group search for innovative ideas that incorporate everyone's points of view. This can be a challenging task – the facilitator is often the only person in the room who has even considered the possibility that inclusive alternatives may exist.

To accomplish this goal, a facilitator draws from the knowledge s/he has acquired by studying the theory and practice of collaborative problem solving. Thus s/he knows the steps it takes to build sustainable agreements.

- S/he knows how to help groups break free from restrictive business-as-usual discussions and engage in divergent thinking (see chapter 13).

- S/he can help a group survive the Groan Zone as the members struggle to build a shared framework of understanding (see chapter 14).

- S/he knows how to help a group formulate creative proposals that reflect the weaving-together of several perspectives (see chapter 15).

- S/he knows how to bring agreements to closure (see chapters 16 – 17).

In short, s/he understands the mechanics of building sustainable agreements.

When a facilitator introduces a group to the values and methods that foster inclusive solutions, the impact is profound. Many people scoff at the very suggestion that a group can find meaningful solutions to difficult problems. As they discover the validity of this new way of thinking, they often become more hopeful about their group's potential effectiveness.

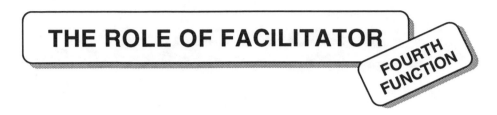

THE ROLE OF FACILITATOR — FOURTH FUNCTION

THE FACILITATOR TEACHES NEW THINKING SKILLS

A Fundamental Problem: Inept Meeting Management

Why are most meetings run so poorly? Many people would answer, "It's my boss. S/he doesn't know what s/he is doing." But this is a misattribution – blaming an individual for what is actually a culture-wide problem. The fact is that *neither* leaders *nor* other members are skilled in collaborative methods. *Very few* people understand the mechanics of group decision-making well enough to organize a group into a productive team of thinkers.

The Facilitator's Contribution

A facilitator has both the opportunity and the responsibility to teach group members how to design and manage an effective decision-making process. Here are four sets of skills a group can learn from a competent facilitator:

Principles for Finding Inclusive Solutions   Most groups need help learning how to turn Either/Or problems into Both/And solutions. A facilitator can teach people to develop innovative ideas that take everyone's needs into account.

Well-Designed Procedures for Running Meetings   Clear, explicit procedures are among the most important thinking skills a group can learn. For example, consider the impact of a badly designed agenda: how can a group be effective when people don't know what they're trying to accomplish? A facilitator can teach an array of procedures for running successful meetings.

Structured Thinking Activities   Sometimes a group needs help focusing on the same thing at the same time. At those times, a structured thinking activity – *formal brainstorming*, for example – can be very helpful. Seasoned facilitators develop a repertoire of structured thinking activities that can be offered to groups at appropriate times.

Clear Language to Describe Group Dynamics   When a facilitator teaches a model like the Diamond of Participatory Decision-Making, s/he provides group members with shared points of reference and shared language. This enables a group to step back from the *content* of their discussion and talk about their *process,* so they can improve the dynamics of their meeting.

FACILITATOR SKILLS
FOR PARTICIPATORY DECISION MAKING

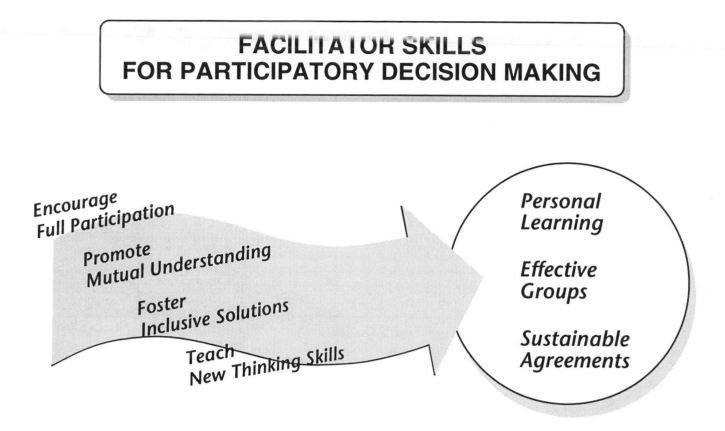

The facilitator's mission is to support everyone to do their best thinking. Participatory values support intelligent thinking – serious, creative thinking by engaged, committed individuals who can work together to make wise decisions.

For the first three chapters of this book, the focus has been on the *what* and the *why* of supporting groups to do their best thinking. The *how* has not been discussed. Beginning with the next chapter, the focus shifts to methods, skills and tools.

Facilitation skills can be grouped into two sets: those which are useful in virtually every stage of a thinking process, and those which are useful primarily at a specific stage. This distinction is the key to the organization of the rest of the book.

The skills that are useful *throughout* a process are presented in the next eight chapters, which comprise *Part Two: Facilitator Fundamentals*. The skills that are useful primarily in a specific stage are presented in the final eight chapters, *Part Three: Building Sustainable Agreements*.

Part Two

FACILITATOR FUNDAMENTALS

FACILITATIVE LISTENING SKILLS

TECHNIQUES FOR HONORING ALL POINTS OF VIEW

- ▶ Diverse Communication Styles
- ▶ Paraphrasing
- ▶ Drawing People Out
- ▶ Mirroring
- ▶ Gathering Ideas
- ▶ Stacking
- ▶ Tracking
- ▶ Encouraging
- ▶ Balancing
- ▶ Making Space
- ▶ Intentional Silence
- ▶ Listening for Common Ground

THE CALCULUS OF DIVERSITY

THE LIMITS OF TOLERANCE

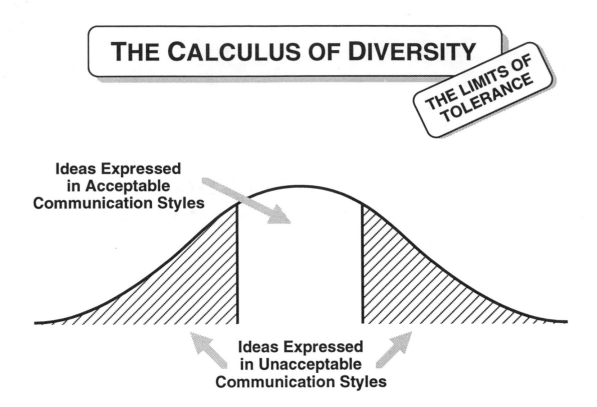

Ideas Expressed in Acceptable Communication Styles

Ideas Expressed in Unacceptable Communication Styles

Of all the ideas that are put forth in the course of a meeting, some gain quite a bit of attention while others disappear from awareness as if they had never been spoken. One of the major reasons for this phenomenon is explained by the diagram. Here is the principle: an idea that is expressed in an acceptable communication style will be taken more seriously by more people. Conversely, ideas that are presented poorly or offensively are harder for people to hear.

For example, many people want everyone's statements to be succinct, not repetitious. Others can be impatient with shy or nervous members who speak in broken sentences. Others may not want to listen to exaggerations, distortions, or unfounded pronouncements. Some people refuse to respond to someone who interrupts a discussion in order to raise a completely different subject. And some people are profoundly uncomfortable with anyone who shows too much feeling. In any of these cases, some listeners will probably ignore the substance of the ideas being expressed, no matter how valuable those ideas might be.

There are a great many groups whose members genuinely want each other to voice their opinions, share their insights, and come up with interesting new ideas. But the range and the richness of their discussion will be limited by the degree to which they can tolerate diverse communication styles.

THE CALCULUS OF DIVERSITY

STRETCHING THE LIMITS

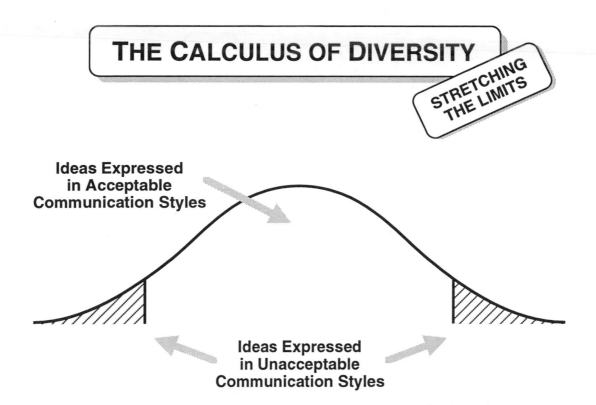

Ideas Expressed in Acceptable Communication Styles

Ideas Expressed in Unacceptable Communication Styles

This diagram shows the range of ideas available to groups that make the effort to tolerate diverse communication styles. By using good listening skills, a facilitator can be an excellent support to such groups. For example:

- When someone is being repetitious, a facilitator can use paraphrasing to help that person summarize his/her thinking.

- A facilitator can help those who speak in awkward, broken sentences by slowing them down and drawing them out.

- Similarly, a facilitator can validate the central point of an exaggeration or distortion without quarreling over its accuracy.

- A facilitator can treat interruptions firmly yet respectfully, by assuring the speaker that when the current discussion ends, the facilitator will ask the group what to do with the new topic.

- When someone expresses him/herself with intense feeling, a facilitator can acknowledge the emotion, then make sure the speaker's point does not get lost.

These situations demonstrate how important it is for a facilitator to listen skillfully and respectfully to *everyone.*

PARAPHRASING

WHY:

- *Paraphrasing* is a fundamental listening skill. It is the foundation for many other facilitative listening skills, including *mirroring, gathering,* and *drawing people out.*

- *Paraphrasing* has both a calming effect and a clarifying effect. It reassures the speaker that his or her ideas are worth listening to. And it provides the speaker with a chance to hear how his/her ideas are being heard by others.

- *Paraphrasing* is especially useful on occasions when a speaker's statements are convoluted or confusing. At such times, the paraphrase will help the speaker gauge how well his/her ideas are getting across.

- In sum, *paraphrasing* is the tool of choice for supporting people to think out loud.

HOW:

- Use your own words to say what you think the speaker said.

- If the speaker's statement is one or two sentences, use roughly the same number of words when you paraphrase it.

- If the speaker's statement is many sentences long, summarize it.

- Preface your paraphrase with a comment like one of these:
  "It sounds like what you're saying is . . ."
  "This is what I'm hearing you say . . ."
  "Let me see if I'm understanding you . . ."

- When you have completed the paraphrase, look for the speaker's reaction. Say something like, "Did I get it?" Verbally or nonverbally, s/he will indicate whether or not s/he feels understood. If not, *keep asking for clarification until you understand what s/he meant.*

DRAWING PEOPLE OUT

WHY:

- *Drawing people out* is a way of supporting people to take the next step in clarifying and refining their ideas. It sends the speaker this message, "I'm with you; I understand you so far. Now tell me a little more."

- *Drawing people out* is particularly useful in two circumstances: 1) when someone is having difficulty clarifying an idea; 2) when someone thinks s/he is being clear, but the thought is actually vague or confusing to the listener.

- *Drawing people out* sends the message, "Take your time and get your idea *all the way out*."

- When deciding whether to draw someone out, ask yourself this question: "Do I think I understand the core of what s/he is trying to say?" If the answer is "no," then draw the speaker out.

HOW:

- *Drawing people out* is most effectively used *along with paraphrasing,* not *instead of paraphrasing.*
  Example: The speaker says, "I think it's really fair to say that most people are pretty uncomfortable with change." The listener paraphrases, (e.g., "So it sounds like you're saying that change is hard for most people.") Then the listener asks, "Can you give me an example of what you mean?"

- The most basic technique of *drawing people out* is to paraphrase the speaker's statement, then ask open-ended, nondirective questions.
  Examples: "Can you say more about that?" or "What do you mean by . . .?" or "How so?"

- Here is a less common method that also works well. First, paraphrase the speaker's statement, then use *connectors* such as, "So . . ." or "And . . ."
  Example: "You're saying to wait six more weeks before we sign the contract, because . . ."

MIRRORING

WHY:

- *Mirroring* captures people's exact words. It is a highly formal version of *paraphrasing,* in which the facilitator repeats the speaker's exact words. Some people need this degree of precision in order to feel that they are truly being heard.

- Newly-formed groups, and groups unfamiliar with using a facilitator, often benefit from the trust-building effects of *mirroring*.

- In general, the more a facilitator feels the need to establish his/her neutrality, the more frequently s/he should *mirror* rather than paraphrase.

- *Mirroring* speeds up the tempo of a slow-moving discussion. Thus it is the *tool of choice* when facilitating a brainstorming process.

HOW:

- If the speaker has said a single sentence, repeat it back verbatim.

- If the speaker has said more than one sentence, repeat back key words or phrases.

- In either case, *use their words not your words.*

- Mirroring the speaker's words and mirroring the speaker's tone of voice are *two different things.* You want your tone of voice to remain warm and accepting, regardless of what the speaker's voice sounds like.

- Be yourself with your gestures and tone of voice; don't be wooden or phony. Remember, a key purpose of *mirroring* is building trust.

GATHERING IDEAS

WHY:

- To help a group build a list of ideas at a fast moving pace, you want to *gather* ideas, *not discuss* them.

- *Gathering* is a skill that combines *mirroring* and *paraphrasing* with physical gestures. Listening skills acknowledge people's thoughts and reduce their inclination to defend their ideas. Physical gestures – waving an arm or walking around – serve as "energy boosters" that keep people feeling involved.

- In order to set a fast, lively pace, use *mirroring* more than *paraphrasing*. When you repeat their exact words, many participants get into the groove of expressing their ideas in short phrases – typically three to five words. These are much easier to record on flipcharts than long sentences.

HOW:

- Effective *gathering* starts with a concise description of the task. For example, "For the next ten minutes, please evaluate this proposal by calling out 'pros' and 'cons.' First I'll ask for someone to call out a 'pro' reaction. Then I'll ask for a 'con,' and so on. We'll build both lists at the same time."

- If it's the group's first time listing ideas, spend a little time teaching them *suspended judgment*. Example: "For this next activity, I'd like everyone to feel free to express their ideas, even the off-beat or unpopular ones. So please let this be a time for generating ideas, not judging them. The discussion can come as soon as you finish making the list."

- Now have the group begin. As members call out their items, mirror or paraphrase whatever is said.

- Honor all points of view. If someone says something that sounds "off the wall," just mirror it and keep moving.

STACKING

WHY:	HOW:

WHY:

- *Stacking* is a procedure for helping people take turns when several people want to speak at once.

- *Stacking* lets everyone know that they are, in fact, going to have their turn to speak. So instead of competing for air time, people are free to listen without distraction.

- In contrast, when people don't know when or even whether their turn will come, they can't help but vie for position. This leads to various expressions of impatience and disrespect – especially interruptions.

- When a facilitator does not stack, s/he has to privately keep track of who has spoken and who is waiting to speak. *Stacking* relieves the facilitator of this responsibility; everyone knows when his/her turn is coming.

HOW:

- *Stacking* is a four-step procedure. First, the facilitator asks those who want to speak to raise their hands. Then s/he creates a speaking order by assigning a number to each person. Third, s/he calls on people when their turn to speak arrives. Then, when the last person has spoken, the facilitator checks to see if anyone else wants to speak. If so, the facilitator does another round of *stacking*. Here's an example of each step:

- Step 1. "Would all those who want to speak, please raise your hands."

- Step 2. "Susan, you're first. Deb, you're second. Bill, you're third."

- Step 3. [*When Susan has finished*] "Who was second? Was it you Deb? OK, go ahead."

- Step 4. [*After the last person has spoken*] "Does anyone else have something to say?"

TRACKING

WHY:

- *Tracking* means keeping track of the various lines of thought that are going on simultaneously within a single discussion. For example, suppose a group is discussing a plan to hire a new employee. Two people are talking about roles and responsibilities. Two others are discussing financial implications, and another two are reviewing their experiences with the previous employee. In such cases, people need help keeping track of all that's going on, because they are focused primarily on clarifying their own ideas.

- People often act as though the particular issue that interests *them* is the one that *everyone* should focus on. *Tracking* lets the group see that several elements of the topic are being discussed, and treats all as equally valid.

- *Tracking* relieves the anxiety felt by someone who wonders why the group isn't responding to his/her ideas.

HOW:

- *Tracking* is a three-step process. First, the facilitator indicates that s/he is going to step back from the conversation and *summarize* it. Then s/he names the different conversations that have been in play. Last, s/he checks for accuracy with the group. Here's an example of each step:

- Step 1. "It sounds like there are three conversations going on right now. I want to make sure I'm tracking them."

- Step 2. "It sounds like one conversation is about roles and responsibilities. Another is about finances. And a third is about what you've learned by working with the last person who held this job."

- Step 3. "Am I getting it right?"

- People generally respond well to these questions. If someone tries to clarify what was important about *their* issue, be supportive. But don't play favorites – ask for clarifications from others too.

ENCOURAGING

WHY:

- *Encouraging* is the art of creating an opening for people to participate, without putting any one individual on the spot.

- There are times in a meeting when someone may appear to be "sitting back and letting others do all the work." This doesn't necessarily mean that they are lazy or irresponsible. Instead, it may be that they are not feeling engaged by the discussion. With a little encouragement to participate, they often discover an aspect of the topic that holds meaning for them.

- *Encouraging* is especially helpful during the *early stage of a discussion,* while members are still warming up. As people get more engaged, they don't need as much encouragement to participate.

HOW:

Here are some examples of the technique of *encouraging:*

- "Who else has an idea?"

- "Is there a student's perspective on this issue?"

- "Does anyone have a 'war story' you're willing to share?"

- "A lot of women have been talking. Let's hear from the men."

- "Jim just offered us an idea that he called a 'general principle.' Can anyone give us an example of this principle in action?"

- "What was said at table two?"

- "Is this discussion raising questions for anyone?"

- "Let's hear from someone who hasn't spoken for awhile."

BALANCING

WHY:

- The direction of a discussion often follows the lead set by the first few people who speak on that topic. Using *balancing*, a facilitator helps a group round out its discussion by asking for other views that may be present but unexpressed.

- *Balancing* undercuts the common myth that "silence means consent." In doing so, it provides welcome assistance to individuals who don't feel safe enough to express views that they perceive as minority positions.

- *Balancing* not only assists individual members who need a little support at that moment; it *also* has strong positive effects on the norms of the group as a whole. It sends the message, "It is acceptable here for people to speak their mind, no matter what opinions they hold."

HOW:

Here are some examples of *balancing:*

- "Okay, now we know where three people stand; does anyone else have a different position?"

- "Are there other ways of looking at this?"

- "What do others think?"

- "Does everyone else agree with this?"

- "So, we've heard the 'x' point of view, and the 'y' point of view. Is there a third way of looking at this?"

- "Let's see how many people stand on each side of this issue. We're not making a decision, and I'm not asking you to vote. This is just an 'opinion poll' to find out how much controversy we've got in the room. Ready? How many people think it would be good if . . .?"

MAKING SPACE

WHY:

- *Making space* sends the quiet person this message: "If you don't wish to talk now, that's fine. But if you *would* like to speak, here's an opportunity."

- Every group has some members who are highly verbal and other members who speak less frequently. When a group has a fast-paced discussion style, quiet members and slower thinkers may have trouble getting a word in edgewise.

- Some people habitually keep out of the limelight because they are afraid of being perceived as rude or competitive. Others might hold back when they're new to a group and unsure of what's acceptable and what's not. Still others keep their thoughts to themselves because they're convinced their ideas aren't "as good as" those of others. In all of these cases, people benefit from a facilitator who makes space for them to participate.

HOW:

- Keep an eye on the quiet members. Be on the lookout for body language or facial expressions that may indicate their desire to speak.

- Invite them to speak. For example, "Was there a thought you wanted to express?" or "Did you want to add anything?" or "You look like you might be about to say something . . ."

- If they decline, be gracious and move on. No one likes being put on the spot and everyone is entitled to make his/her own choice about whether and when to participate.

- If necessary, hold others off. For example, if a quiet member makes a move to speak but someone jumps in ahead say, "Let's go one at a time. Rita, why don't you go first?"

- Note: if participation is *very* uneven, suggest a structured go-around to give each person a chance to speak.

INTENTIONAL SILENCE

WHY:

- *Intentional silence* is highly underrated. It consists of a pause, usually lasting no more than a few seconds, and it is done to give the speaker that brief extra "quiet time" to discover what they want to say.

- Some people need the momentary silence because they are not fully in touch with what they're thinking or feeling. Others need it because they are wrestling over whether or not to say something that might be risky. Still others need the silence to organize their thoughts into a coherent communication.

- *Intentional silence* is also powerful when a group member's remark seems too pat, too easy. The facilitator's silent attention allows that person to reflect on what s/he just said, and express his/her thoughts in more depth.

HOW:

- Five seconds of silence can seem a lot longer than it really is. Thus, the ability to tolerate the awkwardness most people feel during silence is the most important element of this listening skill. If the facilitator can survive it, everyone else will too.

- With eye contact and body language, stay focused on the speaker.

- Say nothing, not even "hmm" or "uh huh." Do not even nod or shake your head. Just stay relaxed and pay attention.

- If necessary, hold up a hand to keep others from breaking the silence.

- Sometimes everyone in the group is confused or agitated or having trouble focusing. At such times, silence may be very helpful. Say, "Let's take a minute of silence to think what this means to each of us."

LISTENING FOR COMMON GROUND

WHY:

- *Listening for common ground* is a powerful intervention when group members are polarized. It validates the group's areas of disagreement and focuses the group on their areas of agreement.

- Many disputes contain elements of agreement. For example, civil rights activists often argue vehemently over priorities and tactics, even while they agree on broad goals. When disagreements cause the members of a group to take polarized positions, it becomes hard for people to recognize that they have *anything* in common. This isolation can sometimes be overcome when the facilitator validates *both* the differences in the group *and* the areas of common ground.

- *Listening for common ground* is also a tool for instilling hope. People who believe they are opposed on every front may discover that they share a value, a belief or a goal.

HOW:

- *Listening for common ground* is a four-step process. First, indicate that you are going to *summarize the group's differences and similarities*. Second, summarize the differences. Third, note areas of common ground. Last, check for accuracy.

- Step 1. "Let me summarize what I'm hearing from each of you – I'm hearing a lot of differences but also some similarities."

- Step 2. "It sounds like one group wants to leave work early during the holiday season, and the other group would prefer to take a few days of vacation."

- Step 3. "Even so, you all seem to agree that you want *some* time off before New Year's."

- Step 4. "Have I got it right?"

- A variation is to *highlight an area of likely agreement*. "Several of you say this plan would cost too much. Do others think so?" Look around the room for nods of confirmation. "Well, *there's* something you all agree on."

5

FACILITATING
OPEN DISCUSSION

TECHNIQUES FOR SUPPORTING A
FREE-FLOWING EXCHANGE OF IDEAS

- ▶ Determining Who Goes When

- ▶ Stacking: Advantages & Limitations

- ▶ Interrupting a Stack

- ▶ Helping Individuals Make Their
  Points

- ▶ Managing Divergent Perspectives

- ▶ Focusing the Discussion

- ▶ Tracking Different Lines of Thought

- ▶ Tolerating Silences

- ▶ Explaining the Facilitator's Role
  During an Open Discussion

FACILITATING OPEN DISCUSSION

INTRODUCTION

Open discussion is the unstructured, conversational, familiar way of talking in groups. People speak up when they want to, and talk for as long as they choose. Open discussion serves many purposes. If someone raises an issue that is important to everyone, the entire group can discuss it. And if the issue does *not* engage the group, someone else can switch topics simply by voicing a new line of thought. Stakeholders can express diverse perspectives. Points of dispute can be clarified, analyses can be deepened, proposals can be sharpened. At its best, open discussion can be very effective.

But in reality, most open discussions are hard to sit through. Sometimes the conversation meanders or drifts. Sometimes a few individuals dominate. Sometimes people talk past one another without even attempting to link their ideas to the previous speaker's statements. All in all, the term "open discussion" is often a synonym for "Groan Zone."

Nonetheless, it is absolutely essential to know how to facilitate an open discussion – it is by far the most common approach to thinking in groups.

THE FACILITATOR'S TWO CENTRAL QUESTIONS

When facilitating an open discussion a facilitator is making decisions constantly. How much should s/he say? When should s/he say it? In most cases, these decisions are simply judgment calls. But underlying such judgments are two central questions. The first question involves deciding *who talks when*. The second involves deciding *what content* to support.

DETERMINING WHO TALKS WHEN Should the facilitator keep attention focused on the person currently speaking? Or should the facilitator move the focus away from that speaker and call upon others? The theory and technique of making this choice are discussed in the sections, "Organizing the Flow of a Discussion" and "Helping Individuals Make Their Points."

FOCUSING THE DISCUSSION Should the facilitator keep the focus on the specific points being made by the current speaker? Or should the facilitator help the group move away from those specific points and move on to an entirely different line of thought? The theory and technique of making this choice is discussed in the section, "Managing Diverse Perspectives."

FACILITATING OPEN DISCUSSION

ORGANIZING THE FLOW OF A DISCUSSION

A BASIC PROBLEM   When an open discussion is underway, many groups have trouble determining whose turn it is to speak next. Usually the decision is left to individual members: "Speak up whenever you have something you want to say." This principle may seem reasonable but in practice it creates confusion and inequity. Those who think it is polite to wait for a lull in the conversation usually end up waiting much longer than those who start talking whenever the preceding speaker takes a breath. Moreover, those who are more assertive may come across to some of their co-members as rude or domineering, while those who are more tentative may be perceived as having fewer ideas to contribute. Accordingly, one of the most straightforward and valuable contributions a facilitator can make is to help group members know when it is their turn to speak.

STACKING   The technique of *stacking* is a highly effective yet easy-to-master method for directing the traffic of an open discussion. To stack, a facilitator simply inquires of the group, "Would you please raise your hand if you'd like to speak?" As the participants' hands go up, the facilitator assigns each one a number. "You'll be first . . . You're second . . . You'll go third . . . " and so on. Then whenever someone finishes speaking, the facilitator calls on the person who is next in line. "Who was third – was it you, Jean? Okay, your turn – please go ahead." After the stack is complete, the facilitator asks, "Does anyone else want to speak? If so, please raise your hand now."

INTERRUPTING THE STACK   The problem with stacking is that it impedes spontaneity – no one has the opportunity to make an immediate response to someone else's remarks. No matter how provocative those remarks might be, one must wait till the end of the current stack in order to raise one's hand and respond. Many minutes could elapse, during which time the other speakers' comments might significantly water down the group's attention span. If the facilitator observes a sudden flurry of hand-waving or agitated body language, these are indicators that people may feel more-than-usual pressure to respond quickly to an important remark. To handle this problem, the facilitator can adopt a technique called *interrupting the stack*. S/he can say, "I'm going to interrupt the stack for a couple of minutes and let two or three people respond to this last comment. For those of you who are already in line to speak, don't worry – I won't forget about you. I will definitely return to the designated speaking order soon."

Interrupting the stack allows a group to spontaneously intensify a discussion. But it can also create the appearance of a facilitator who plays favorites. To prevent this a facilitator should, *when s/he first asks for raised hands,* state that s/he might interrupt the stack to permit a few responses to a hot topic.

FACILITATING OPEN DISCUSSION

ADVANTAGES AND LIMITATIONS OF STACKING   Facilitators who rely too heavily on stacking often receive comments like these: "I felt you were being very fair and even-handed with us, but I wish you had done more to help us stay focused. There were too many different topics on the floor – I couldn't follow the discussion." Or, "I wanted us to be able to get deeper into the meat of the controversy, and I felt like you were too intent on having everyone participate. I would have liked it if two or three people could have just debated each other for awhile."

As these statements illustrate, *stacking* alone is not sufficient. If overdone, it can become tiresome. But it is nonetheless a very important intervention. Often it is *stacking* that enables a group to break habitual patterns of deference and favoritism. For example, *stacking* is sometimes the simplest way to help a rigidly hierarchical group make room for participation from low-status members. In the final analysis, *stacking* is the clearest and the most explicit – and therefore the most accessible – technique for organizing the flow of an open discussion.

INFORMAL TECHNIQUES FOR BROADENING PARTICIPATION

THE PROBLEM   Not all groups benefit from *stacking.* For example, some groups have a fast-paced, almost competitive style of interacting. For them, *stacking* would seem artificial and forced. As another example, *stacking* is too structured for very small groups – consisting of, say, five or six members. Yet members of such groups may still need help knowing when they can speak. This problem becomes acute whenever the flow of discussion falls under the spell of two or three high-participating speakers, who are allowed to dominate the proceedings. At those times, a facilitator can use informal methods to shift the focus away from the frequent contributors and create opportunities for less frequent contributors to speak. Four such methods – *encouraging, balancing, making space,* and *using the clock* – are discussed below.

ENCOURAGING   When using the technique of *encouraging,* a facilitator says, "Who else wants to say something?" or "Could we hear from someone who hasn't talked for awhile?" The assumption that underlies this technique is that some people may need a little nudge to speak up. *Encouraging* is thus a means of providing extra support to those who need it. The entire group can benefit from this intervention, because it takes pressure off everyone. Frequent participators are freed to speak without fear that their contributions will overpower the others; infrequent participators feel more invited to offer their ideas without fear of appearing rude or aggressive.

FACILITATING OPEN DISCUSSION

BALANCING   The technique of *balancing* is useful when most members of a group appear reticent to disagree with the opinion of the person who has just spoken. For example, suppose a member of the group's senior management says, "Internal politics is not a problem here. If your work has merit, you will be rewarded appropriately." Using *balancing*, a facilitator could say, "As we all know, there are many times when different people have entirely different perspectives on the same situation. In this case, there has been a statement that internal politics is not a problem. Does *everyone* see it that way, or are there other points of view?" Under less threatening circumstances a facilitator can ask, simply, "What are some other ways of looking at this?" Or, "Does anyone have a different point of view?" All of these accomplish the same goal: they lend some support to people who do not agree with the mainstream point of view.

MAKING SPACE   The technique of *making space* involves questions or supportive statements that are aimed at specific individuals. For example, a facilitator may say, "Frankie, you look like you want to speak – do you?" Or, "Lonnie, did you have something you wanted to say?" Invitations like these work best when a participant has made a gesture indicating s/he may want to speak. For example, some people lift their index finger without raising their hand. Others raise their chin in a sort of reverse nod. Someone else might look directly at a facilitator and crinkle their nose or purse their lips as if to say, "No, I don't agree with what was just said."

Of course, it's always a little dicey to call on people by name. Many people do not want to be singled out. Thus a facilitator should use this technique sparingly – only when s/he sees a gesture that appears to mean, "May I talk?" or "I have an opinion too."

USING THE CLOCK   The technique of *using the clock* involves statements like these: "We have five minutes left. I want to make sure we've heard from everyone who wants to speak – particularly those who haven't had a chance yet. Who wants to speak?" Or, "We only have time for one or two more comments – perhaps we should hear from someone who hasn't spoken for awhile." These interventions communicate that the stakes have gone up a little – if you want to speak, now is your chance.

Another way of *using the clock* is aimed at situations when a few people have become highly engaged in a conversation. To give other members an opportunity to participate, a facilitator can say, "We still have more than fifteen minutes left in this discussion. How about if we hear from someone who hasn't spoken for awhile?"

FACILITATING OPEN DISCUSSION

HELPING INDIVIDUALS MAKE THEIR POINTS

REFLECTIVE LISTENING   Through the use of *paraphrasing* and *mirroring*, the facilitator can help a speaker feel understood. This keeps the focus of attention on the individual who was just speaking, but the facilitator does not push the speaker for any particular behavior. The speaker is left to decide for him/herself whether to continue talking or stop.

When a facilitator engages in *reflective listening*, it is important that s/he do it for as many participants as possible. Otherwise, some people will wonder why the facilitator seems to be playing favorites.

But continual *reflective listening* during an open discussion can become tiresome and annoying. It slows down the pace and interferes with spontaneity. Therefore, many facilitators do not use *reflective listening* during an open discussion, except as a way to help speakers who are clearly having difficulty expressing themselves, and whose need for support would be obvious to other participants.

DRAWING PEOPLE OUT   By asking questions or even by saying, simply, "Can you say more about that?" the facilitator helps a speaker develop a line of thought. This move also keeps the focus of attention on the individual who was just speaking. Note, however, that it is much more directive than *reflective listening;* the speaker is explicitly being invited to continue talking.

Thus, when a facilitator decides to draw someone out, s/he is in effect making a judgment that it would benefit the group to hear more from the person who has just been speaking. In this way, the facilitator has a subtle but very real influence over who gets how much air time – and whose ideas will develop more, become better organized, better articulated, and ultimately more accessible to other members.

Therefore, it is imperative that facilitators *resist the temptation to draw out the people whose ideas sound the most promising*. This would violate the cardinal rule of impartiality; soon group members would suspect that the facilitator had a hidden agenda. Instead, a good rule of thumb is to draw someone out only when that person's ideas are hard to understand – regardless of whether or not the ideas are interesting or realistic.

FACILITATING OPEN DISCUSSION

MANAGING DIVERGENT PERSPECTIVES

THE PROBLEM: MULTIPLE FRAMES OF REFERENCE   Broad participation in a discussion usually produces a divergence of perspectives. This diversity can cause serious misunderstandings.

EXAMPLE   The owner of several large parking garages met with his nine managers to discuss a reorganization of duties that would take place in another month, after automated ticket-payment machines were installed in each garage. Part way through the meeting the owner raised the problem of customers who lose their tickets. He asked for suggestions. Someone quickly responded with an idea. Someone else showed why that idea wouldn't work. A third person then wondered if the cashiers would cooperate. He pointed out that many of the cashiers would realize that their jobs were in jeopardy. This speaker concluded by proposing that the whole idea of payment by machine be reconsidered – perhaps even abandoned. A fourth person said that she wasn't in favor of abandoning the project, but she did have some concerns about the reliability of the equipment. She said, "Maybe we could test the new equipment in one or two smaller locations and get the bugs out of the system before the major installation." At this point the owner became impatient and scolded everyone for failing to stay on topic.

What the owner did not understand is that in a discussion like this one, each person must approach the topic from his/her own individual frame of reference. The person who suggested considering the question from the cashiers' perspective was thinking out loud. As he did so he realized that he was going to have to deal with laying people off. The person who suggested testing the equipment was remembering her last job, where a computer system had been installed without adequate preparation – causing a plunge in her company's efficiency and morale.

Through the owner's impatience and his irritation, he signaled to the employees that they were doing something wrong. Yet they were not being disloyal to the owner; *they were doing their best to get their ideas formulated*. Each person was working hard to answer the question the owner had posed – but they were all working from their own frames of reference. They could not respond to the exhortation to stay on topic; they felt they *were* on topic. This is a perfect example of the confusions that arise from the inevitable presence of divergent perspectives.

FACILITATING OPEN DISCUSSION

THE FACILITATOR'S CHALLENGE   Situations like the one described on the previous page occur often – and some facilitators don't handle them well. It's tempting to say something like, "It sounds like we're getting off track." or "I think we should return to the topic of lost tickets." These interventions sound good, but they are usually ineffective. They tell participants, in effect, "Don't think from your own frame of reference."

Everyone approaches a discussion from his/her own individual frame of reference. The meaning, the significance and the priority of any given point of view are all matters of interpretation. And each participant arrives with different instincts about such matters. *It's essential for a facilitator to recognize that this is not unhealthy.*

The *goal* of a good discussion is to produce more harmony among individually different perspectives – to reconcile the diversity through a process of mutual understanding. But many people seem to think that participants in a discussion should *start out* with a shared framework. When they hear statements they consider to be tangential, they seek to solve the problem of divergent perspectives through a process of persuasion or control. "That's a side issue." "Let's get back to the point." "Would everyone please get focused?" These statements may cause a speaker to stop talking, but they certainly don't help the speaker to feel understood.

The point is that people of goodwill can – and do – differ on such matters as what's important and what's not; what's on track and what's off track; what's useful and what's useless. When these differences occur, discomfort arises. This is normal and healthy – it means people are participating. But the discomfort can deepen – even to the point of ruining a group's ability to think together – when participants don't realize that their individual frames of reference are biasing their assessment of the value of one another's contributions. At such times, people become impatient with one another, they say things they regret, they stop listening, they act childishly.

SEQUENCING   What can a facilitator do to prevent this deterioration? The simplest and most straightforward method is *sequencing*. With this technique, a facilitator validates each perspective and then directs a group to focus on each line of thought in sequence, one at a time.

The next page gives an example that illustrates both the need for and the correct use of a sequencing intervention.

FACILITATING OPEN DISCUSSION

EXAMPLE   A group of teachers met monthly to discuss the school's curriculum. Carter, a second-year teacher, made a controversial statement. Toni, the librarian, had a private reaction to that statement. "I hope Carter stops talking soon," thought Toni. "He's going on a tangent and it's wasting our time." But the next person to speak responded to Carter's points in earnest. After a few minutes, Toni said, "Okay folks, we need to get this discussion back on track." Someone else then said, "Thanks, Toni. I, too, thought we'd drifted away from our topic." This was a critical juncture. Carter felt he had been put down. Toni felt irritated and guilty. Both stopped participating and the meeting ended on a sour note.

If a facilitator had been present, a simple *sequencing* intervention might have produced an entirely different result. The facilitator could have intervened at the critical juncture and said, "We appear to have two conversations going on simultaneously. Some of you want to respond to Carter's statement. At the same time, others of you would prefer to return to the previous topic. So here's what I'm going to do. I'm going to take two or three more comments on Carter's statements, and then I'm going to ask Tony to re-introduce the other line of thought. We'll spend at least a few minutes on *that* topic-area. Then, if necessary, we can take stock and see what seems most important to focus on at that point."

This example demonstrates how *sequencing* works. Step 1: Validate both perspectives. Step 2: Help the group pay attention to one line of thought for a few minutes. Step 3: Help the group pay attention to a *different* line of thought for the next few minutes.

ADVANTAGES AND LIMITATIONS OF SEQUENCING   When a facilitator sequences two conversations that are underway simultaneously, s/he is keeping a discussion focused without taking sides. This intervention usually earns a group's appreciation. By validating both perspectives, the facilitator establishes a greater sense of safety for everyone. By identifying and labeling two separate lines of thought, the facilitator helps members keep track of what is going on. And by organizing the group's participation – first a few minutes on one idea, then a few minutes on the other – the facilitator demonstrates that s/he can guide the group through the Groan Zone.

But *sequencing* only works when there are two perspectives.   When a discussion heads down three or four different tracks – as in the example of the parking garage – the chances are great that the group *would not* appreciate hearing the facilitator say, "First we'll spend a few minutes on Idea A, then we'll shift to Idea B, then we'll go to Idea C and then to Idea D." That sequence would seem *too* controlled and too tedious to sit through.

FACILITATING OPEN DISCUSSION

CALLING FOR RESPONSES At times a facilitator may say something like, "Does anyone have a reaction to what Erin just said?" Or, "After listening to the previous three speakers, does anyone have any questions for them?" Questions like these guide whoever speaks next to remain on the same track as the person who has just spoken. *Calling for responses* is thus a method for preserving the focus of the discussion, even though it also encourages participation from new speakers.

This technique has the same effect as drawing someone out: the ideas that receive a facilitator's support are likely to be more fully discussed. Yet since the facilitator is asking for broader participation, this move is rarely opposed or even distrusted. Participants tend to view *calling for responses* as a neutral effort to keep the discussion moving. This tends to be true even when it is apparent that the facilitator has made a choice between two or more topics. So long as a facilitator makes the choice in good faith – not for the sake of favoring certain ideas but rather to keep the discussion balanced – most group members will give the facilitator the benefit of the doubt.

DELIBERATE REFOCUSING When the facilitator deliberately refocuses the conversation s/he says things like, "For the past ten minutes you have been discussing Topic ABC. But some of you indicated that you wanted the group to discuss Topic DEF too. Is now a good time to switch?" Or, "A while ago Robin raised an issue, but no one responded. Before we lose that thought altogether, I just want to check: does *anyone* have a comment for Robin?" As these examples illustrate, *deliberate refocusing* is another method for keeping the discussion balanced. Rather than permit one content-area to dominate, the facilitator refocuses the conversation in order to provide fair opportunities for other issues. One of the most effective, and least offensive, occasions for *deliberate refocusing* is when a group has allowed two or three speakers to monopolize the discussion for several minutes or longer.

Of all the techniques described in these pages, *deliberate refocusing* is the most directive. It pushes people to move away from one track of discussion and move onto another track, at the same time as it encourages everyone to move their attention away from one set of speakers and give their attention to a different set of speakers. Accordingly, the bias that is built into this technique is more noticeable. When a facilitator refocuses a discussion s/he runs the risk of being perceived as non-neutral – as choosing to cut off discussion perhaps before the group has completed a train of thought. Therefore, it is recommended that this technique be used sparingly.

FACILITATING OPEN DISCUSSION

TRACKING   As illustrated by the case of the parking garage managers, open discussions often branch into several distinct subconversations. *Tracking* means keeping track of those various lines of thought. A facilitator *tracks* by saying things like, "I think you are discussing several issues at the same time. Here they are. . . " Then s/he identifies each track. Thus a facilitator might have said to the parking garage managers, "I think you are discussing four issues. First: how to deal with customers who lose tickets. Second: will cashiers cooperate? Third: should you reconsider the *very idea* of payment by machines? Fourth: concern about the reliability of the equipment."

Tracking is valuable when a discussion is at its most competitive, its most unruly – when people are least likely to be listening to each other. These are precisely the times when directive methods like *sequencing* don't work. When everyone is tensely pushing their own agenda, suggestions by the facilitator are hard to hear and respond to. At such times, a facilitator must refrain from prioritizing or structuring the discussion. Instead, s/he remains neutral and alert to the necessity for supporting every speaker. *Tracking* reassures everyone that at least *someone* is listening.

COMPLETING A TRACKING INTERVENTION   After showing a group the themes they have been discussing, how should a facilitator complete the intervention? The most effective method is to ask for accuracy and then do no more. Ask, "Have I captured all the themes?" Someone may answer, "No! You missed *my* ideas." If so, correct the omission, and finish with a summary. "So there you are – discussing five topics all at once." Then stop.

A COMMON MISTAKE OF TECHNIQUE   Many facilitators are tempted to complete a *tracking* intervention by asking "Which topic would you like to focus on, now?" But it is nearly impossible for a group to *answer* that question. Typically, the members then go into a tailspin as they dicker over the most suitable focus, becoming mired in talking about what to talk about.

If a facilitator refrains from asking what people want to focus on, a group generally responds to a tracking intervention in one of two ways.   The most common response is an *integrative* one. Someone combines a few of the tracks named by the facilitator and makes a clever proposal or offers an insightful analysis or raises a provocative question. In other words, someone integrates and advances the group's thinking. The second most common response is a *persistent* one: someone returns to his/her pet theme. At times the members will follow that person's lead, in which case the group has created its new focus – at least temporarily. At other times a quarrel ensues. "I don't *want* to talk about that issue now." In those cases the facilitator can be an honest broker and propose a simple *sequence*. "Can we spend a few minutes on this issue, then shift to some of the other themes?"

FACILITATING OPEN DISCUSSION

ASKING FOR THEMES   This technique is quite similar to *tracking,* with one major difference: the lines of thought are identified by group members, not by the facilitator. To *ask for themes,* a facilitator first says, "You are now discussing several issues, all at the same time." S/he then asks, "Can anyone identify any of the themes or topic-areas currently being discussed?" As people call out their responses, the facilitator writes them on a flipchart.

When people have finished listing themes, the facilitator can say, "Now let's return to open discussion and see what happens in the next few minutes. If necessary we'll come back to this list and structure it more. But we might be able to skip that step altogether – let's find out. Does anyone have any comments about *any* of these themes?" As with *tracking,* the next response will probably be either an integrative response or a persistent one.

FRAMING   As with the two preceding interventions, the facilitator begins by pointing out that several subconversations are underway. The facilitator then says, "Let's remember how this discussion began." S/he then restates the discussion's original purpose. For example, "Originally, Susan asked for input into next month's agenda. The conversation has now branched out in several directions. Some might be important to pursue right now; perhaps others can be deferred. Which ones do *you* think are relevant?" The remaining steps are the same ones taken when a facilitator *asks for themes.* Record the group's answers, then return the group to open discussion.

FURTHER CONSIDERATIONS

TOLERATING SILENCES   A typical silence during an open discussion lasts about three to five seconds. A painfully long silence lasts ten or fifteen seconds. Those silences mean that *people are thinking.* For example, people may need a few seconds to form an analysis of a complex problem. Or in a tense meeting, participants might become quiet while they search for tactful ways to express difficult feelings. Silence is not dysfunctional; it occurs when participants turn inward. Yet some facilitators find it exceedingly hard to tolerate silences of those lengths. This has little to do with the needs of the group. Rather it reflects the facilitator's *own* discomfort with silence.

To discern *your* level of discomfort, ask a friend to help with this experiment: during a conversation, say "Okay, let's be quiet now." Allow five seconds to elapse. Now discuss how that felt. Repeat the experiment with a lapse-time of fifteen seconds. *Tolerating silence* is like any other skill – it is acquired through practice. Let *someone else* break the silences in your conversations.

FACILITATING OPEN DISCUSSION

SWITCHING FROM OPEN DISCUSSION TO A DIFFERENT FORMAT   When a discussion becomes tedious and people appear to be restless or bored, the wisest choice might be to end the open discussion and switch to another format. Alternative formats include working in small groups, individual writing, structured go-arounds, formal brainstorming, and many more. These are discussed in great detail in chapter 6.

INTRODUCING AN OPEN DISCUSSION   When a facilitator works with a group for the first time, s/he should briefly explain his/her approach so they can cooperate with it. Unusual interventions like *stacking* and *interrupting the stack* require more explanation than self-evident ones like *sequencing*.

Here is a sample of an effective introduction. "We're about to spend half an hour in open discussion. Since we haven't done this before, I want to tell you how I work. I see an open discussion as a free-flowing opportunity for an interchange of ideas between each participant and the entire group. My basic plan, therefore, is to stay out of your way so you can talk to each other.

"If more than one person wants to talk at the same time, I'll ask you to raise hands and I'll number you off. That way, you'll know when your turn is coming and you won't have to keep waving your hand to get my attention. Once in a while, if someone makes a statement that produces immediate reactions, I might take a few comments from people who weren't in line to speak. But I'll only do that when it's an obvious choice. And if I *do* let anyone take a cut, I will *definitely* return to those who were in line.

"There are two other ways I might intervene to reduce confusion. If an individual is having a lot of trouble expressing his/her thoughts clearly, I might ask a question or two, to draw out his/her thinking. And if the whole discussion becomes tangled somehow, I'll do *something* to help people keep track of what's being said. Okay, that's it from me. Any questions?"

The preceding introduction takes roughly a minute and ten seconds to deliver. That is a long time for a facilitator to be speaking. But unless s/he introduces his/her approach, the group may not be capable of cooperating.

IN CONCLUSION   Open discussion is the most common of all the formats for thinking in groups. But the power and the effectiveness of an open discussion can vary widely, depending to a large degree on the facilitator's mastery of the participatory techniques described in this chapter.

6

ALTERNATIVES TO OPEN DISCUSSION

VARYING PARTICIPATION FORMATS
TO BUILD GROUP MOMENTUM

▶ Presentations and Reports

▶ Idea-Listing

▶ Working in Small Groups

▶ Individual Writing

▶ Structured Go-Arounds

▶ Computer Assisted Meetings

▶ Experiential Learning

▶ Multi-Tasking

▶ Debriefing a Structured Activity

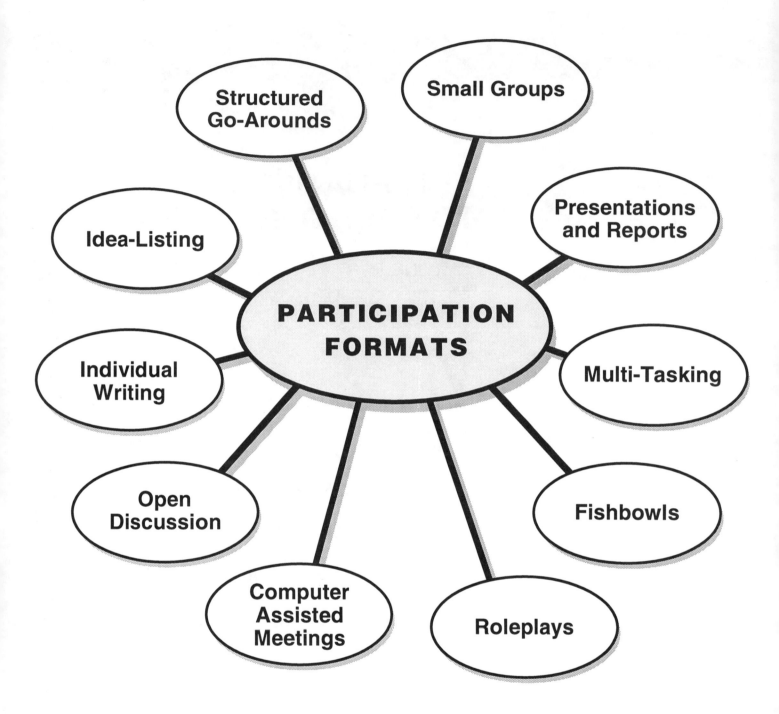

Most groups rely heavily on *open discussion* and *presentations and reports,* seldom using the other formats shown above. Ironically, open discussion and presentations and reports are the two formats that place the most pressure on people to appear polished and conclusive when they speak. By contrast, the other formats give people latitude to do rough-draft thinking. Learning when and how to use these formats is the focus of this chapter.

IMPROVING PRESENTATIONS AND REPORTS

PROBLEM		SOLUTION
Disorganized, complicated reports that group members cannot follow.	⇨	Encourage the presenter to take a few minutes ahead of time to think through the logic of his/her report.
Tedious, rambling, repetitive reports.	⇨	Have the presenter jot down his/her key points on paper before s/he begins speaking.
Group members do not appear to understand the report's central point.	⇨	Before the meeting, encourage the presenter to state the most important point in the first sentence, and to restate it in the summary.
People look dazed and uncomprehending, as though they were in a fog.	⇨	Ask the presenter to set aside time for questions and answers. Then strongly encourage group members to use it.
Confusion about what the listeners are expected to do with the information presented.	⇨	Encourage the presenter to tell people what s/he expects them to do with the information. For example, "Please communicate these ideas to your peers."
Reports that barrage the listeners with details, details, details, causing people to get overloaded and shut down.	⇨	Encourage the presenter to use visual aids. Slick, glossy overheads are rarely necessary. Hand-drawn diagrams on flipcharts usually work fine.
Presenters pass out written materials, then keep on talking. Participants stop listening in order to look over the handouts.	⇨	Advise the presenter to either distribute material and then pause while people look it over, or wait to hand out written material until the report is done.

IDEA-LISTING

RECOMMENDED USES

1. *Jumpstarting a discussion.* Idea-listing will help a group to rapidly identify many aspects of the subject, even when they're just beginning to think about it.

2. *Showing the members of a polarized group that there are actually more than two competing opinions in the room.* Idea-listing will draw out a wide range of thoughts on a given topic. This tends to happen even when there is an "us versus them" atmosphere in the group.

3. *Searching for a better understanding of the causes or elements of a problem.* When a problem is more complicated than it originally appeared, use idea-listing to explore questions like "What's really going on here?" or "What are some influences we have not yet considered?"

4. *Generating a list of innovative or unconventional solutions to a difficult problem.*

5. *Bringing a large group back together after people have been working in small groups.* Idea-listing is the fastest way to collect the fruits of their various discussions. The group then has more time to go into depth on topics of interest.

6. *Providing structure when a topic feels overwhelming, unwieldy, or out of control.* By listing ideas, participants can see the breadth of the whole group's thinking. They can start sorting out the issues, and prioritizing the elements they want to tackle first. Thus, idea-listing is often an important first step in reducing the complexity of a difficult task.

IDEA-LISTING

PROCEDURE

1. *Hang large sheets of paper on the wall.* Hang more paper than you think you will need because groups often produce many more ideas than you expect.

2. *Ask for a volunteer to serve as the chartwriter.* The job of the chartwriter is to write down everyone's ideas without censoring or improving anything.

3. *Go over the following ground rules with the group:*

- Anyone may put anything on the list that seems relevant to them.

- No arguing about whether or not something belongs on the list.

- No discussion, just call out ideas – participants will have time for discussion after the idea-listing is finished.

4. *State the group's task in the form of a question.* For example, "What are our options for reducing our budget?"

5. *Start listing ideas.* Ask people to call out their ideas one at a time. If anyone begins arguing or discussing an item, politely remind the whole group of the ground rules.

6. *Don't panic when the pace slows down.* This is often temporary. It usually means people have emptied their minds of the obvious ideas and they are becoming more thoughtful as they search for less obvious ideas. If you push people at this stage, they often feel pressured, and many people will stop thinking.

7. *Toward the end of the allotted time, announce "Two more minutes."* This often produces one final burst of ideas.

WORKING IN SMALL GROUPS

RECOMMENDED USES

1. *Breaking the ice — making it feel safer to participate.* People feel less reticent in small groups; it seems less public.

2. *Keeping the energy up.* It's physically energizing to get out of a chair and move around. Furthermore, working in small groups allows everyone to talk. Active involvement energizes people.

3. *Deepening everyone's understanding of a topic.* In small groups, each person has more time to explore and develop each other's ideas.

4. *Exploring different aspects of an issue quickly.* Small groups can work on several components of a single problem simultaneously. This is a very powerful use of small groups.

5. *Building relationships.* Small groups provide more opportunity for people to get to know one another personally.

6. *Greater commitment to the outcome.* Small groups support more participation. More participation means more opportunity to influence the outcome. When the outcome incorporates *everyone's* thinking, participants have a deeper understanding of its logic and nuance, and they are more likely to feel committed to its effective implementation. This is what is meant by "ownership" of the outcome.

BREAKING INTO SMALL GROUPS

PROCEDURE

1. *Give a one sentence overview of the purpose of the next task.* Example: "Now we're going to discuss our reactions to Dr. Stone's last lecture." Leave the instructions vague for now. (Clarify them in step 4.)

2. *Tell the participants how to find partners for their small groups.* Examples: "Turn to the person next to you," or "Find two people you don't know very well."

3. *Wait till everyone has formed their small group before giving further instructions.*

4. *After everyone has settled down, clarify the task at hand.* State the topic people will be discussing, then state the expected outcome. Example: "Dr. Stone claimed that married managers and single managers are treated very differently. Do you agree? What has *your* experience been? See if each of you can come up with two or three examples that have arisen at your place of work."

5. *If you have any instructions about specific ground rules or procedures, give them now.* Example: "One person should be 'the speaker' while the other person is 'the listener.' Then reverse roles when I give the signal."

6. *Tell people how much time has been allotted for this activity.*

7. *As the process unfolds, announce the time remaining.* Example: "Three more minutes!" When time is almost up, give a final warning. Say, "Just a few more seconds."

8. *Reconvene the large group by asking a few people to share their thoughts and learnings.*

INDIVIDUAL WRITING

RECOMMENDED USES

1. *Giving members a chance to collect their thoughts in preparation for open discussion.*

2. *Reflecting privately on something unusual or noteworthy that happened recently in the group.*

3. *Preserving anonymity.* People may hesitate to speak freely when their superiors or subordinates are present, or when they fear other group members will disapprove of their comments. Sometimes members are more willing to share their thoughts when they can submit them anonymously to the group.

4. *Allowing group members to collect their thoughts and feelings after tempers have flared.* When emotions go out of control, people can benefit from taking five minutes to write about the hurt and anger they may be feeling.

5. *Producing a first draft of a written product, such as a letter or a mission statement.* Each person writes his/her own rough draft version of the product. Then, those who like what they've written can share their drafts with the group.

6. *Obtaining one last round of input from everyone that the final decision-maker can consider after the meeting is over.*

7. *Evaluating a meeting, when time is scarce but constructive criticism is needed.*

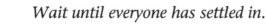

INDIVIDUAL WRITING

PROCEDURE

1. *Give an overview of the task.* For example, "We're going to take five minutes writing our thoughts about the problems with our performance review process."

2. *Ask everyone to take out a pen and paper.* (Note: Bring extra pens and paper. It's surprising how many people don't bring writing materials to meetings.)

3. *Wait until everyone has settled in.*

4. *Give detailed instructions about the task.* For example, "Many people are not satisfied with our performance review process. Your task is to clarify specifically what you don't like about it. First, write two or three problems with the policy as it now stands. Then, write about the ways you have been adversely affected by that policy." Be sure to let people know whether or not they will be expected to show their work to someone else. Note: It is very reassuring to say, "You won't have to show this to anyone. This is intended solely to help you clarify your own thinking."

5. *Let people know how much time has been allotted for individual writing, then begin.*

6. *Give a one-minute warning when time is almost up.*

7. *When time runs out, reconvene the group.* Allow ample time for discussion of the material that was generated during the writing period.

STRUCTURED GO-AROUNDS

RECOMMENDED USES

1. *Warming up a newly formed group.* New groups usually need a more structured activity because the safety level is low.

2. *Structuring a complex discussion.* During open discussion, there are often several subconversations going on simultaneously. A structured go-around acknowledges this fact, and allows each person's pet topic to become the focus of group attention for a brief period of time.

3. *Making room for quiet members.* A go-around supports those who have trouble breaking into conversations.

4. *Gathering diverse perspectives when the membership consists of varied interest groups.* Go-arounds restrain members from arguing about the validity of each others' frames of reference.

5. *Giving initial reactions to a controversial topic.* When a topic provokes anxiety, many people turn inward; they rehearse thoughts to themselves to try to find the "right way" to say something risky. Meanwhile, the few who do speak up take all the heat. A go-around gives everyone time to collect their thoughts so they can share the risk.

6. *Returning from a break after a heated disagreement.* After any disturbing episode, a break followed by a go-around is an ideal method for allowing everyone to voice reactions to what occurred before the break.

7. *Closing a meeting.* This gives each member a final chance to express thoughts and feelings that might otherwise not be spoken – at least, not in front of everyone.

STRUCTURED GO-AROUNDS

PROCEDURE

1. *Have group members pull their chairs together to form a circle.* It is important in a go-around that every member see every other member's face.

2. *Give a one sentence overview of the topic to be addressed.* Example: "In a moment we'll each have a chance to give our reactions to the presentation we just heard."

3. *Explain the process.* Example: "We'll go clockwise from whoever speaks first. While someone is talking, no one may interrupt. When you're through speaking, say 'pass' or 'I'm done'."

4. *If there are particular variations in the ground rules, go over them now.* For example, some facilitators give people explicit permission to pass without speaking when it is their turn.

5. *After having gone over the ground rules, restate the topic.* If a more detailed explanation is needed, give it now.

6. *Give people an idea of how much time to take.* Example 1: "This will work best if each of you spends about a minute sharing your reactions." Example 2: "Take as much time as you like to give your impressions of why this problem keeps reappearing."

GO-AROUND VARIATIONS

The Standard Structured Go-Around

Go clockwise – or counterclockwise – from whoever speaks first.

Toss the Beanbag

When the speaker is done, s/he tosses an object (an eraser, or whatever) to someone else, who speaks next.

Seven Words or Less

Everyone evaluates the meeting in seven words or less. Incomplete sentences are fine.

Two or Three Feeling Words

Each person uses two or three *feeling words* to describe his/her mood. (Examples: "satisfied and tired" or "confused, worried, cranky.")

Talking Stick

To speak, a group member picks up the *talking stick.* No one else may speak until the stick has been set down.

Popcorn

Everyone takes their turn when they choose, not in any particular order – but only after the preceding speaker has said "pass."

These are all variations of the basic go-around. They all have two ground rules in common: (1) one person speaks at a time, and (2) the speaker indicates when s/he's done speaking – for example, by saying "pass." All the variations encourage and equalize participation.

The use of a go-around is also a wonderful way to close a meeting because it gives people a final opportunity to express themselves.

COMPUTER ASSISTED MEETINGS

LAPTOP COMPUTERS AND FACE-TO-FACE MEETINGS

A growing number of facilitators use laptops to enhance participation. The computers are linked together on a network, allowing participants to communicate with one another in writing, as the meeting progresses. This technology is particularly effective as a brainstorming device: it can handle simultaneous contributions from dozens – or even hundreds – of members. Each participant types his or her ideas into a computer, and the ideas are instantaneously transmitted throughout the room to all other computers. Thus a person can go back and forth between writing his/her own thoughts and reading what everyone else has written. Each person can write responses or make additions to the list, whenever s/he feels moved to do so.

GROUPWARE

In order to utilize the capabilities of this technology, a facilitator must become conversant with a special class of computer software, called "groupware." One of the most effective groupware systems is *Council*,* written by facilitation expert Jim Ewing. As an engineer turned organization development specialist, Jim was uniquely positioned to create an easy to use groupware that supports and enhances face-to-face dialogue. Its key properties are the anonymous and simultaneous entry of ideas, and the capacity to support very large groups to think cohesively. Other groupware systems include *GroupSystems V, MeetingWorks, VisionQuest* and *CAFacilitator*.

APPLICATIONS

Anonymity can make a crucial difference to people who feel too threatened to state their opinions out loud. *Simultaneity* allows everyone to express their first thoughts rapidly. Everyone can then view the group's collective output by scrolling through the list of items on their individual monitors. Once everyone sees the range of initial thinking, people can shift away from using the computers altogether, and enter face-to-face discussion of the ideas that seem most challenging and compelling. Because of these properties, groupware is fast becoming one of the most effective meeting-formats for conducting meaningful discussions, particularly in large-sized groups.

---

* For further information about *Council,* call co-author Lenny Lind at 800-318-3521.

TWO FORMATS FOR EXPERIENTIAL LEARNING

FISHBOWLS

1. Briefly describe the activity. Then ask for five or six volunteers to be "in the fishbowl."

2. Have the volunteers sit in a circle in the middle of the room. Have everyone else sit in an outer circle.

3. Give the volunteers their specific instructions. Set a time limit, then start the activity. Make sure those in the outer circle remain quiet.

4. When time is up, break the room into small groups to discuss their observations and feelings about what happened in Step 3.

5. Reconvene the large group. Ask those who were in the fishbowl to share their experiences. Then ask those who were on the outside to share their observations.

ROLEPLAYS

1. Start by explaining the purpose of the roleplay. For example, "This activity will help us gain insight into some communication problems between managers and employees."

2. Break into small groups.

3. Assign a role to each participant and provide some background to bring that role to life. For example, "Your boss gave you an impossible task and you were afraid to challenge him."

4. Give any specific instructions that might be needed. For example, "In this roleplay, you must explain why you did not finish the task, to a boss who may react defensively."

4. Clarify the time limits, then begin.

5. When finished, reconvene the large group and debrief the activity.

TWO FORMATS FOR MULTI-TASKING

SIMULTANEOUS COMMITTEES

1. Divide the group into committees and assign a different task to each committee. For example, suppose the group is planning a conference. They might divide into three small groups: one committee makes a list of people to invite; a second lists topics to discuss; a third identifies logistics to handle.

2. Have each committee select people to play three roles: discussion leader, recorder, and presenter.

3. Specify the time limit for working in committee. Then begin. Give a 10-minute warning before ending.

4. Reconvene the large group. Ask for a report from one of the presenters. Allow 5-10 minutes for questions. Obtain reports from all committees.

THE GALLERY TOUR

1. Divide the group into committees.

2. Give flipcharts and markers to each committee and send them to their "stations" – separate rooms, or corners of the room. Tell them to record their work on flipcharts and post the charts on the nearest walls.

3. When time is up, reconvene the large group. Now form "tour groups." Each tour group must have members from every committee.

4. Tell the groups to take a 7-minute tour of each station. The charts should be explained by someone who was in that committee.

DEBRIEFING A STRUCTURED ACTIVITY

WHY

Structured activities, like idea-listing or breaking into small groups, usually produce a wide range of perspectives. When an activity ends, it is often helpful to give the group an opportunity to reflect on the discussion as a whole, rather than focusing on one or two specific points that were raised. For example, people may want to say, "I never realized that there were so many different ways of looking at this issue!" or, "Now I'm starting to understand why this is such a problem."

This tool provides a facilitator with a straightforward procedure for conducting a debriefing. All questions listed below work equally well.

HOW

1. Before starting, select a question from the following list:

   "Now that we've heard what everyone has said,
   - What have I learned?
   - What concerns has this raised for me?
   - What feelings am I having?
   - What am I noticing about our group?
   - What do I think of our prospects for success?
   - Have I heard anything I didn't already know?
   - What is my reaction to the presence of so many different points of view?"

2. Have people go around and answer the question.

3. Upon completion of the go-around, have the group discuss, "Where do we go from here?"

   Note: Before answering this question, it's often useful to take a ten minute break.

7

CHARTWRITING TECHNIQUE

USING MARKERS AND FLIPCHARTS
TO SUPPORT FULL PARTICIPATION

▶ The ChartWriter's Job Description

▶ Lettering

▶ Colors

▶ Symbols

▶ Layout

▶ Formats

▶ Deciding How Much to Write

▶ ChartWriting in Action

▶ After the Meeting

In many groups, participation is not balanced. A few people do most of the talking, while others sit and listen. This pattern shifts dramatically when people's ideas are written on flipcharts where they can be seen by everyone.

ChartWriting strengthens full participation in several ways. First, *it validates.* Recording people's words gives them the message, "This is a valuable idea." And when their *ideas* are valued, *people* feel valued. This is the central benefit of ChartWriting: it lays a foundation for a spirit of mutual respect.

Second, ChartWriting *provides participants with a group memory* * – a written record that can be kept visible throughout the meeting. *This extends the limits of the human brain.* A vast amount of scientific research has shown that most people can retain roughly seven items of information in their short-term memory. Once a person's short term memory is full, s/he simply cannot absorb another idea – nor can s/he easily create new ideas – without forgetting something. (For example, you can probably remember a new friend's seven-digit phone number by repeating it over and over; but try remembering two new phone numbers at once!) In a meeting this can pose a real problem. Typically, people hang onto the ideas they care about, and let the rest float in one ear and out the other. ChartWriting solves this problem. Participants know that if they forget something, they can look it up on the chart. This frees the mind and supports people to keep thinking. (For a detailed discussion on the benefits of using a group memory, see "The Case For A Group Memory" by Michael Doyle and David Straus in *How To Make Meetings Work,* pages 38-48, New York: Jove Press, 1982.)

It is important to recognize that ChartWriting is not merely a tool for keeping the record of a meeting. Primarily it is a vehicle for encouraging full participation. It equalizes and balances. It enlivens the discussion. It helps people work toward understanding and integrating each other's points of view. In summary, it is one of the facilitator's most fundamental tools for supporting groups to do their best thinking.

* The term "group memory" was coined by Geoff Ball, a California specialist in multi-party conflict resolution. He is the founder of RESOLVE, one of the nation's first consulting firms to promote collaborative problem-solving as an alternative to litigation.

LETTERING

1. PRINT YOUR LETTERS

UNIFORM, CAPITAL LETTERS are easiest to read quickly. Using upper and lower case letters is fine if your penmanship is legible. Writing in cursive may be slightly faster, but taking a few extra seconds to print will make your text much easier to read.

2. MAKE **THICK-LINED** LETTERS

Use the *wide end* of the marker tip. Press firmly against the paper. Firm, thick-lined lettering is much more visible from a distance than soft, thin-lined lettering.

3. WRITE STRAIGHT UP AND DOWN

Straight lettering is easier to read than *slanted* lettering.

4. CLOSE YOUR LETTERS

Don't leave gaps in letters like B and P. Letters without gaps are easier on the eyes. Closing your letters helps people read more before they get tired.

5. USE PLAIN, BLOCK LETTERS

Letters without curlicues are easier on the eyes. *Fancy script slows down reading time,* so it should be saved for occasional special effects.

6. PRACTICE MAKES PERFECT

If your printing isn't perfect, don't panic – practice!

A painless way to improve lettering is to practice whenever you might otherwise be doodling or taking notes, or writing grocery lists, memos, love letters – whatever. Habits you develop with pen and paper *will transfer* to the flipchart.*

* Thanks to Jennifer Hammond-Landau, noted San Francisco graphic facilitator, who gave us this tip in 1982!

COLORS

1. ALTERNATE COLORS

People read faster, retain more, and have a longer concentration span when the text is written in two or three colors, so alternate colors frequently. But remember: it's not necessary to follow a pattern in your alternation. The goal is simply to break up the monotony.

2. USE *EARTH TONES* FOR TEXT

The earth tones, also called the "soft colors," are blue, brown, purple and green. They are easier on the eyes.

3. USE HOT COLORS FOR HIGHLIGHTING

The "hot colors" are orange, red, yellow, and pink. They are harder on the eyes and should be reserved for borders, shading, underlining, and for special symbols like arrows or stars. Note also that yellow is very difficult to see at a distance.

4. AVOID **BLACK**

Reserve black for numbering pages. It's too heavy and dense for much else.

5. BEWARE OF COLOR CODING

Beginners often try to organize their work by color coding – one color for headings, a second color for key points, a third for sub points, etc. This usually turns into a mixed-up mess. A group's thinking process is generative and dynamic – its categories keep shifting as people build on each other's ideas. *"Rough-draft thinking" is not the time for color coding.* By contrast, color coding is very effective with documents like agendas that are created before the meeting begins, or whenever the content of the document is known in advance.

6. USE THE *CHARTWRITER'S GRIP* TO HOLD 4 MARKERS AT ONCE

The *ChartWriter's grip* involves sticking a marker between each finger on the hand you don't write with. Keep the tops off and point the ink-tips outward. This way you are ready for action with any color!

SYMBOLS

1. BULLETS

Bullets are big dots that make items stand apart from one another. Use them often – especially when listing ideas.

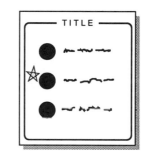

2. STARS

A star indicates that something is especially noteworthy.

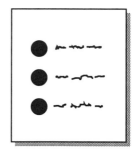

3. BORDERS

Borders have a pleasant visual impact. They can be used to frame a whole page, or to highlight certain blocks of text, or a title. Pink or orange borders work beautifully.

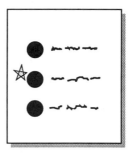

4. CIRCLES

Circles can do many things, such as:
- lasso one idea and connect it with another;
- draw attention to a decision that has been made;
- highlight the most important issue on the page;
- separate and categorize information on the page;
- break up the visual monotony of a page full of text.

SYMBOLS

5. ARROWS

An arrow is a very powerful symbol. For example, you can use arrows to demonstrate that:

- Idea A and Idea B are a vicious cycle;
- Idea 1 comes first, Idea 2 comes second;
- Ideas X, Y and Z all belong to Topic Q.

Arrows create automatic connections. Make sure the connections are actually being suggested by group members. If the group thinks you are connecting ideas for them, you will lose your neutrality. They may resent you or feel manipulated.

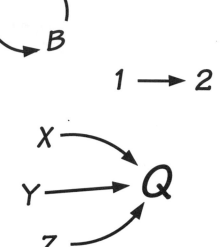

6. OTHER SYMBOLS

Many ideas can be expressed with simple drawings.

* The "Star-Person" was created by David Sibbet, who has developed a large family of easy-to-draw Star-People. See David's *Fundamentals of Graphic Language Practice Book*, San Francisco: Grove Consultants, 1991.

LAYOUT: SPACING

1. LETTER SIZE

One inch is a good height for letters. If the group is very large, some people will be sitting far away and you may have to write larger.

2. MARGINS

Margins should be at least two inches on all four sides of the page. Having empty space near each line of text encourages members to edit, or add to their previous ideas. This space is also useful for tallying votes – as, for example, when group members prioritize a long list of ideas.

3. BETWEEN LINES

Leave at least one inch between lines of text.

4. INDENTING

Indenting is nice looking and easy to read – especially when each indented line starts with a bullet.

5. UNDERLINING

Leave three inches below underlined words.

6. WHITE SPACE

White space is your friend. An open, spacious page looks inviting and gives the group a breezy feeling about its work. Crowded pages look hectic and heavy. Use as much paper as you need to give the group an expansive canvas upon which to paint their thinking.

7. DON'T CROWD THE BOTTOM OF THE PAGE

Make sure the size and spacing of your writing is the same at the bottom of the page as it is at the top.

Start a new page before you really need to, because a group will lower their output at the end of a page. Participants often behave as if the task is finished once the page is full. If you start a new page, it is amazing how frequently people catch a second wind and start generating new material.

LAYOUT: FORMAT

1. THE LIST

The list is the most common format. It consists of a title, or heading, followed by a series of items. A list often has subtitles with items under each one. Put a bullet in front of each item.

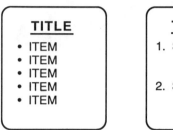

2. THE MATRIX

A matrix is a grid with headings placed both horizontally (across the top) and vertically (along the left side). A matrix can be used to help a group discuss relationships between two or more variables.

	PRO'S	CON'S
IDEA 1		
IDEA 2		
IDEA 3		

3. THE FLOW CHART

A flow chart can describe how something works, or it can show a sequence of events.

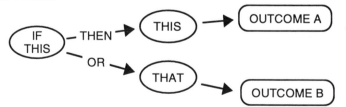

LAYOUT: FORMAT

4. THE ORBIT DIAGRAM

An orbit diagram can highlight a key point and describe others in a less linear way.

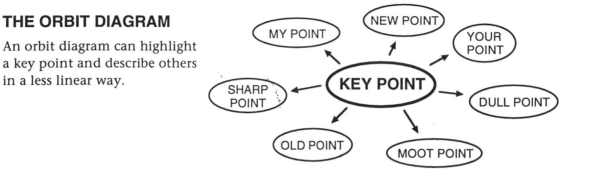

5. FORMATS FOR OPEN DISCUSSION

If you are recording an unstructured, open discussion, you may not be able to use a structured format.

When you are using a pad of paper on an easel, the safest approach is to *skip three or four lines* after each new thought. As the conversation goes along, you will often want to go back to fill in the blank spaces.

When you are cutting sheets from rolls of paper and have lots of space, you may find the following approach valuable:

- Mentally divide the sheet of paper into five sections. Do not actually draw the sections on the paper. (The illustration below is only meant to show you, the reader, the arrangement of the sections.)

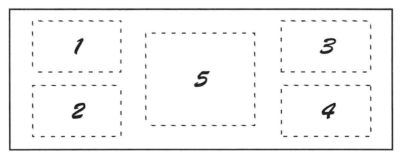

- As you record the discussion, put each completely new theme into a different section. Within each section, record using the list format. *Leave the center section blank.*

- As the discussion moves along, group members often notice that they can use the center space to list central themes of the discussion.

DECIDING HOW MUCH TO WRITE

WHAT TO LISTEN FOR   **HOW TO WRITE IT**

Suggestions

Example: "Let's check in daily
between now and the conference."

CHECK IN DAILY
TILL CONFERENCE

Logical Connections

Example: "In this organization,
it's clear to me that absences
and low morale are related to
one another."

ABSENCES   →   LOW
               MORALE

Summary Statements

Example: "So what we're saying is
that we want this program to target
both teachers and parents."

TARGET GROUP:
TEACHERS AND PARENTS

Unanswered Questions

Example: "I know this is off the
subject, but I'm still confused about
whether we're ever going to hire a
new financial assistant."

☆ HIRE FINANCIAL ASS'T?

 OPEN QUESTION

Don't worry about capturing every word a speaker says – just be sure to
preserve the meaning of what has been said.

CHARTWRITING IN ACTION

1. SENTENCES ARE EASY TO READ

"Send note to caterer" is much easier to understand than "note to caterer" because it includes a noun and a verb. Here's the guideline: *will this be understandable in a week?*

2. DON'T BE SHY—WRITE "WE" AND "I"

Some beginners feel awkward using these pronouns. For example, instead of writing "We want a meeting," a beginner might write "They want a meeting" or "You want a meeting." Remember: it's the group's record – write with their voice.

3. VERBS AND NOUNS ARE HIGH PRIORITY

Example: If you hear "I hope we remember to write a warm thank you note to that great caterer," get the key verbs and nouns first – "Remember: send note to caterer."

4. ADJECTIVES AND ADVERBS ARE LOW PRIORITY

It's fine to write the adjectives and adverbs – like "warm" and "great" in the example above – but only if you have the time.

5. USE ONLY STANDARD ABBREVIATIONS

Do not invent abbreviations in order to write faster. For example, do not write "defnt" for "definite," or "expl" for "explain." Here's the guideline: *will this be understandable to someone who is not at the meeting?*

6. TITLE EVERY PAGE

Every page needs a title, even if it says "[title of previous page] continued."

7. ENCOURAGE PROOFREADING

Invite people to read over your work. Accept corrections gladly – even if it messes up your beautiful chart.

AFTER THE MEETING

1. CHECK PAGE NUMBERS

Make sure all pages are ordered and numbered understandably.

2. CHECK TITLES

Add titles if you didn't have a chance during the meeting.

3. PUT THE LIDS BACK ON YOUR MARKERS

If you don't, they'll dry out! At more than a dollar per marker, that's a lot of ink to waste. Besides, nothing is more irritating than getting ready for a session, only to discover at the last moment that your brown or blue marker doesn't work.

4. ROLL UP THE PAGES TOGETHER, AND LABEL THEM

Flipcharts are often brought back to the next meeting. It is difficult to hang pages that have fold-creases in them. It's also difficult to read them. Therefore, when you're taking charts off the wall, roll rather than fold.

Label the ouside of the rolled-up paper with three items of information:
- Name of the meeting
- Date of the meeting
- Topics

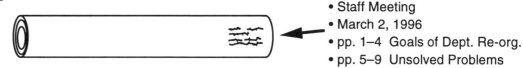

- Staff Meeting
- March 2, 1996
- pp. 1–4 Goals of Dept. Re-org.
- pp. 5–9 Unsolved Problems

5. SECURE THE PAGES WITH TWO RUBBER BANDS

6. GIVE THE CHARTS TO WHOMEVER WILL USE THEM NEXT

Hand the charts to the appropriate person, rather than putting them down. Similarly, don't carry the charts away unless you have been assigned that responsibility.

7. CONDUCT YOURSELF PROFESSIONALLY

Each of the previous six steps is an excellent opportunity to demonstrate thoroughness and efficiency. Group members will notice it. They may not acknowledge it verbally, but they will recognize that they are working with a professional.

8

BRAINSTORMING

THE THEORY AND TECHNIQUE OF SUSPENDED JUDGMENT

- ▶ The Cost of Premature Criticism

- ▶ Suspended Judgment

- ▶ Ground Rules for Brainstorming

- ▶ Facilitator's Do's and Don'ts for Brainstorming

- ▶ The Many Uses of Brainstorming

THE COST OF PREMATURE CRITICISM

Rough-draft thinking is just like rough-draft writing – it needs encouragement, not evaluation. Many people don't understand this – if they notice a flaw in someone's thinking, they point it out. They think they've been helpful. But rough-draft ideas need to be clarified, researched, and modified before being subjected to critical evaluation. The timing of critical evaluation can make the difference between the life and death of a new idea.

EXAMPLE

A small but growing law firm was looking for office space. The firm's administrator researched the possibilities, then offered a proposal: "I found 8,000 square feet on the north side of town for $10,000 per month for a one-year lease. The owner will lower the rent to $8,000 if we sign a five-year lease. We could offset our rent by subletting to the current tenant. The north side isn't great at night, but it's near public transportation and has plenty of parking. I think we should seriously consider this location." This was a fully-developed proposal, ready to be critiqued. If it contained any flaws, now was the time to find them.

However, several months earlier, the group had shot down the administrator's initial proposal. "Since larger spaces are cheaper," the administrator had said, "what if we rented a big office and sublet some of it?" Someone responded, "Forget it, we don't have time or energy to find people to sublet." Someone else said, "I don't want to be responsible for too much space. After all, every landlord in town will make us sign a five-year lease – we could really get stuck."

Note that these quick reactions were based on erroneous assumptions. It did not require much effort to find a sublet, and the firm did not have to sign a five-year lease. Nonetheless, some participants were so quick to criticize the administrator's thinking that they killed the idea before the group had a chance to develop it. After the first discussion, the administrator stopped looking for places that required sublets. But six months later, after looking and looking for a smaller office at a good rent, he remembered his original idea and pursued it.

Premature criticism is often inaccurate. And stifling. When ideas are criticized before they are fully formed, many people feel discouraged and stop trying. Furthermore, they may become unwilling to volunteer their rough-draft thinking at future meetings. They anticipate objections and keep quiet unless they can invent a counterargument. Thus, people learn to practice self-censorship. A group is then deprived of access to its most valuable natural resource: the creative thinking of its members.

SUSPENDED JUDGMENT
COMMON QUESTIONS & ANSWERS

1. **How can I suspend my judgment if I truly do not agree with what someone else is saying?**

Suspended judgment does not imply agreement; it implies tolerance. You don't have to let go of *anything* – you're just making room for other people to express *their* ideas.

2. **What if I know that an idea won't work?**

Suspended judgment encourages people to use their creative imagination. This often produces impossible ideas. For example, "If we were all 20 feet tall we could save lots of gasoline by walking more." You don't have to believe an idea is *true*; just let yourself "try it on" and see what your imagination produces. After all, "if humans could fly" was a crazy idea until the twentieth century.

3. **Isn't collecting silly ideas a waste of time? Wouldn't it be more efficient for us to focus on the realistic options?**

Suspended judgment comes into play precisely when the so-called "realistic" options have all been found lacking. In other words, creative thinking is the most efficient use of a group's time when nothing else works!

4. **Doesn't suspended judgment produce chaotic discussions that go off in a dozen directions?**

Only if the process is handled poorly. To use suspended judgment effectively, the group should establish clear ground rules and a clear time limit. To paraphrase de Bono,* the more informality you want your group to achieve with the *content* of your thinking, the more structured formality you need in the *process* of your thinking.

5. **If I suspend judgment of an idea I think is wrong, how will I get a chance to critique that idea?**

Suspended judgment is *temporary*, not permanent. Most processes that call for suspended judgment are designed to last no more than thirty minutes. *Suspended* does not mean *abandoned*.

* Source: *Lateral Thinking*, E. de Bono, New York: Harper & Row, 1970, p. 151.

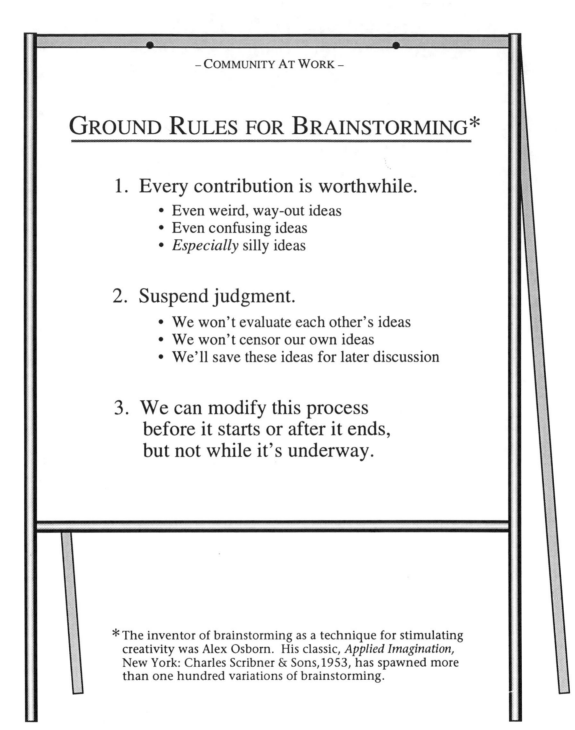

– COMMUNITY AT WORK –

GROUND RULES FOR BRAINSTORMING*

1. Every contribution is worthwhile.

- Even weird, way-out ideas
- Even confusing ideas
- *Especially* silly ideas

2. Suspend judgment.

- We won't evaluate each other's ideas
- We won't censor our own ideas
- We'll save these ideas for later discussion

3. We can modify this process before it starts or after it ends, but not while it's underway.

*The inventor of brainstorming as a technique for stimulating creativity was Alex Osborn. His classic, *Applied Imagination*, New York: Charles Scribner & Sons, 1953, has spawned more than one hundred variations of brainstorming.

When introducing the technique of formal brainstorming to a group, spend a little time discussing the value of *suspended judgment*. Then ask each participant if s/he is willing to follow these ground rules. If one or more members are not, encourage the group to modify the ground rules to fit the needs of all members.

FACILITATOR TIPS FOR BRAINSTORMING

DO

- Do a lot of *mirroring* to keep things moving at a fast clip.

- Do encourage people to take turns.

- Do treat silly ideas the same as serious ideas.

- Do move around to create a lively feeling.

- Do say, "Let's see if I've got it right so far" if a person is difficult to follow.

- Do repeat the purpose often: "Who else can explain why our office systems are so inefficient?"

- Do start a new flipchart page before the previous one is full.

- Do give a warning that the end is approaching.

- Do expect a second wind of creative ideas after the obvious ones are exhausted.

DON'T

- Don't interrupt.

- Don't say, "We've already got that one."

- Don't say, "Ooh, good one!"

- Don't say, "Hey, you don't really want me to write that one, do you?"

- Don't favor the "best" thinkers.

- Don't use frowns, raised eyebrows or other nonverbal gestures that signal disapproval.

- Don't give up the first time the group seems stuck.

- Don't simultaneously be the leader, the facilitator, and the chartwriter.

- Don't start the process without clearly setting the time limit.

- Don't rush or pressure the group. Silence usually means that people are thinking.

THE WIDE WORLD OF BRAINSTORMING

Most groups use brainstorming for very limited purposes – generating solutions to a problem or creating new products. But brainstorming can be put to a much greater variety of uses. It can be used to help build lists of such things as:

- NEW GOALS

- UNDERLYING CAUSES OF A PROBLEM

- POINTS OF VIEW HELD BY PERSONS NOT IN THE ROOM

- UNEXPRESSED CONCERNS

- HELPFUL PEOPLE OR RESOURCES

- WAYS TO BUILD TEAMWORK

- NEW DIRECTIONS OF INQUIRY

- LESSONS FROM THE PAST

- OBSTACLES TO MEETING A GOAL

- WAYS TO IMPROVE HOW A MEETING IS RUN

- HIDDEN BELIEFS OR ASSUMPTIONS

- SOURCES OF INSPIRATION

Groups members' willingness to *suspend judgment* will probably free them to list ideas or perspectives they would not otherwise consider.

9

TOOLS FOR MANAGING LONG LISTS

ORGANIZING DIVERGENT STRANDS
OF THOUGHT

▶ What to Do After the Brainstorm

▶ Theory and Technique
of Categorizing

▶ Methods for Selecting Priorities

▶ Formats for Selecting Priorities

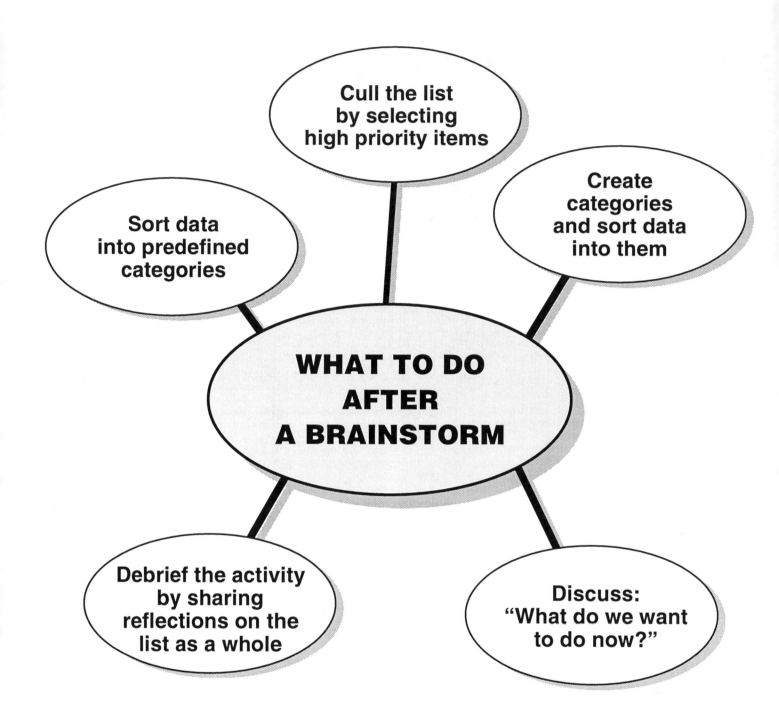

It's easy to get overwhelmed by the sheer volume of ideas that are generated by a divergent-thinking process. Many people respond to this dilemma by glomming onto one idea and pushing the group to focus on it. This knee-jerk reaction almost always plunges a group into the Groan Zone, because different people usually want to focus on different items. Several better options are indicated above. Techniques for culling and categorizing are discussed in detail on the following pages.

CATEGORIZING IN THE REAL WORLD

INTRODUCTION

When a group has finished a brainstorming process, they often want to categorize the resulting list of items. This is natural. Most people cannot hold long lists in their head; they get overwhelmed. The group has to find some way of reducing the list to a manageable number of items, and many people think categorizing is the easiest way to get all that data under control. But categorizing involves two separate mental tasks – *creating categories* and *sorting items into categories* – and groups easily confuse these two tasks.

Creating categories is a relatively challenging task for a group, because people don't easily reach agreement on the meaning or the importance of a given category. Therefore, this task takes time. *Sorting,* on the other hand, is comparatively straightforward once the categories are well-defined. The problem is that most groups want to do the task of creating categories, but they want it to *feel* as simple and easy as the task of sorting items into categories. This problem is illustrated by the following case study.

CASE STUDY

A group of front-line supervisors brainstormed a list of "Ways To Get More Training." They decided to categorize the list. First they created four categories: *Workshops; Apprenticeships; Readings;* and *Finding Mentors.* Then they began to sort each item into the four categories.

Soon someone suggested that some of the items might better fit into a new category, *Going Back to School.* This elicited a debate on whether or not *Going Back to School* was the same as *Workshops.* The discussion ended with an agreement to add the new category. Then the group immediately got caught in a disagreement over where to place the item "take classes on computer skills." Should it be placed in *Workshops* or in *Going Back to*

School? After a brief squabble, the members decided to put it in both places. But people were starting to get that feeling of "hey I don't care, let's just get on with it."

Then someone pointed out that many of their ideas for apprenticeships involved mentors. "Don't all apprenticeships," he asked, "require mentoring? I don't know if mentoring should even be a separate category." Several participants now got involved in a spirited discussion about the role of a mentor. They found this issue to be interesting on its own merits. Unfortunately not everyone felt this way. A few members got very antsy. One person, irritation in her voice, asked, "What difference does it make? Come on, *please.*"

This led someone to say, "Let's get focused. What's our purpose here? What are we trying to accomplish by doing this categorizing?" And sure enough, the next three speakers had three different answers to that question.

At this point, forty minutes into what was expected to be a quick-and-easy sorting task, someone said, "Hey folks, we're making this way too hard. Let's just do it and get it over with." And many heads nodded, desperately. From that point on, everyone agreed to anything; the experience had gone sour and people wanted just to be done with it. Five minutes later it was over.

And the finished product? It was typed up and promptly forgotten.

CATEGORIZING IN THE REAL WORLD

INSIGHTS

THE NATURE OF THE PROBLEM

Why is categorizing harder than people expect it to be? First of all, many people tend to assume that crucial terms mean the same thing to everyone. ("Why are we wasting time over the meaning of *Workshops?* Let's just use common sense.") But, in fact, people *don't* share common meanings for the terms they're using, and this causes group members to feel pulled in two opposing directions: should we slow down and make an effort to define our terms or would that just be a waste of precious time? This tension between the desire to clarify meaning and the desire to complete the task creates an uncomfortable undercurrent of ambiguity.

In addition, individuals vary greatly in the *number* of categories they use to organize their perceptions. Some people are detail-oriented. Their minds make a lot of distinctions between things, and as a result they tend to subdivide a list into many categories. Others are global thinkers; they make fewer distinctions because their minds operate at a more general, more abstract level of analysis. Accordingly, they tend to subdivide a list into fewer categories. Neither approach is right or wrong. But when people with both types of cognitive styles try to create categories together, they are destined to disagree on such issues as whether *Workshops* is a separate category from *Go Back to School*.

USING PREDEFINED CATEGORIES

In the case study, it would have been much easier for the group if they had used predefined categories to sort their list. For example, suppose the group sorted their items by *Cost*. Some items would be *Expensive*. Some would be *Mid-range*. And some would be *Cheap*. The sorting would have proceeded more smoothly and produced useful results. After identifying some inexpensive training opportunities and some expensive ones, the group would have been able to discuss next steps.

Sorting the list into predefined categories can usually be done quite adequately by two or three people. When done, they show their work to everyone else for revision. While the small group sorts the list, the large group can take a break. Or the large group could divide into teams that sort the same list into additional predefined categories. For example, one team could sort the list by *Desirability* while another team sorted by *Urgency*.

CATEGORIZING IN THE REAL WORLD

OPTIONS

CREATING CATEGORIES FROM SCRATCH

Creating categories together means having a philosophical discussion. This is both the value and the cost of creating categories from scratch. A philosophical discussion puts a group into the Groan Zone, where they will have to struggle to integrate one another's beliefs and definitions. The process is uncomfortable and frustrating, and people will resist it. Sometimes the result is worth the struggle; often it is not.

When people present and define their own categories, they are essentially presenting their own worldview. Sometimes this is worth doing – such as when group members have not yet discussed their values or goals. Consider, for example, a community planning group made up of teachers, parents and elected officials. The members of this type of group have diverse frames of reference. It may be well worth their time to use a discussion of categories as a way to develop mutual understanding. A similar example in a business setting would be a product-development group consisting of members from marketing, manufacturing, and research and development. In cases like these, the opportunity to define categories can prove very useful.

SUMMARY

Creating categories is a difficult task. It takes a lot of time and can produce a lot of frustration. It should be done when people want to gain a deeper understanding of one another's values and goals. *Sorting items into predefined categories* is a fairly simple task. It should be done whenever the primary reason for categorizing a list is to reduce the list to a mentally manageable number of items. A list of thirty or forty items can be sorted in roughly ten minutes by two or three people. The results can then be reviewed by the whole group and revised as needed.

Because the opportunity to categorize a list arises so frequently in meetings, facilitators must understand the differences between *creating categories* and *sorting.* Those who do can make a real contribution to the development of a group's thinking skills.

TWO METHODS OF CATEGORIZING

CREATING CATEGORIES FROM A LIST OF IDEAS

1. Each person, in turn, proposes his/her own set of categories. It is acceptable to propose one category or many, on each turn.

2. Everyone takes as many turns as they want. Combinations and variations are encouraged.

3. After all sets of categories have been listed, discuss them.

4. Sometimes the group's thinking converges easily into one set of categories. If so, the task is done. If not, be prepared for a lengthy discussion.

SORTING A LIST INTO PREDEFINED CATEGORIES

1. As a group, select one or more predefined categories. Example: "How urgent is each item – high, medium or low?" (See next page.)

2. Recruit two or three people to sort the list.

3. The sorters should review the list item by item, making sure to place every item in a category.

4. Tell the sorters that it is perfectly fine to place one item in more than one category – especially if they disagree about the "right" category.

5. When the list has been sorted, bring it back to the large group.

COMMON PREDEFINED CATEGORIES

CATEGORIES ——————— SUBCATEGORIES ———————

CATEGORIES	SUBCATEGORIES			
URGENCY	High	Medium	Low	Unknown
TIME NEEDED	A lot	Some	Not much	Unknown
COST	Expensive	Mid-range	Cheap	Unknown
FEASIBILITY	Probably will work	Fifty-fifty chance	Probably won't work	Uncertain
DESIRABILITY	Highly desirable	Worth a try	Undesirable	Unknown
USEFULNESS	Highly useful	Useful	Not very useful	Unknown
NEXT STEPS	Collect more info	Talk to boss	Meet with someone	Analyze further

There is nothing sacred about these categories; they are simply useful in many situations. Some situations may call for a category that is not listed on this page. For example, at times it might be useful to sort a list by "likelihood of generating intense emotions." Everyone should feel free to create a category to fit the circumstances.

SELECTING HIGH PRIORITY ITEMS FROM A LONG LIST

METHODS

CAST FIVE STRAWS

1. Each member gets five straw votes. S/he can distribute these straw votes any way s/he wants.

2. It's okay to cast all five for the same item. It's also okay to cast straws for five different items.

3. Half-votes are permitted, but not encouraged.

4. The top five items become the group's high priority list.

GREATEST HITS

1. Divide the number of items on the brainstormed list by three.

2. Each person receives that number of choices to indicate his or her favorite items.

3. Everyone may distribute his or her choices any way s/he wants.

4. The top third of the list – i.e., the items chosen most often – becomes the group's list of greatest hits.

CHOOSE AS MANY AS YOU LIKE

1. Each person votes as many times as s/he wants.

2. Each person casts one vote for every item s/he wants the group to treat as a high priority.

3. All items that receive unanimous or nearly unanimous support become the group's high priority list. (Note: Most groups define near-unanimity as "unanimity minus one" or "unanimity minus two."

SELECTING HIGH PRIORITY ITEMS FROM A LONG LIST

FORMATS

METHOD	HOW TO DO IT	MAJOR ADVANTAGE	MAJOR DRAWBACK
ITEM BY ITEM	The facilitator reads down the list one item at a time, noting how many people raise their hands for each item. Example: "Okay, how many people like item #3? How many like item #4?" and so on.	Reduces awareness of the preferences of influential members.	With lengthy lists of options, this is usually a tedious, draining experience.
PERSON BY PERSON	Each person takes a turn to state his/her preferences. Often a go-around is the simplest way to get this done.	Gives people permission to be assertive.	Those who go last have an unfair advantage – they can revise their preferences based on what others have said.
EVERYONE AT THE WALL	Everyone stands up, takes a colored marker, and puts dots beside his/her preferences.	People get out of their chair and move around. This often has a positive, energizing affect on the group's mood.	With short lists, this method is often overkill.
SECRET BALLOT	All items on the list are numbered. Participants indicate their preference by writing their chosen numbers privately on paper. Results are tabulated by two or more people.	Useful in highly controversial situations, especially when someone might make a different choice if his/her vote were going to be made public.	Reinforces the perception that it is not safe for people to reveal their preferences openly.

TEN COMMON TACTICS
FOR MISHANDLING A LENGTHY LIST

☑

☐ 1. Roll up the flipcharts and put them under your desk.

☐ 2. Take a break and never come back.

☐ 3. Say, "Let's categorize these quickly, then move on." And then, two hours later . . .

☐ 4. Publish the list in the next newsletter, to show everyone that your group is making progress.

☐ 5. Vaguely recall a similar list that was generated at a meeting last year, then postpone further consideration of the current list until the old one can be found. "After all, we don't want to do the same work all over again."

☐ 6. Have someone go away and sort the list – then at the next meeting forget to put that person on the agenda.

☐ 7. Give the flipcharts to the secretary to type up.

☐ 8. Assume that every item is now taking care of itself. Later, complain bitterly about the problems that still exist. "I thought we decided . . ."

☐ 9. Try to shorten the list by combining items, then argue over the meaning of each new item.

☐ 10. Congratulate yourself on a very productive meeting.

10

DEALING WITH
DIFFICULT DYNAMICS

SUPPORTIVE INTERVENTIONS
THAT DON'T MAKE ANYONE WRONG

- ▶ Understanding the Phenomenon of "The Difficult Person"

- ▶ Inventory of Typical Mistakes and Effective Interventions

- ▶ Overcoming the Tendency to Defer to Authority

- ▶ Handling Out-of-Context Distractions

- ▶ Stepping Back from the Discussion to Talk about the Process

- ▶ Discussing Difficult Dynamics

DIFFICULT DYNAMICS PRODUCE DIFFICULT PEOPLE

Periods of misunderstanding and confusion are normal when a group has to wrestle with a difficult problem. These periods are characterized by feelings of tedium, tension and a general sense of impatience and frustration. Even though these are normal experiences, they are nonetheless unpleasant.

Staying focused at such times is an enormous challenge. Clear-headed thinking deteriorates as emotional urgency intensifies. Some people get so exasperated and overwhelmed they can barely pay attention. Others feel compelled to take over the leadership of the discussion, whether or not they know how to do it effectively. Some people just want to withdraw and get away. And others, feeling their anger rise, struggle privately to stay cool – when what they *really* want to do is pick a fight.

Despite the rise in tension, many people continue making efforts to stay present and committed to the task. They keep trying – but they're trying under pressure. This can't help but affect their moods, their presentation styles, and their thinking abilities. Their behavior toward others may be less than sensitive. They might blurt out their ideas with less tact than usual. They might go on and on – oblivious to the effect they're having on their audience – because they feel they're on the verge of an important line of thought. These are a few of the countless examples of the symptoms people exhibit when trying to contribute their best thinking under stress.

The expression of these symptoms makes many people uncomfortable. If there is a facilitator, people usually look to the facilitator to "save them" from their anguish. Indeed, many popular books* claim that the facilitator's proper response to difficult dynamics is to "control those difficult people." For example, it's conventional wisdom to talk to such a person during the break and ask him or her to tone it down. Similarly, most people expect a facilitator to interrupt people who deviate from a topic and exhort them to "get back on track." We believe, however, that so-called solutions like these are based on a faulty line of analysis – namely, that eliminating a symptom will somehow remove the cause of the distress.

This chapter offers the reader a different perspective. Difficult dynamics are treated as group situations that can be handled supportively rather than as individual personalities which need to be fixed. On the first four pages, advice is given for handling twelve common "difficult" situations. The remaining pages provide tools that help group members work together to tackle *any* pattern they may wish to change.

* For example, see *Dinosaur Brains*, A. Bernstein, New York: Balantine, 1990.

DEALING WITH DIFFICULT DYNAMICS

PROBLEM	TYPICAL MISTAKE	EFFECTIVE RESPONSE
DOMINATION BY A HIGHLY VERBAL MEMBER	Inexperienced facilitators often try to control this person. "Excuse me, Mr. Q, do you mind if I let someone else take a turn?" Or, even worse, "Excuse me, Ms. Q, you're taking up a lot of the group's time . . ."	When one person is over-participating, everyone else is under-participating. So, focus your efforts on the passive majority. Encourage *them* to participate more. Trying to change the dominant person merely gives that person all the more attention.
GOOFING AROUND IN THE MIDST OF A DISCUSSION	It's tempting to try to "organize" people by getting into a power struggle with them. "Okay, everybody, let's get refocused." This only works when the problem isn't very serious.	*Aim for a break as soon as possible.* People have become undisciplined because they are overloaded or worn out. After a breather, they will be much better able to focus.
LOW PARTICIPATION BY THE ENTIRE GROUP	Low participation can create the impression that a lot of work is getting done in a hurry. This leads to one of the worst errors a facilitator can make: assume that silence means consent, and *do nothing* to encourage more participation.	Switch from large-group open discussion to a different format that lowers the anxiety level. Often, idea-listing is the perfect remedy. If safety is a major concern, small group activities are very important.

DEALING WITH DIFFICULT DYNAMICS

PROBLEM	TYPICAL MISTAKE	EFFECTIVE RESPONSE
TWO PEOPLE LOCKING HORNS	A lot of time can get wasted trying to "resolve a conflict" between two people who have no intention of reaching agreement. People often use one another as sparring partners, in order to clarify their own ideas.	Reach out to other members and say, "Who else has an opinion on this issue?" or, "Let's step back for a minute – are there any other issues that need to be discussed?" Remember: don't focus your attention on the dominant minority, focus on the passive majority.
ONE OR TWO SILENT MEMBERS IN A GROUP WHOSE OTHER MEMBERS PARTICIPATE ACTIVELY	"Mr. Z, you haven't talked much today. Is there anything you'd like to add?" This may work when a shy member has non-verbally indicated a wish to speak. But all too often, the quiet person feels put on the spot and withdraws further.	"I'd like to get opinions from those who haven't talked for a while." Breaking into small groups works even better. Small groups allow shy members to speak up without having to compete for "air time."
WHISPERING AND SIDE JOKES	Facilitators commonly ignore this behavior in the hope that it will go away. Sometimes it does, but it frequently gets worse.	With warmth and humor, make an appeal for decorum. "As you know, those who don't hear the joke often wonder if someone is laughing at *them*." If the problem persists, assume there's a reason. Has the topic become boring and stale? Do people need a break? Or the reverse – maybe *everyone* needs time for small group discussion.

DEALING WITH DIFFICULT DYNAMICS

PROBLEM	TYPICAL MISTAKE	EFFECTIVE RESPONSE
MINIMAL PARTICIPATION BY MEMBERS WHO DON'T FEEL INVESTED IN THE TOPIC	Act as though silence signifies agreement with what's been said. Ignore them and be thankful they're not making trouble.	Look for an opportunity to have a discussion on "What's important to me about this topic?" Have people break into small groups to begin the discussion. This gives everyone time to explore their own stake in the outcome.
POOR FOLLOW-THROUGH ON ASSIGNMENTS	Give an ineffective pep-talk. Ignore it. "We didn't really need that information anyway." Put most of the responsibility on one or two people.	Have people do assignments in teams. Build in a report-back process at a midpoint before the assignment is due. This gives anyone having trouble a chance to get help.
FAILURE TO START ON TIME AND END ON TIME	Wait for the arrival of all the "people who count." This obviously means starting late – but hey, what else can you do? When it's time to end, go overtime without asking. If anyone has to leave, they should tiptoe out.	Start when you say you're going to start. (Waiting encourages lateness.) If you must go overtime, call a break so people can "phone home." If going overtime is recurrent, improve your agenda planning.

DEALING WITH DIFFICULT DYNAMICS

PROBLEM	TYPICAL MISTAKE	EFFECTIVE RESPONSE
QUIBBLING ABOUT TRIVIAL PROCEDURES	Lecture the group about wasting time and "spinning our wheels." Space out, doodle and think to yourself, "It's their fault we're not getting anything done."	Have the group step back from the content of the issue and talk about the process. Ask the group, "What is really going on here?"
SOMEONE BECOMES STRIDENT AND REPETITIVE	At lunch, talk behind the person's back. Tell the person-in-charge that s/he must take more control. Confront the person during a break. Then, when the meeting resumes, act surprised when his/her anxiety goes through the roof!	People repeat themselves because they don't feel heard. Summarize the person's point of view until s/he feels understood. Encourage participants to state the views of group members whose views are different from their own.
SOMEONE DISCOVERS A COMPLETELY NEW PROBLEM THAT NO ONE HAD PREVIOUSLY NOTED	Try to come up with reasons why the group would not need to focus on that issue. Pretend not to hear the person's comments.	Wake up! This may be what you've been waiting for – the doorway into a new way of thinking about the whole situation.

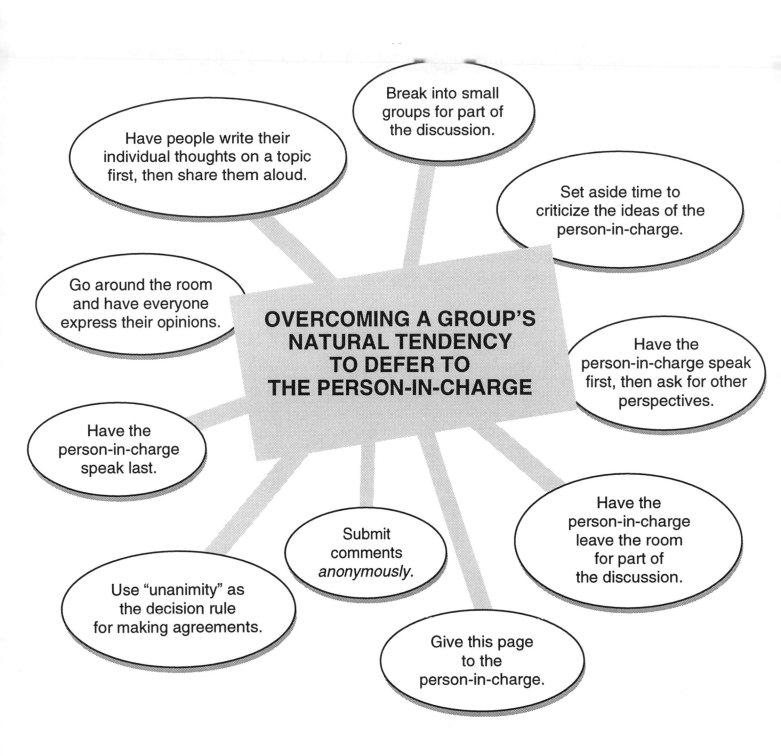

The most straightforward way to overcome a group's tendency to defer to the person-in-charge is to *identify the tendency and educate the group.* Acknowledge that it takes courage to speak truthfully in a hierarchy. Ask people to discuss what they might say differently if the person-in-charge were not in the room. Some people will respond defensively; others will be surprisingly honest. Remember that everyone – from the boldest risk-taker to the most cautious diplomat – will need the facilitator's respect and support.

ACKNOWLEDGING DISTRACTIONS

THE SITUATION

Current events sometimes interfere with a group's ability to concentrate. After a terrible storm, for example, people need to talk about their flooded basements and leaking roofs. After an election, people need to discover how they feel about the potential impacts. During an organizational transition – a massive layoff, say – people need to let off steam and express their anxieties.

What should a group do when faced with distractions like these? Many people believe that the best response is to ignore their existence. This belief is grounded in value judgments however, not in empirical fact. Realistically, the presence of a serious distraction will lower a group's efficiency *regardless of what group members are officially allowed to talk about.*

This activity gives people the chance to spend a well-structured period of time talking about what's really on their minds. After expressing themselves, people are often better able to concentrate on the work at hand.

THE TECHNIQUE

1. If it's obvious that the group is having trouble focusing on the topic at hand, suggest that people talk about whatever might be the source of distraction. For example, "I notice we're having a hard time concentrating on this subject, and I'm aware that [the recent event] is on a lot of people's minds. Could we step back and spend a few minutes talking about [the event]?"

2. After securing agreement from the group to proceed, pose an open-ended question, such as "What *are* people feeling about [the event]?" Ask everyone to respond.

3. When everyone has spoken, suggest a sequence for making the transition back to the main topic. For example, "What if we spend a few more minutes in this conversation, then take a short break and return to the main topic after the break?"

STEP BACK FROM THE DISCUSSION AND TALK ABOUT THE PROCESS

THE SITUATION

Meetings sometimes get bogged down for unknown reasons. For example, during a discussion some people keep bringing up a topic about which the group had already made a decision. At such times a facilitator may be tempted to ask the group, "What's going on here? We appear to be stuck; does anyone have any ideas why?"

One might expect such a comment to help a group reflect on their process. But it seldom works. The sudden "level shift" is too confusing. A few people will respond to the facilitator, but most will keep discussing the original topic. The problem is that some people don't realize they are being asked to step back from the discussion and talk about their process.

Here's a better strategy. First, point out that something isn't working. Next, obtain the group's agreement to step back from the discussion and talk about their process. *This is the crucial step.* Once members signal their readiness to proceed, everyone together can explore what's blocking them.

THE TECHNIQUE

1. Describe the predicament. Use facts to support your observations. "The group is having trouble staying on topic. Three people have asked us to stay focused on the budget, but someone keeps changing the subject."

2. Obtain agreement to proceed. "It might be useful to step back from the discussion for a moment and explore what's getting in the way. I have a simple way to do this and would like your agreement to proceed."

3. When agreement is obtained, ask a question that focuses on the process, not the content, of the preceding discussion. For example, "Does anyone have any thoughts about the way we are working together?"

4. After three or four responses ask a more pointed question. For example, "What might be blocking us from working more effectively?"

5. When participants seem ready to return to the original task, prepare the group to make the shift. Ask, "Before you return to [the topic], are there any further reactions to what has just been said?"

6. Option: Call a short break at this point. The group's leadership will probably use the time to rethink the agenda.

DISCUSSING DIFFICULT DYNAMICS

STRENGTHS & IMPROVABLES

1. Hang two sheets of paper. Title one page, "Strengths." Title the other page, "Improvables." *

2. Ask someone to call out a strength. Then ask someone else to call out an improvable. Build the two lists simultaneously.

3. Encourage participants to speak frankly in the spirit of constructive learning.

4. While the lists are being made, the ground rule of suspended judgment is in effect – no defending, explaining or apologizing.

LEARNING FROM LAST WEEK'S EXPERIENCE

1. Ask participants to look back on their last meeting and recall anything that made them feel uncomfortable.

2. Brainstorm a list: What can we do to handle this better in the future?

3. If everyone agrees to abide by one or more items on the list, fine. Often, however, agreement does not come easily because unresolved feelings may still be present. Rather than attempt to force an agreement prematurely, treat steps 1 and 2 as a consciousness-raising activity. Often, simply naming a problem goes a long way toward changing it.

* Many facilitators substitute "+" for "Strengths," and "Δ" (the Greek symbol for change) for "Improvables."

11

DESIGNING REALISTIC AGENDAS

CONCEPTS AND METHODS
FOR THINKING INTO THE FUTURE

- ▶ Planning an Agenda:
  Critical Components

- ▶ Distinguishing Topics from Outcomes

- ▶ Agenda Planning in a Larger Context

- ▶ Options for Work Between Meetings

- ▶ Preventing an Overcrowded Agenda

- ▶ Agenda Planning: Process Design

- ▶ Agenda Planning Roles

SURE-FIRE METHODS FOR CREATING A PATHETIC AGENDA

☑

1. Time the agenda right down to the minute, and assume the meeting will start exactly on time.

2. Assume that everybody will know what you're trying to accomplish at the meeting – if they don't, they'll ask.

3. Plan to spend the first half of the meeting prioritizing what to do in the second half of the meeting.

4. Keep the meeting interesting by making sure the people who give reports use overheads and pie charts.

5. If you've got an agenda of difficult and important items, improve efficiency by skipping breaks and shortening lunch.

6. When the most important discussion is likely to be emotionally charged, save it for last. Maybe the group will be more ready to deal with it by then.

7. Since everyone prefers their meetings to stay on track, assume that no one will raise a topic that's not on the agenda.

8. When you know the agenda is too packed, assume the meeting will run overtime. But don't tell anyone in advance – people sometimes do their best thinking under pressure.

9. To maintain your flexibility, don't put the agenda in writing.

10. Don't waste time planning an agenda. Things never go the way you expect them to.

GOOD AGENDA PLANNING
TWO CRITICAL COMPONENTS

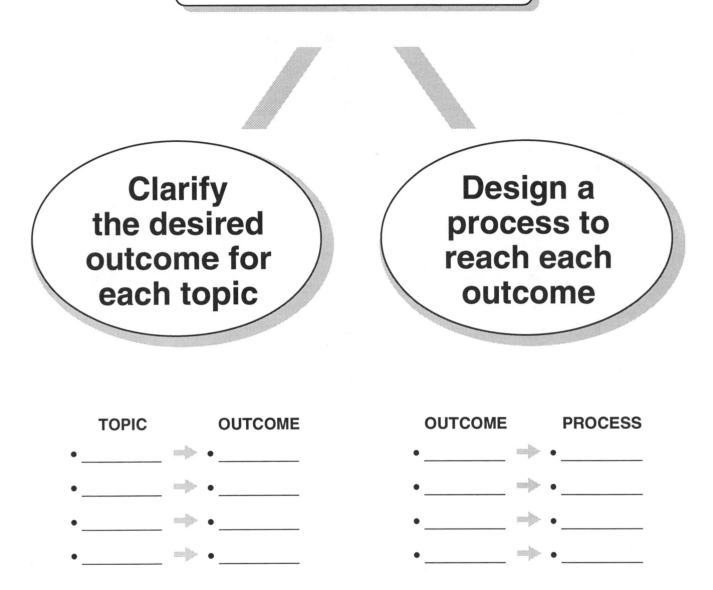

Clarify the desired outcome for each topic

Design a process to reach each outcome

TOPIC		OUTCOME
• _____	➡	• _____
• _____	➡	• _____
• _____	➡	• _____
• _____	➡	• _____

OUTCOME		PROCESS
• _____	➡	• _____
• _____	➡	• _____
• _____	➡	• _____
• _____	➡	• _____

When discussion of a new topic begins, participants need to know what they are expected to achieve during the meeting.

Many topics would be handled more effectively if the process were subdivided into two or three different participation formats.

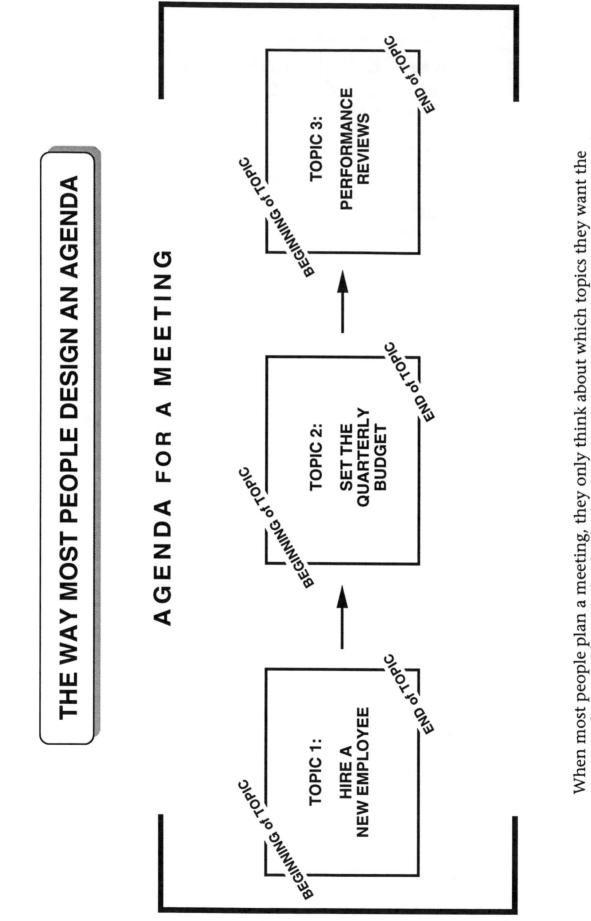

THE WAY MOST PEOPLE DESIGN AN AGENDA

AGENDA FOR A MEETING

BEGINNING of TOPIC

TOPIC 1:

HIRE A NEW EMPLOYEE

END of TOPIC

BEGINNING of TOPIC

TOPIC 2:

SET THE QUARTERLY BUDGET

END of TOPIC

BEGINNING of TOPIC

TOPIC 3:

PERFORMANCE REVIEWS

END of TOPIC

When most people plan a meeting, they only think about which topics they want the group to discuss. They rarely clarify the desired outcomes for each topic. This is a good way to confuse participants at the meeting.

COMMUNITY AT WORK © 1996

A TOPIC CAN HAVE MANY DIFFERENT OUTCOMES

MEETING FOR TODAY'S POSSIBLE OUTCOMES	**TOPIC 1: HIRE A NEW EMPLOYEE**	**TOPIC 2: NEXT QUARTER'S BUDGET**	**TOPIC 3: PERFORMANCE REVIEWS**
	• Reach group agreement on the criteria for an ideal candidate.	• Review this quarter's budget and ask participants to come to the next meeting having identified items that need further discussion.	• Decide whether to schedule performance reviews this quarter or next quarter.
	• First, agree on the criteria for an ideal candidate; then, write a job description.	• Identify items that need further discussion, then assign people to prepare background reports for the next meeting.	• Get out appointment calendars and set up the meeting dates.
	• Both of the above, then assign someone to direct the recruiting process.	• Review this quarter's budget; identify questionable items; discuss; decide on changes.	• Evaluate how well the performance reviews are working; make list of possible improvements.

This chart illustrates the reason it is important for an agenda planner to clarify the desired outcome for each topic s/he places on the agenda. If s/he merely names a topic without stating the expected outcomes, people will make their own assumptions about what they're being asked to accomplish. *This will cause problems.* People who think they have a lot to get done will push for brief discussions and quick decisions. Others, thinking they have more time, may talk at length. What a mess!

COMMUNITY AT WORK © 1996

AGENDA PLANNING IN A LARGER CONTEXT

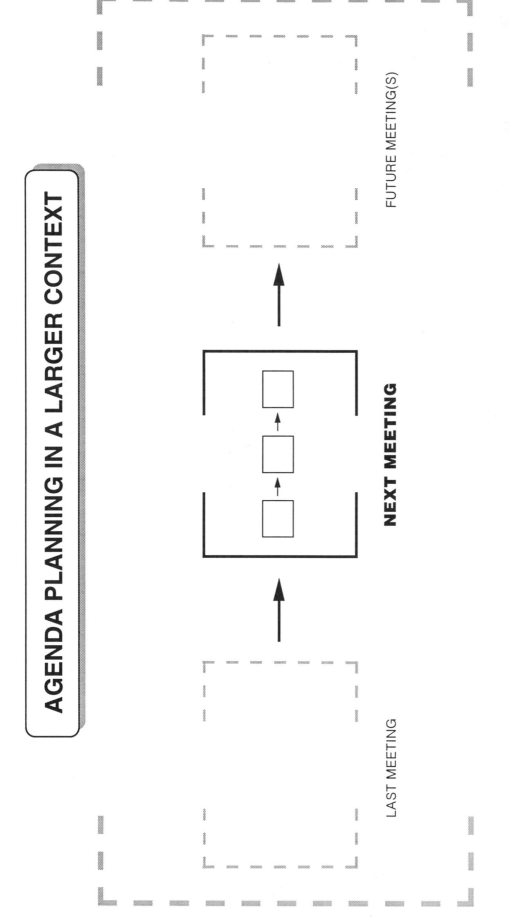

LAST MEETING

NEXT MEETING

FUTURE MEETING(S)

Narrow objectives can be accomplished in single meetings; significant goals take more time. People who do not understand this principle often confuse their overall goals with what they can reasonably expect to accomplish in a short time frame. For example, many boards of directors believe it's possible to plan their agency's five-year goals and objectives at a one-day retreat. Effective agenda-planners, by contrast, clarify the "big picture goals," then spread out the work over a series of meetings.

COMMUNITY AT WORK © 1996

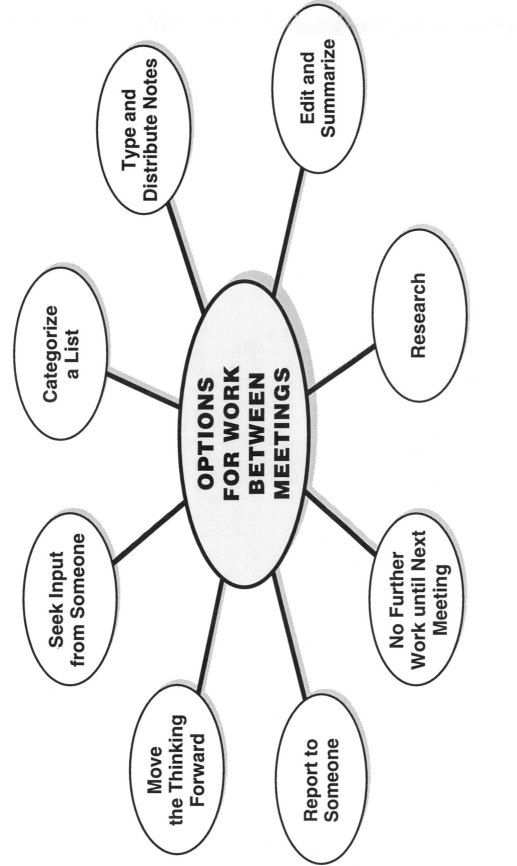

OPTIONS FOR WORK BETWEEN MEETINGS

- Type and Distribute Notes
- Edit and Summarize
- Categorize a List
- Research
- Seek Input from Someone
- Move the Thinking Forward
- Report to Someone
- No Further Work until Next Meeting

Plenty of work can be accomplished between meetings. A planner who understands this principle can look a few meetings into the future and create a more sophisticated design for achieving the overall goal. Furthermore, when a planner knows that s/he can plan for work to get done between meetings, s/he may not feel as much pressure to design an unrealistic agenda that attempts to "get it all done" in a single meeting.

COMMUNITY AT WORK © 1996

PREVENTING AN OVERCROWDED AGENDA

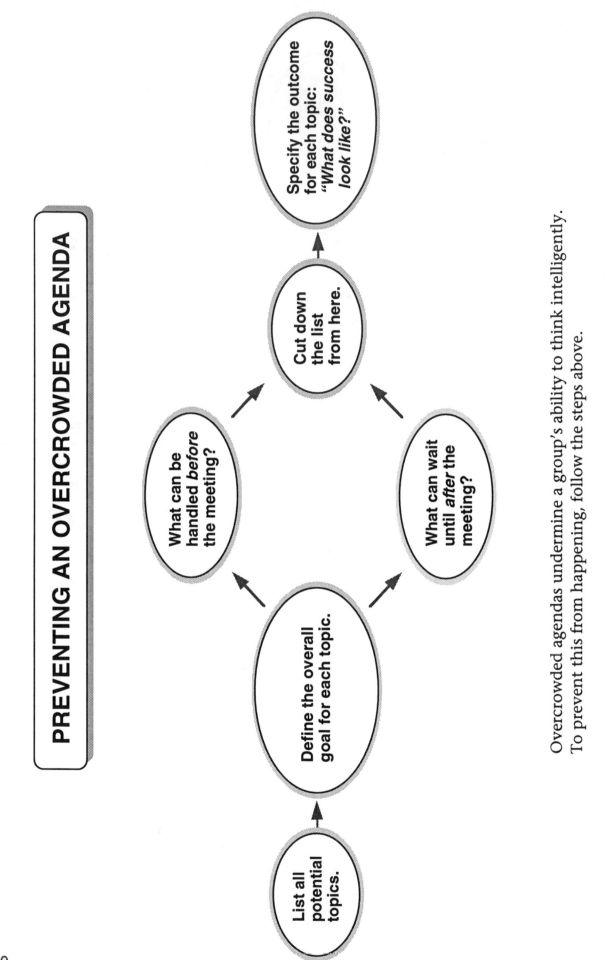

List all potential topics.

Define the overall goal for each topic.

What can be handled *before* the meeting?

What can wait until *after* the meeting?

Cut down the list from here.

Specify the outcome for each topic: *"What does success look like?"*

Overcrowded agendas undermine a group's ability to think intelligently. To prevent this from happening, follow the steps above.

COMMUNITY AT WORK © 1996

AGENDA PLANNING SESSIONS

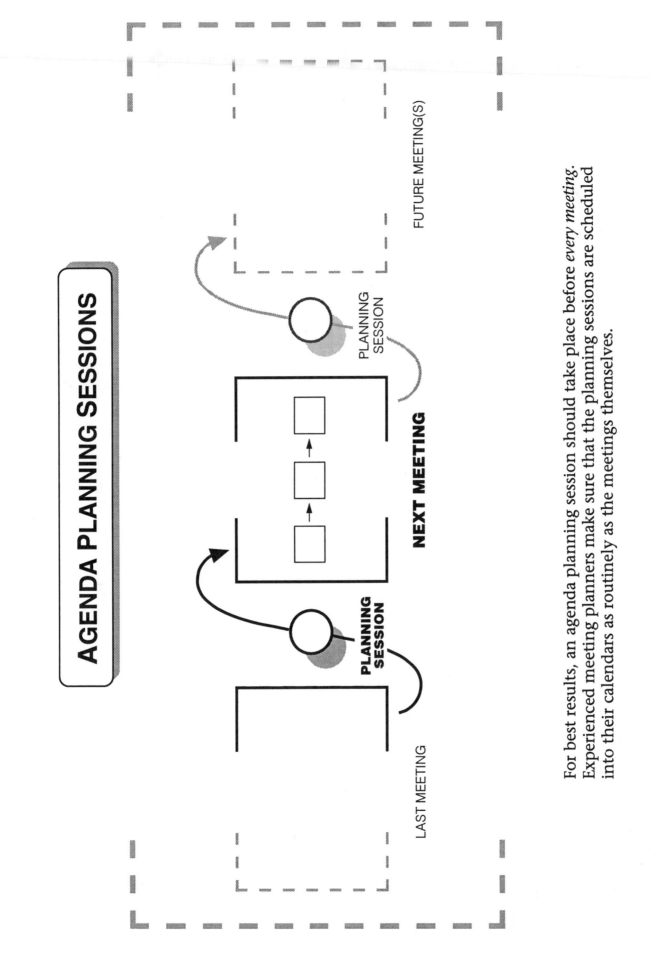

LAST MEETING

**PLANNING
SESSION**

NEXT MEETING

PLANNING
SESSION

FUTURE MEETING(S)

For best results, an agenda planning session should take place before *every meeting*. Experienced meeting planners make sure that the planning sessions are scheduled into their calendars as routinely as the meetings themselves.

COMMUNITY AT WORK ©1996

THE WAY MOST PEOPLE VIEW THE PROCESS OF A MEETING

AGENDA FOR A MEETING

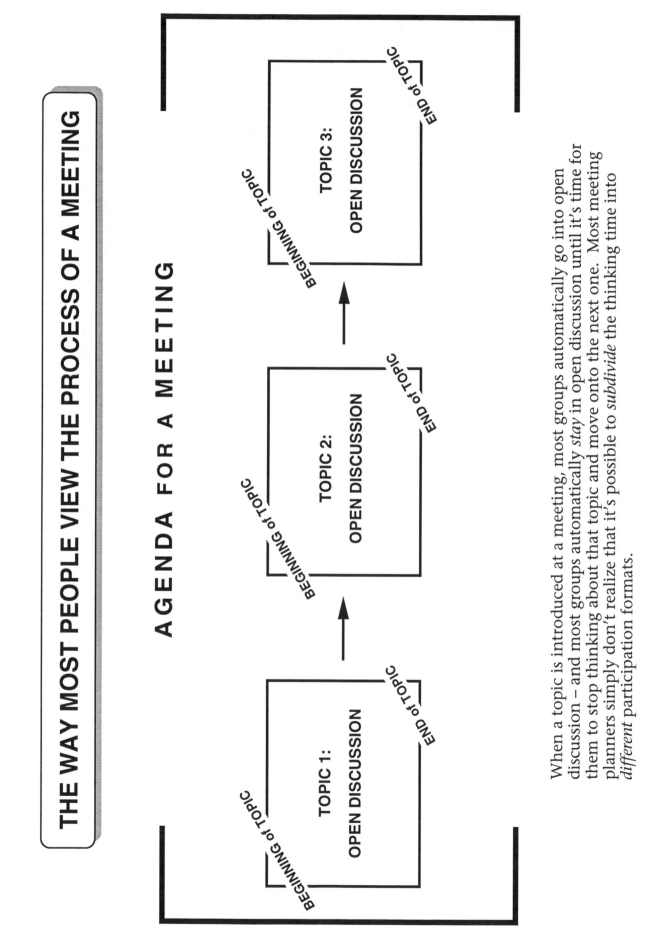

TOPIC 1:
OPEN DISCUSSION

BEGINNING of TOPIC

END of TOPIC

TOPIC 2:
OPEN DISCUSSION

BEGINNING of TOPIC

END of TOPIC

TOPIC 3:
OPEN DISCUSSION

BEGINNING of TOPIC

END of TOPIC

When a topic is introduced at a meeting, most groups automatically go into open discussion – and most groups automatically *stay* in open discussion until it's time for them to stop thinking about that topic and move onto the next one. Most meeting planners simply don't realize that it's possible to *subdivide* the thinking time into *different* participation formats.

COMMUNITY AT WORK © 1996

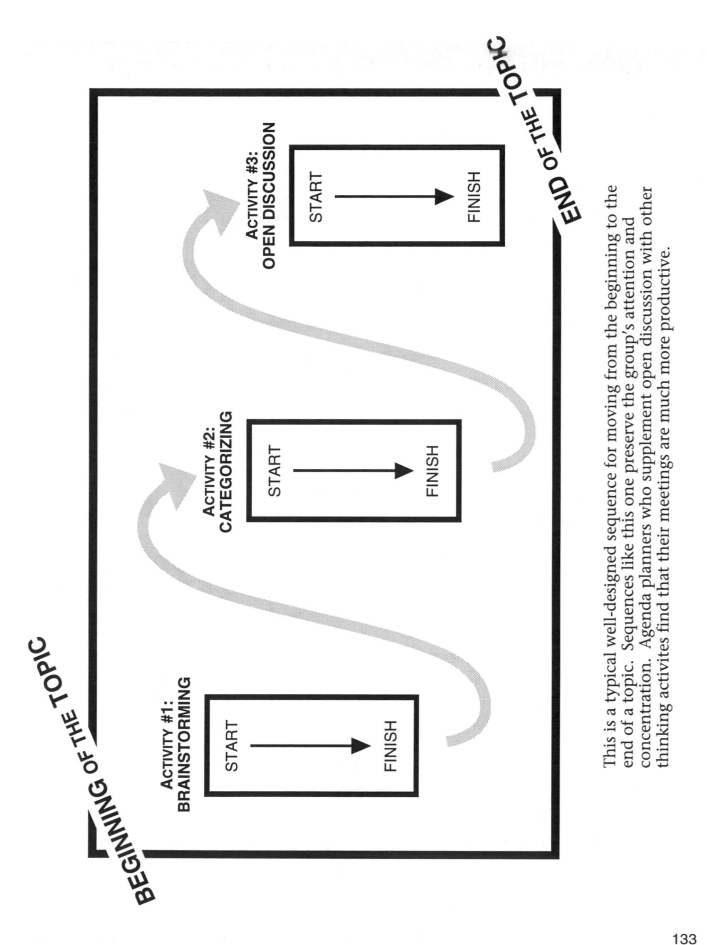

BEGINNING OF THE TOPIC

END OF THE TOPIC

ACTIVITY #1:
BRAINSTORMING

START ➔ FINISH

ACTIVITY #2:
CATEGORIZING

START ➔ FINISH

ACTIVITY #3:
OPEN DISCUSSION

START ➔ FINISH

This is a typical well-designed sequence for moving from the beginning to the end of a topic. Sequences like this one preserve the group's attention and concentration. Agenda planners who supplement open discussion with other thinking activites find that their meetings are much more productive.

COMMUNITY AT WORK © 1996

SOME OF THE MANY POSSIBLE THINKING ACTIVITIES

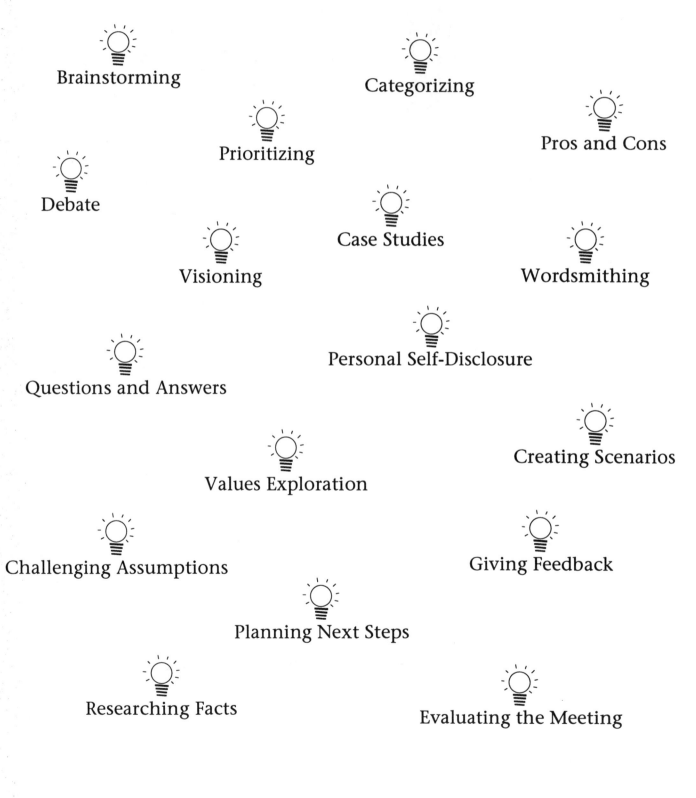

Brainstorming

Categorizing

Prioritizing

Pros and Cons

Debate

Case Studies

Visioning

Wordsmithing

Personal Self-Disclosure

Questions and Answers

Creating Scenarios

Values Exploration

Challenging Assumptions

Giving Feedback

Planning Next Steps

Researching Facts

Evaluating the Meeting

AGENDA PLANNING: PROCESS DESIGN

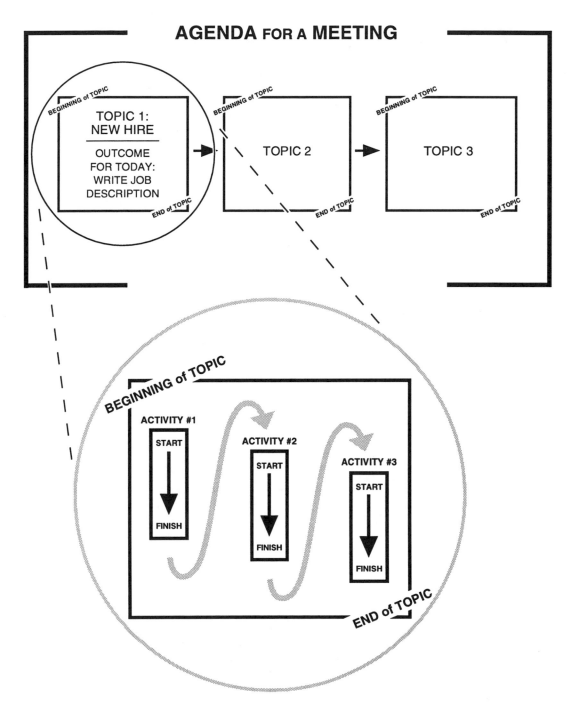

AGENDA FOR A MEETING

Once the desired outcome is clear, a suitable process is usually easy to design. For example, to write a job description: first a group could list attributes of the job; then sort the list into themes; then break into small groups to write up each theme.

AGENDA PLANNING ROLES

THE FACILITATOR	THE PERSON-IN-CHARGE
Explains the importance of reserving time to plan the agenda.	Decides how much time to invest on agenda planning.
Asks the person-in-charge to list all possible topics.	Identifies possible topics.
Asks the person-in-charge to set the overall goal for each topic.	Clarifies the overall goal for each topic.
Encourages the person-in-charge to specify the outcomes s/he wants the group to reach at the next meeting.	Sets a specific outcome for each topic on next meeting's agenda.
Suggests process options for moving from the beginning to the end of each topic.	Considers options and makes decisions regarding the process design for each topic.
Does not present the agenda to the group at the meeting. This prevents confusion about whether the person-in-charge fully endorses the agenda.	Presents the agenda at the meeting and explains the objectives for each item.

Part Three

BUILDING SUSTAINABLE AGREEMENTS

12

PRINCIPLES FOR BUILDING SUSTAINABLE AGREEMENTS

MAKING DECISIONS THAT INCORPORATE
EVERYONE'S POINT OF VIEW

- ▸ What Makes an Agreement Sustainable

- ▸ Case Example: A Typical Tale of Woe

- ▸ Case Example: Success Story

- ▸ Business-as-Usual Compared with Participatory Decision-Making

- ▸ Two Mindsets: Either/Or and Both/And

- ▸ Facilitating Sustainable Agreements

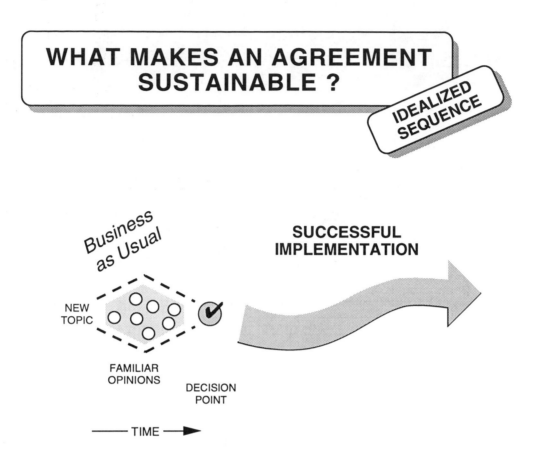

WHAT MAKES AN AGREEMENT SUSTAINABLE ?

IDEALIZED SEQUENCE

Business as Usual

SUCCESSFUL IMPLEMENTATION

NEW TOPIC

FAMILIAR OPINIONS

DECISION POINT

◄── TIME ──►

The diagram shown above represents an idealized sequence of the relationship between the discussion that precedes a decision, and the implementation that follows a decision. The discussion is quick and direct, and the implementation is straightforward.

Many people – perhaps most people – really do believe in this model. No struggle. No Groan Zone. No problems. Just a clean, linear, predictable forward movement from the inception of an idea to the end of its implementation.

And the reason the model is so widely credible is simple: *most of the time, it works!* In other words, most of the decisions a group makes *are* routine. The issues are familiar; the solutions are obvious; and the implementation can be accomplished with a bare minimum of planning and organizing.

Not all problems are routine, though. And what most people don't realize is that *this model does not work when the problem is a difficult one.*

WHAT MAKES AN AGREEMENT SUSTAINABLE ?

TOUGH PROBLEMS DON'T SOLVE EASILY

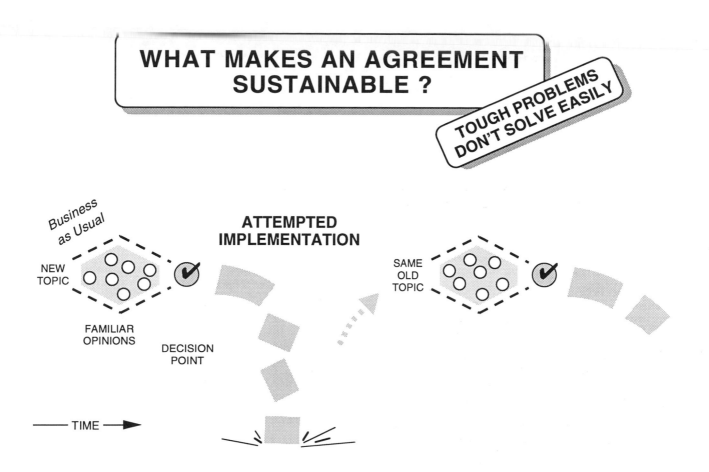

When a group attempts to solve a *difficult* problem as though it were a routine problem, they will very likely make a decision that simply does not work. The implementation will break down and the group will find itself, sooner or later, back where it began.

Groups that pressure themselves to solve a tough problem with a conventional, business-as-usual discussion frequently produce "pseudo-solutions" – ideas that sound good at the time, but are ridiculous in retrospect. Here are some common pseudo-solutions:

- Agree on the top 20 priorities
- Delegate a job to someone who is already too overworked to do it
- Establish a policy that has no accountability built into it
- Create a committee to do the same work all over again
- Create a program and don't fund it
- Make an agreement that will be vetoed by someone who is not present
- Agree to "try harder" from now on

Pseudo-solutions don't solve anything; they merely provide participants with an illusory feeling of closure – so people can believe they accomplished something without having to go through the Groan Zone.

UNSUSTAINABLE AGREEMENTS

A TYPICAL TALE OF WOE

It's a mistake to expect a business-as-usual discussion to solve a difficult problem. Here's a case in point.

CASE STUDY

The owner of a large urban department store had a problem: his salespeople were consistently late for work. The owner had tried everything he could think of – fines, threats, pleading – but nothing worked. So he called a store-wide staff meeting to tackle the problem.

The meeting began in good spirits. Many participants had an opinion about what the "real problem" was, and they were eager to state their views.

Basically there were two camps. One group, including most floor managers and supervisors, believed that the owner hired too many students to work part-time. Students, they said, are transient – not committed to the long-term health of the business. If supervisors were free to hire more full-time employees, they could instill the staff with more loyalty, better morale and higher standards of discipline.

The other group, including most salespeople, said that the problem was caused by the way they were paid. They were on commission, and very few shoppers appeared before mid-morning. Therefore, said the salespeople, they rarely earned any money for the first hour of the day. They recommended that those who opened the store should be paid a few extra dollars per day for their work.

The store owner listened as the two sides debated each other. After a while, people's patience began to wear thin. No one seemed to be changing their mind, and the group hadn't found any new ideas. The group saw no point in continuing. Someone said, "Everyone can't always get what they want. Sometimes there are winners and losers, and we just have to bite the bullet." So the owner said, "Here's my proposal. For the next four months, everyone who works on the first floor will be paid extra for coming on time. If it works, I will do it storewide. If it doesn't work, I will switch policies and hire more full-time employees. How does this sound?" A few people said, "Fine" or "Let's try it." The owner asked for objections, got none, and said, "All right, we're agreed."

After the meeting most people felt that the salespeople "won" and the managers "lost." The salespeople were glad for the extra pay and pleased that their concerns had been heard. But the supervisors were irritated. They felt the owner had not respected their judgment and that their authority had been undermined.

Over the next few months, the part-time students were treated very poorly. If someone asked to work Thursday and Friday, they were scheduled to work Monday and Tuesday. If they asked to work evenings, they got mornings. The students reacted predictably: by taking long breaks; by spending too much time on personal phone calls; by calling in sick at the last minute; by quitting on two day's notice. The full-time sales staff saw what was happening and reacted by complaining more than ever. Morale on the first floor dropped to an all-time low.

Four months later, the owner ended the experiment and told the managers to hire more full-time staff. They were relieved. Now, with a better workforce, they could move forward on their goals of improving morale and loyalty and instilling higher standards of discipline. But the sales staff were resentful. They felt they'd been robbed of extra income by a management that had sabotaged the agreement. They told newly hired employees, "Don't trust your boss; he is a jerk." Tensions lingered for years. And the original problem – coming to work late – got worse than ever.

SUSTAINABLE AGREEMENTS

SUCCESS STORY

Group decision-making *does work,* as long as it is properly planned. It can produce meaningful, integrated, broadly supported solutions to exceedingly difficult problems. The key is to stay committed to a participatory process.

CASE STUDY

In Mendocino County, California, local authorities brought together a group of loggers, environmentalists and government officials to try to resolve a longstanding quarrel over the fate of privately-owned redwood groves.

Until 1975 the property tax on privately-owned forest land was based on the number of standing trees. The more trees on your property, the more tax you paid. To give the lumber companies an incentive to replant, all redwood trees under forty years old were exempt from the tax. But this policy had an unintended consequence: it created an incentive to cut down all older redwood trees, including ancient redwoods, whether or not the wood was in demand.

Environmentalists proposed taxing *all* redwoods, regardless of age. Lumber companies opposed this proposal. They argued that it would discourage them from replanting. Further, it would induce them to cut down even more trees – fewer standing trees would mean fewer taxes. Many residents of Mendocino County were advocates for preserving old-growth forests, and the county politicians felt pressured to find a workable solution.

Accordingly they created a task force with representatives from all factions. The task force was charged with developing a proposal for revising the tax code. The proposal would then be submitted to the California State legislature for approval.

The first meetings of the task force were polarized. The loggers insisted that the environmentalists' proposal would wreak havoc on the local economy, which depended heavily on the viability of the lumber business. Environmentalists retorted that the lumber companies were mercenary and short-sighted, and that they failed to protect the needs of the local ecosystem.

Many observers doubted that the group could produce a proposal that would make it through the legislative gauntlet. (Ten committees had to approve the bill – providing special-interest lobbyists ample opportunity to stall a proposal they didn't agree with.) But the conveners of the task force were determined to overcome the odds. They provided encouragement and staff support, so the group could keep working to find a solution that would be agreeable to all parties. They knew that letting

the dispute persist would lead to costly legal battles, a divided community and various potential disruptions in the local economy.

Over the next few months, the task force met regularly. They gradually relaxed their posturing and became more willing to search for common ground. As they became more familiar with each other's points of view, their discussion became more interesting and more insightful.

It took them several months, but they found a creative framework: what if they stopped calculating property tax based on standing trees and switched to a tax based on *cut lumber?* This would discourage lumber companies from logging more than they could immediately market. By removing the tax on standing trees, land owners were no longer penalized for preserving ancient redwoods.

They developed a formal proposal and sent it to the legislature. Since it was supported by all sides, the proposal sailed through all ten legislative committees without opposition. The bill passed quickly, became law, and the entire community benefited.

Source: This case study was told to Sam Kaner by a former lumber industry lobbyist who was a member of the task force described above.

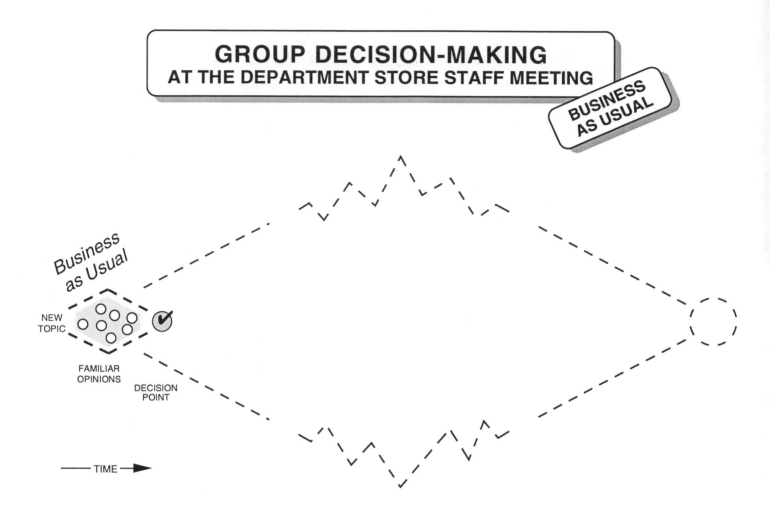

What went wrong at the department store staff meeting? Not only did the participants fail to solve the tardiness problem, but their course of action bred long-lasting animosity and cynicism. The above diagram offers insight into the reasons their meeting produced such poor outcomes.

Not realizing how much effort it would take to find a sustainable agreement, the group engaged in a *business-as-usual* decision-making process. They arrived at a decision without ever breaking out of the narrow band of familiar opinions to hunt for creative options. No one, for example, even raised the possibility of opening the store an hour later. Nor did anyone suggest simple but off-beat ideas, such as offering free cappuccinos to early-morning shoppers. Rather than search for alternatives, the group focused on two conventional options that were easy to discuss – people stated their own points of view without thinking too deeply about the larger implications of their opinions. People repeated their arguments until nothing new was being said; no one attempted to take the other side's needs into account. The owner, who expected to reach closure at that meeting, suggested a proposal and then made a superficial effort to check for group agreement. Thus the group reached a quick decision – quick, but entirely ineffective.

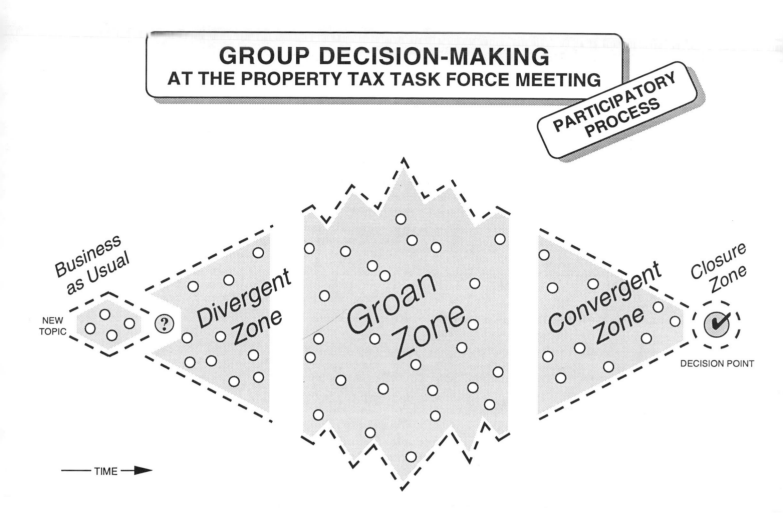

GROUP DECISION-MAKING
AT THE PROPERTY TAX TASK FORCE MEETING

PARTICIPATORY PROCESS

Business as Usual

NEW TOPIC

Divergent Zone

Groan Zone

Convergent Zone

Closure Zone

DECISION POINT

TIME ➤

What made the second case turn out so differently? The problem itself was much more difficult: the stakes were higher, the competing interest groups were more powerful, and the overall structure for reaching closure was incomparably more complicated. Yet the parties were able to find a creative solution that was genuinely acceptable to all sets of stakeholders. The diagram above is a rough schematic representation of the type of decision-making process *this* group engaged in.

Recognizing that they had a difficult problem on their hands, this group did not try to solve the problem in a meeting or two; instead they created a structure that allowed them to keep working for as long as it took to solve the problem. As for the decision-making authority, they saw that all parties would have to agree to the final decision or it wouldn't work. This, in turn, allowed them to survive the rocky start. Once they broke out of the narrow band – which in their case was marked by arguments between factions – it was inevitable that they would enter the Groan Zone. They had to struggle, sometimes for whole days, to understand one another's perspectives. Over time, they built a shared framework of understanding, which allowed them to create a solution that incorporated everyone's point of view.

TWO MINDSETS FOR SOLVING PROBLEMS

Why did the results of the department store staff meeting turn out so poorly, compared to the results of the property tax task force? Part of the answer to this question is obvious: *they organized themselves differently.* The people at the department store held a single meeting: business as usual. They gave themselves a chance to air familiar opinions, then they brought the issue to closure. In contrast, the members of the property tax task force designed a participatory process that allowed their problem solving process to unfold in stages. They, too, began by airing familiar opinions – but they created a structure that supported people to move beyond their starting positions and build a shared framework of understanding.

But this tells us *what* they did, not *why* they did it. Why, in other words, did the two groups organize themselves so differently? The answer is that each group was operating from a different *mindset* for solving problems: one group had an *Either/Or Mindset*; the other group had a *Both/And Mindset*.

From the perspective of an *Either/Or Mindset*, solving a problem is a matter of making a choice among competing alternatives. Either you choose option "A" or you choose option "B" – someone wins and someone loses, and that's how it goes. From the perspective of a *Both/And Mindset*, solving a problem is a matter of finding an inclusive solution – one that encompasses everyone's point of view. Rather than choosing between options "A" and "B," you search for a brand new alternative that is satisfactory to everyone.

Groups that operate from an *Either/Or Mindset* are in a hurry. They want to get the decision over with. Naturally – what's the point of going over and over the same territory? Once the range of options has been clarified, further discussion becomes irrelevant. But groups that operate from a *Both/And Mindset* place a higher value on effectiveness than on expedience. If the original range of options can provide the group with a workable solution, then great! Decisions that can be made quickly *should* be made quickly. But if the original range of options does not provide a workable solution, then more work lies ahead. The goal in such groups is not merely to reach a decision, but to reach a *sustainable agreement* – that is, to find a solution that works.

Several characteristics of these two mindsets are contrasted on the next page.

TWO MINDSETS FOR SOLVING PROBLEMS

	EITHER / OR	BOTH / AND
VALUE SYSTEM	Competitive	Collaborative
TYPE OF OUTCOME EXPECTED	Win / Lose	Win / Win
ATTITUDE TOWARD "WINNING"	To the victor goes the spoils.	Your success is my success.
ATTITUDE TOWARD "LOSING"	Someone has to lose.	If someone loses everyone loses.
ATTITUDE TOWARD MINORITY OPINIONS	Get with the program.	Everyone has a piece of the truth.
WHY EXPLORE DIFFERENCES BETWEEN COMPETING POSITIONS?	To search for bargaining chips, in preparation for horsetrading and compromise.	To build a shared framework of understanding, in preparation for mutual creative thinking.
ESSENTIAL MENTAL ACTIVITY	Analyze: break wholes into parts	Synthesize: integrate parts into wholes
HOW LONG IT TAKES	It's usually faster in the short run.	It's usually faster in the long run.
WHEN TO USE IT	When expedience is more important than durability, *Either/Or thinking* will usually produce satisfactory results.	When all parties have the power to block any decision, and the issue is for high stakes, *Both/And thinking* is usually the only hope for resolution.
UNDERLYING PHILOSOPHY	Survival of the fittest	Interdependence of all things

WHAT MAKES AN AGREEMENT SUSTAINABLE ?

SHARED UNDERSTANDING

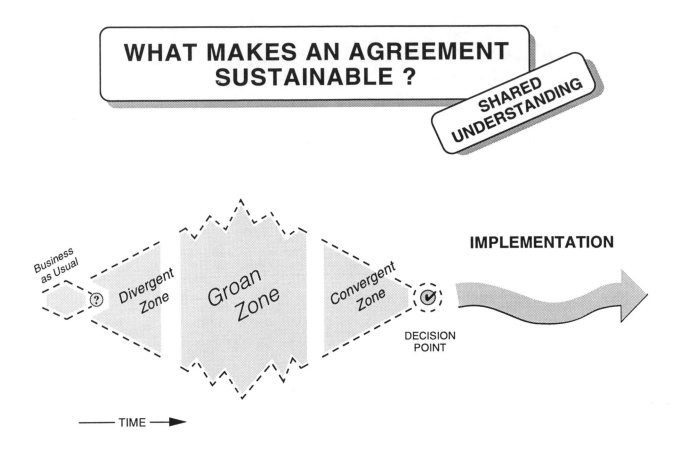

The diagram shown above represents the process of building sustainable agreements. Up to the point of decision, progress is slow – much slower than anyone expects – as the members of the group struggle to develop a shared framework of understanding. The implementation, on the other hand, is often interesting, exciting and challenging in a positive, stimulating way – rather than painful. Bringing a sustainable agreement to fruition is like swimming with the tide instead of against it. People feel confident that their efforts are headed toward results.

What is it that makes a sustainable agreement sustainable? The answer is that the agreement is based a solution that incorporates everyone's point of view. Participants would say, "Yes, this works! From my perspective, this proposal actually does solve the problem."

How does a group achieve this? By patient, persistent effort. People keep working to understand one another's goals and needs and fears and frames of reference. They face conflicts and overcome them; they explore possibilities by putting themselves in each other's shoes; they challenge their underlying assumptions; they search for imaginative solutions. And they share responsibility for reaching a result that works for everyone.

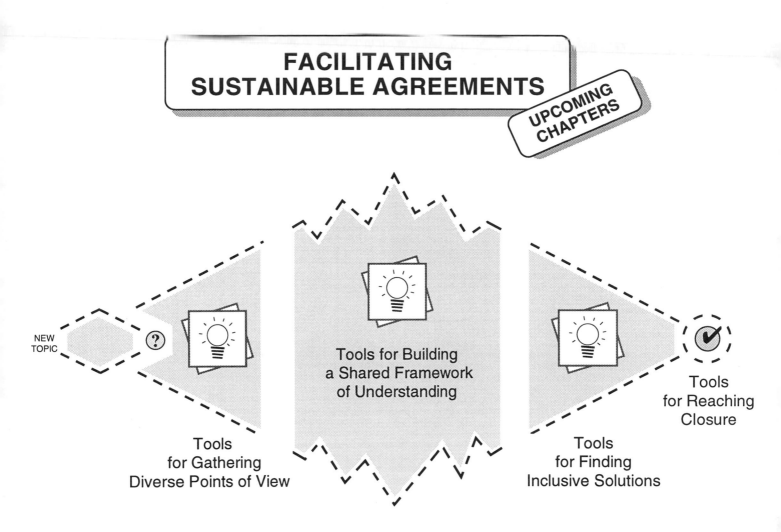

FACILITATING SUSTAINABLE AGREEMENTS

UPCOMING CHAPTERS

NEW TOPIC

Tools for Building a Shared Framework of Understanding

Tools for Gathering Diverse Points of View

Tools for Finding Inclusive Solutions

Tools for Reaching Closure

Groups need different types of support at different points in the process. Facilitators who understand this will vary their technique accordingly. Different zones call for different tools and skills.

For example, it is unwise to promote convergent thinking in a group whose members have not yet built a shared framework of understanding – they will probably not trust solutions proposed by their opponents, because they do not yet feel personally understood by one another. On the other hand, if members are *able* to take each others' needs into account, they might benefit greatly from a structured thinking activity that helps them hunt for inclusive solutions.

The preceding chapters of this book have introduced the reader to the fundamental skills of group facilitation. Skills like listening, chartwriting and process management are useful in *every* zone. But there are also many facilitation tools that are designed to work in a *specific* zone. Dozens of these tools are presented in the next five chapters.

13

GATHERING DIVERSE POINTS OF VIEW

PRINCIPLES AND TOOLS THAT PROMOTE FREE EXPRESSION

- ▶ **Introduction to the Divergent Zone**

- ▶ **Six Tools for Surveying the Territory**

- ▶ **Six Tools for Generating Alternatives**

- ▶ **Three Tools for Raising Difficult Issues**

- ▶ **Summary**

GATHERING DIVERSE POINTS OF VIEW

INTRODUCTION

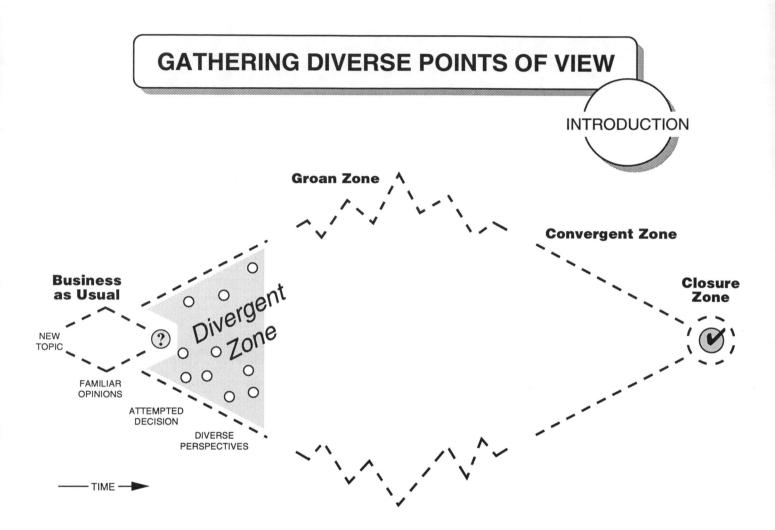

The facilitator's main task in the Divergent Zone is to create opportunities for everyone to express their views on the topic at hand. At this phase of the discussion, the facilitator does not even try to resolve disagreements. S/he honors everything everyone says and refrains from asking anyone to revise or reconsider their opinions.

Structured thinking activities like the ones presented in this chapter can be very helpful in the Divergent Zone. Structure serves as a container – it can allow members to express a wide range of opinions without fearing that their diversity will overwhelm the group's resources. People sense this, and they feel relief at the thought that the process is "under control." For this reason, many groups are pleased to be given an opportunity to do structured thinking in the Divergent Zone. Facilitators can offer their suggestions with confidence that they will usually be well received.

GATHERING DIVERSE POINTS OF VIEW

THREE TYPES OF THINKING IN THE DIVERGENT ZONE

Whenever a group is engaged in divergent thinking, the members are *increasing the diversity* of the material they can work with. Divergent thinking expands the range of the ideas that can be discussed further. This principle holds true whether group members are engaged in a boisterous round of brainstorming or whether they are nervously sharing their individual reactions to a painful controversy. In either case, their activity will result in the emergence of a greater diversity of perspectives. This is the defining property of the Divergent Zone.

Nonetheless, not all divergent thinking is the same. There are different *types* of divergent thinking, and each has its own characteristics. The three most common types are: *Surveying The Territory; Searching For Alternatives;* and *Raising Difficult Issues*.

Type 1: Surveying the Territory

Surveying the Territory involves identifying the components of the problem under discussion. For example, suppose a group is facing a contentious dispute. If every group member takes a turn stating his or her position, everyone will get an initial impression of the complexity of the conflict. The essence of this type of divergent thinking is *collecting perspectives*.

Type 2: Searching for Alternatives

Searching for Alternatives refers to the creative activity of listing unusual, innovative ideas. Some ideas on the list will prove to be realistic, many will not. The essence of this type of divergent thinking is *generating*.

Type 3: Raising Difficult Issues

Raising Difficult Issues involves the discussion of a troubling – often threatening – subject. Some groups treat the members who raise difficult issues as troublemakers; deviations from the party line are squelched. But other groups make an effort to respond to someone who raises a difficult issue by sharing the risk and encouraging everyone to disclose his/her own individual perspective. The ensuing discussion usually turns out to be quite meaningful. The essence of this type of divergent thinking is *speaking freely*.

SURVEYING THE TERRITORY
DIVERGENT ZONE THINKING ACTIVITY TYPE 1

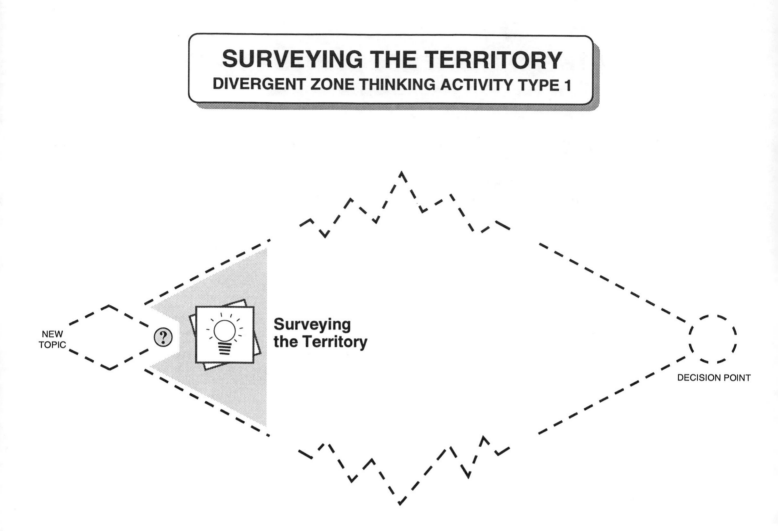

NEW TOPIC

Surveying
the Territory

DECISION POINT

Surveying the Territory involves identifying the components of the problem under discussion. The basic question on people's minds is something like, "How complex *is* this problem?" or "What are we dealing with here?"

The simplest way to help a group survey the territory is by suggesting a go-around. This gives people a chance to hear every member's perspective. While the go-around is in progress, many members will subconsciously be asking themselves questions like these: "Is there a majority view on the issue or is the group splintered into many different factions? Does the person-in-charge (if there is one) have much support for his/her position?" By the time the go-around ends, group members have acquired a reasonably good picture of the scope of the problem they're dealing with.

Sometimes a simple go-around will not provide the group with enough direction. For example, one group might need to find out whether there are different goals in the room; another group might need to find out whether the right people are in the room. This is a perfect opportunity for you, as facilitator, to suggest a structured thinking activity.

SURVEYING THE TERRITORY

SPEAK FROM
YOUR OWN PERSPECTIVE

WHY

This is a basic, straightforward activity which encourages participants to offer their own points of view on the topic at hand.

The purpose of this activity is to enable members to quickly gain a picture of the breadth of the group's thinking. By seeing all the parts, the group gains a sense of the whole.

Another purpose of the activity is to legitimize and validate every perspective. By allowing the group to hear each person's contribution, this activity sends the message, "everyone has something to offer."

HOW

1. Pose an open-ended question such as:

   • How would you describe what's going on?
   • How does this problem impact you?
   • What is your position on this matter?
   • Why, in your opinion, is this happening?

2. Ask each person to answer the question without commenting on each other's ideas.

3. Close the activity by asking participants for their reactions, general comments and learnings.

4. Optional Step:
   When everyone has had a chance to express their views, ask,
   "Is there anyone absent today who might have a significantly different perspective? What might that person tell us?"

— SURVEYING THE TERRITORY —

SPECIFYING REQUIREMENTS

WHY

When tackling a difficult problem, different stakeholders bring different requirements to the table. To be sustainable, the eventual solution must take into account every stakeholder's requirements. For example, an appliance manufacturing company held a product-design meeting to discuss the development of a new, low energy light bulb. The purchasing department wanted the bulb to be built from parts and materials that were readily available. The marketing department insisted that the shape of the bulb had to fit in standardized packaging. The engineering department wanted precise timetables from research and development so they would know how to schedule their staff. And the company president wanted assurance that the new product would be a saleable commodity.

For groups like these, the challenge is to take stock of *all* requirements before getting bogged down in specifics. This activity helps a group to gain a preliminary understanding of everyone's conditions for success.

HOW

1. Hang two sheets of chart paper, titled "Requirements and Necessary Conditions" and "Topics for Further Discussion."

2. Break the group into pairs. Ask each member to describe his/her own requirements and necessary conditions.

3. Reconvene the large group. Give each person three minutes to state his/her requirements and five minutes to answer questions. Record each requirement on the chart paper. Questions that would require further discussion are also recorded.

4. After repeating Step 3 for each person, have the group examine the lists and decide how to organize the subsequent discussion.

WHO, WHAT, WHEN, WHERE AND HOW?

WHY

When solving problems in groups, people come to the table with *very different questions* based on their individual perspectives. Since everyone wants their own questions answered, they often have trouble recognizing that many, many questions – not just their own – need to be answered. This element of divergent thinking is one of the most difficult aspects of group decision-making.

At a recent meeting, for example, one person who was mystified by the budgeting process requested clarifications and explanations repeatedly. Another asked several questions about the reasons why certain people had been invited to the meeting while others had not. A third person appeared to understand everything but one little detail, about which he kept asking questions. Each could barely see that others were struggling with completely different questions.

This activity supports a group to get *all the questions out* so people can see the whole range before they get hooked on any single question.

HOW

1. Hang five sheets of paper titled respectively, "Who?", "What?", "When?", "Where?", and "How?"

2. Start by naming the general topic. For example, "We're now going to work on the planning for the annual staff retreat."

3. On the "Who?" page, brainstorm a list of questions that begin with "Who?" For example, "Who will set the agenda?" "Who knows someone who can rent us a conference room?" "Who should be invited?" "Who said we can't spend more than $500?"

4. Repeat Step 3 for each of the other sheets.

5. When all five lists are complete, identify the easy questions and answer them. Then make a plan to answer the rest.

This tool was inspired by an exercise called "Five W's and H", in *Techniques of Structured Problem Solving,* 2nd ed., A. B. VanGundy, Jr., New York: Van Nostrand Reinhold, 1988, p. 46.

SURVEYING THE TERRITORY
FACTS AND OPINIONS

WHY

This activity enables a group to trade a lot of information without getting bogged down in a discussion of who is right or what is true.

For example, suppose a group needed to begin thinking about next year's budget. The Facts and Opinions tool would help them to generate numerical statistics ("last year we spent $4,000 on legal fees") and speculation ("we might want to initiate two new lawsuits next year") both within a short period of time.

Note that in this example, Facts and Opinions postpones the debate over the budget. Instead, the thrust of the exercise is to gather a lot of material on many different subjects. Once group members see the big picture, they can decide which topics to discuss and in what order.

HOW

1. To prepare for this activity, hang two large pieces of paper on a wall. Title one "Facts" and the other "Opinions." Also, make available sticky-notes in two colors, with enough for every member to receive at least ten of each color.

2. Ask the group members, "What do you know about this topic?" Have each group member write his/her answers on the sticky-notes, using one color for "Facts" and the other color for "Opinions." Note: When someone asks, "How do we know whether something is a fact or an opinion?" answer, "You decide for yourself. If you're not sure, write it both ways."

3. When a person is finished writing, s/he should post his/her sticky-notes on the wall. After reading what others have written, s/he will probably want to add more items. If so, great!

4. After all data has been collected, ask the group for their observations and reflections.

SURVEYING THE TERRITORY

STARTING POSITIONS

WHY

This activity is perfect for helping people deal with a contentious issue – especially when their conflict is fueled by a wide range of opposing perspectives.

When people are brought together to resolve a dispute, many participants arrive with strong opinions and well-rehearsed arguments. They need to be given a chance to express their opinions fully, so they can let everyone else see where they stand.

When people aren't able to speak without being interrupted or discounted, it is predictable that they will insert their positions into the discussion at every opportunity. Conversely, when people *are* supported to state their positions fully, they frequently become more able to listen to one another. This often leads to better mutual understanding, which is a precondition for finding creative solutions to difficult problems.

HOW

1. Introduce the activity by indicating that there may be several diverse perspectives in the room. Encourage everyone to give each other the time and the attention to express their views.

2. Using a go-around format, ask each speaker to take a turn answering the following questions from his/her individual perspective:

   a) What is the problem and what solution is s/he advocating?
   b) What are his/her reasons for taking this particular position?

   Note: This step is often done by having each speaker come up to the front of the room and present his/her ideas standing up.

3. When each person has had a turn, ask the group for observations and reflections.

UNREPRESENTED PERSPECTIVES

WHY

People in a group often share so many assumptions in common that they may not recognize their own blind spots. For example, urban-based environmentalists in the 1980s were notorious for developing rural conservation plans that were not supported locally by the loggers or miners whose livelihoods were being threatened. Such plans almost invariably proved to be unworkable because they had been designed without adequate understanding of the needs and goals of the working people in the affected communities.

This activity assists a group to determine whether there are any stakeholders whose perspective should be represented more effectively at future meetings.

HOW

1. List every group of stakeholders that might be affected by this problem. Don't forget to include less-than-obvious stakeholders. For example, does your issue affect trainees? Suppliers? Neighbors? The families of your employees?

2. One by one, go down the list considering each group in the following way: "How does the situation at hand affect this stakeholder group?" Example: "How does our project expansion for next year affect our trainees?"

3. When the list is complete ask, "Has anyone spotted a problem that wasn't previously identified?" and "Is there someone missing from these meetings who should be included from now on?"

SEARCHING FOR ALTERNATIVES
DIVERGENT ZONE THINKING ACTIVITY TYPE 2

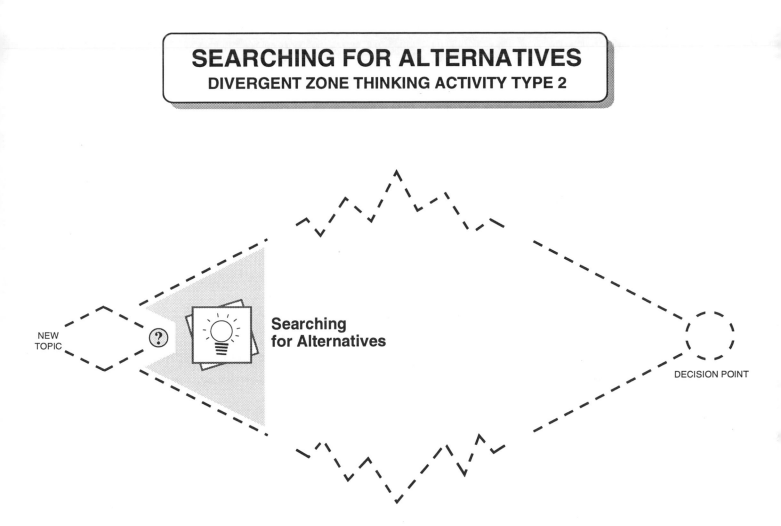

Searching for Alternatives involves generating lists of creative ideas for the purpose of discovering new ways of approaching the problem at hand.

The most straightforward way to help a group search for alternatives is by leading them through a brainstorming session. To do this, begin by asking the group to state the question they want their brainstorm to answer. Write that question at the top of a flipchart page, then review the ground rules of brainstorming, and begin. Have someone else do the chartwriting if possible. Then you can focus on using your facilitative listening skills – *mirroring, paraphrasing* and *gathering ideas*.

Often a brainstorming session will produce exactly what is needed: some new rough ideas that are worth further discussion. But there are times when people are so stuck in their fixed positions, that not even brainstorming can help them break free of their rigid mental models. Many structured creative-thinking activities are available to help you deal effectively with this exact situation. Using a structured thinking activity may provide the group with the added stimulation or provocation it needs. A sampling of these activities are presented on the next pages.

BRAINSTORMING VARIATIONS

THE TRIGGER METHOD

1. Have the group formulate a statement of the problem.

2. Have everyone silently write their questions and/or solutions on sheets of paper for five minutes.

3. Ask someone to read his/her ideas to the group.

4. Have the group discuss these ideas for ten minutes, with the goal of generating variations or totally new ideas. Suspend judgment for this ten-minute period.

5. Repeat steps 3 and 4 for each member.

6. When everyone has had a turn, have the group select the most promising ideas for further analysis.

Source: *Techniques of Structured Problem Solving,* A.B. VanGundy, New York: Van Nostrand Reinhold, 1988.

BRAINWRITING

1. Seat members around a table.

2. Have someone state the problem to be solved.

3. Ask each person to silently write down four ideas for solving the problem on one sheet of paper.

4. Explain to group members that as soon as anyone has listed four ideas, s/he should exchange that page with someone else.

5. When someone has obtained a new sheet of paper, s/he should add one or two more ideas to it. Then trade this page for another.

6. Repeat for fifteen minutes, or until most people run out of ideas.

7. Compare notes and discuss.

Source: *Brainwriting Pool,* in *Chemical Engineering,* H. Geschka, G.R. Schaude, and H. Schlicksupp, August 1973.

SEARCHING FOR ALTERNATIVES

CREATIVE THINKING ACTIVITIES

ROLESTORMING

1. Have everyone select a character. It can be a great leader, a fictional character, a typical customer – anyone who is not in the room.

2. Review the ground rules for brainstorming.

3. Begin brainstorming solutions to the problem at hand. Half the members should participate from the perspective of their imaginary character, while the other half participate as themselves.

4. After a few minutes, switch roles. Thus, the former role-players are now themselves, and vice versa.

5. Debrief. Discuss any insights obtained.

Source: *A Storm of Ideas,* in *Training,* 22:56, R.E. Griggs, December, 1985.

ANALOGIES

1. Have the group generate a list of situations, or actions which are unrelated to the problem at hand, but which are analogous in some way. Example: suppose a group's goal is to increase its funding. The group may generate a list of *other types of growth –* plant growth, growth of a city, etc.

2. Instruct participants to forget the original problem for now. Instead, have them select one of the analogies and describe it in detail. List functions, parts, uses. *Focus on action phrases.*

3. Now encourage the group to consider each analogy in light of the original problem. Example: are any new ideas for fundraising suggested by thinking about a plant's seasonal cycles? Its root structure? Its reproduction by seeds?

Source: *Lateral Thinking,* E. de Bono, New York: Harper and Row, 1970.

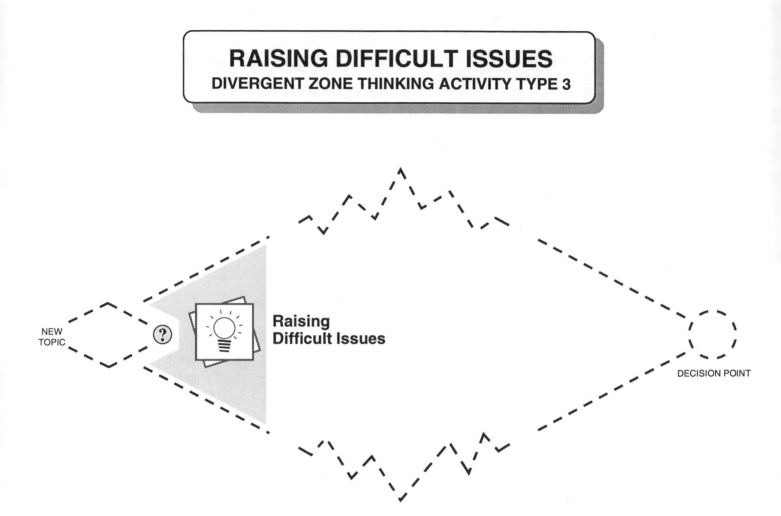

RAISING DIFFICULT ISSUES
DIVERGENT ZONE THINKING ACTIVITY TYPE 3

NEW
TOPIC

?

Raising
Difficult Issues

DECISION POINT

Raising Difficult Issues refers to the discussion of risky subjects – issues that are hard to raise. They are seldom placed on an agenda per se; rather, they surface in the cracks of a related discussion. Someone might say, "Can we talk about what is *really* causing this problem?" Then s/he names the unspeakable issue – the ongoing feud between key parties, the poor decision that no one wants to revisit, or whatever. When this happens, other members *might* participate in exploring this observation – but often they do no such thing! People frequently become anxious and change the subject or withdraw. This places the person who *did* speak up in a tough position – as though s/he were the only one who felt his/her points were relevant.

The following activities provide an alternative. Rather than treat this situation as a dilemma that occurs *after* one person takes a risk, each activity offers participants the opportunity to share the load of *surfacing* difficult issues. Each activity offers a structured, low-pressure forum in which members can speak more freely and explore the difficult topics that might be on their minds.

RAISING DIFFICULT ISSUES

IS THERE ANYTHING I'M NOT SAYING?

WHY

People refrain from saying what they're really thinking for a wide variety of reasons. Sometimes they hold back because the risk is too great. But people also keep quiet because they aren't sure whether their ideas are worth saying; or because they can't turn the kernels of their ideas into fully formed presentations. In other words, there are many occasions when group members – if they were given a little support, a little permission, a little nudge – might go ahead and say what's on their mind. Yet without that support, they often stay quiet.

This activity helps group members take a look at the thoughts they've been having (but not speaking) during a discussion. It also gives members an opportunity to reflect on whether or not the group would be served if they opened up and shared their perspectives.

HOW

1. Describe this activity. Explain why people can benefit from structured activities that give them permission to speak up. Obtain agreement from the group to proceed.

2. Have the group break into pairs. Ask each partner to answer this question: "During this discussion have I had any thoughts I haven't said aloud?" Assure people that no one is required to say anything they don't want to say.

3. Next ask everyone (still in pairs) to answer this question: "Would the group benefit from hearing your partner's thinking?"

4. Return to the large group. Ask for volunteers to share any of their own thoughts that might be useful for others to hear.

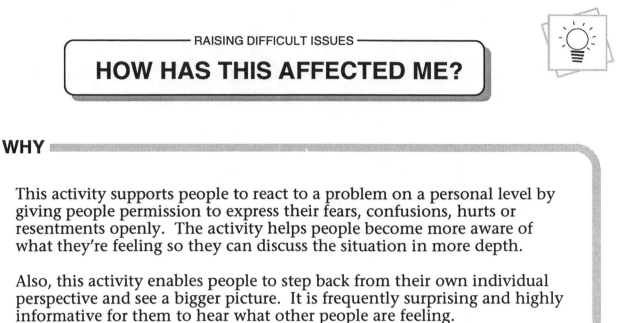

HOW HAS THIS AFFECTED ME?

WHY

This activity supports people to react to a problem on a personal level by giving people permission to express their fears, confusions, hurts or resentments openly. The activity helps people become more aware of what they're feeling so they can discuss the situation in more depth.

Also, this activity enables people to step back from their own individual perspective and see a bigger picture. It is frequently surprising and highly informative for them to hear what other people are feeling.

HOW

1. Ask people to reflect on the following questions:

   a) "How do I feel about this situation?"
   b) "How has it affected me so far?"

2. Ask each person to take a turn sharing his/her reflections and feelings with the whole group. A go-around format works best for this activity because it discourages back-and-forth discussion.

3. When everyone has spoken, ask the whole group, "Now that you have heard from everyone else, what reactions are you having?"

4. If responses indicate that this activity has surfaced a lot of emotion, encourage the group to do a second go-around. Say something like, "Use this time to let the rest of us know whatever is on your mind."

5. End by summarizing the main themes. Validating everyone's self-disclosure helps provide people with a temporary sense of completion, even when the source-problems remain obviously unresolved.

RAISING DIFFICULT ISSUES

THREE COMPLAINTS

WHY

Giving people the opportunity to complain about their situation has two powerful results. When people have a chance to say things that are normally not acceptable, often very useful information is revealed about a situation that would otherwise remain hidden.

Also, when people have a chance to vent their negative feelings instead of stewing in them, they are more able to move forward on a task.

After an activity like Three Complaints, it is common for people to make significant progress on the topic under discussion.

HOW

1. Give the group an overview of the upcoming steps. Then have each individual write on a separate slip of paper three complaints about the situation under discussion.

2. Have everyone throw the slips of paper into a hat.

3. Pull out one note, read it aloud, and ask for comments. The author may or may not wish to identify him/herself.

4. After three or four comments, pull out another complaint and repeat the process.

5. After ten or fifteen minutes, ask the group how much longer they would like this activity to continue.

6. When time runs out, ask people to close by saying what the experience was like for them.

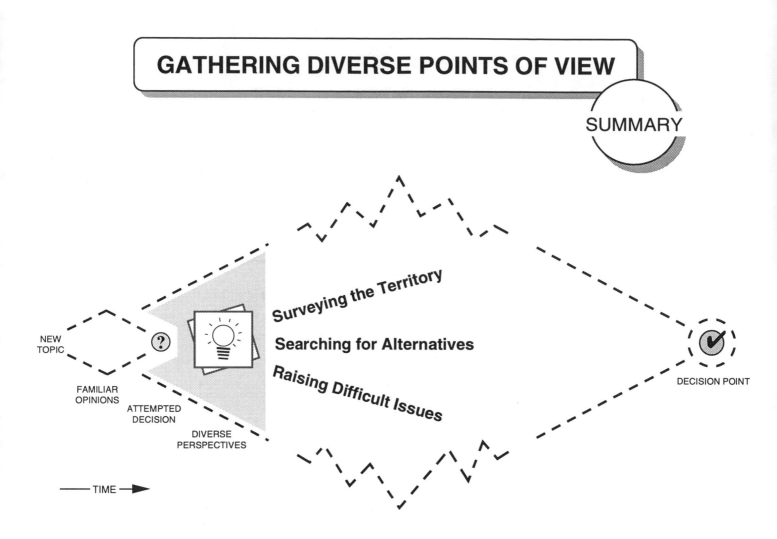

GATHERING DIVERSE POINTS OF VIEW

SUMMARY

NEW TOPIC

FAMILIAR OPINIONS

ATTEMPTED DECISION

DIVERSE PERSPECTIVES

Surveying the Territory

Searching for Alternatives

Raising Difficult Issues

DECISION POINT

TIME

The most common types of divergent thinking are shown above. Each type can be supported by activities like those presented in this chapter. Some activities help a group gain a better picture of the scope of the task at hand. Others enable a group to create a list of unusual ideas. Still others support participants to uncover and then discuss topics that are uncomfortable.

Structured activities are often useful. This does not mean, however, that they are always the best approach. A group can often benefit from using a simple format, like idea-listing or a structured go-around – a format that supports discussion without forcing people to go in any particular direction. And sometimes people simply want to engage in conversation. The facilitator can then rely on facilitative listening skills, such as *stacking*, *encouraging* and *making space*.

No matter what approach s/he takes, the facilitator's main task in the Divergent Zone is to support everyone to speak up and state his or her point of view. This is a prerequisite for building sustainable agreements.

14

BUILDING A SHARED FRAMEWORK OF UNDERSTANDING

PRINCIPLES AND TOOLS THAT
SUPPORT GROUPS TO STRUGGLE
IN THE SERVICE OF INTEGRATION

▶ **Introduction to the Groan Zone**

▶ **Six Tools for Creating Shared Context**

▶ **Six Tools for Strengthening Relationships**

▶ **Summary**

BUILDING A SHARED
FRAMEWORK OF UNDERSTANDING

INTRODUCTION

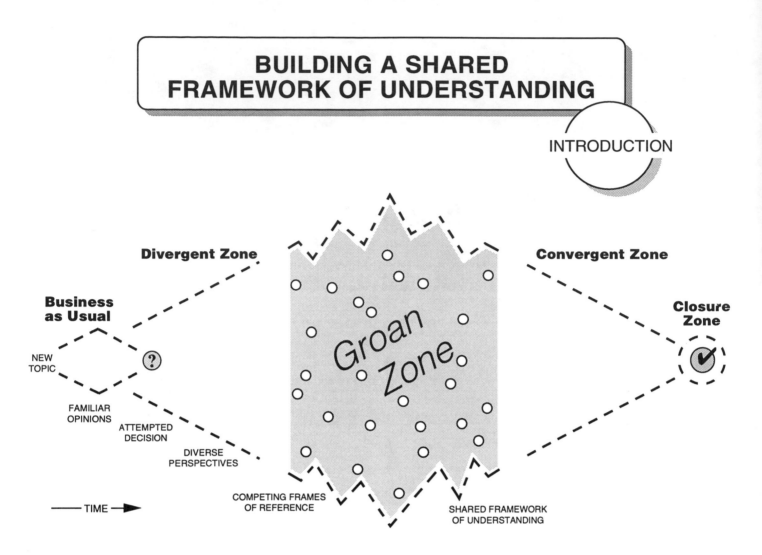

The facilitator's main objective in the Groan Zone is to help the group develop a shared framework of understanding. This is anything but easy. The greater the divergence of opinions in the room, the greater is the chance for confusion and misinterpretation. The facilitator should concentrate on *promoting mutual understanding.* This takes a lot of careful, responsive listening; at times, the facilitator may be the only person in the room who is listening at all.

Whether the facilitator is helping one person stand up to pressure from others, or helping two people clear up a misunderstanding between them, or helping a whole group focus on the same thing at the same time, the overall goal remains constant: *support the group to keep struggling.*

BUILDING A SHARED FRAMEWORK OF UNDERSTANDING

TWO TYPES OF THINKING IN THE GROAN ZONE

After a period of divergent thinking, most groups enter the Groan Zone. Suppose, for example, the members have just finished a brainstorming process. In theory the group's next task seems simple: sift through all the ideas, and discuss a few more in depth. But in practice that task is often grueling. Everyone has his/her own unique frame of reference, and communication can easily break down. Moreover, when people misunderstand one another, their behavior often becomes more confused, more impatient, more self-centered – more unpleasant all around.

This phase of work is truly difficult to tolerate. It is a normal, natural period – but it's still a struggle. The effort to understand one another's perspectives and build a shared framework of understanding – this *struggle in the service of integration* – is the defining work of the Groan Zone.

Most groups flee from the Groan Zone long before they have developed the capacity to think together. This is reflected in the quality of their decisions. Those who *do* persevere discover that what enabled them to survive the struggle were the periods they spent learning to understand each other.

The development of a shared framework of understanding centers around two types of thinking: *Strengthening Relationships,* and *Creating Shared Context.* Both types are discussed in this chapter.

Type 1: Creating Shared Context

Building Shared Context refers to activities that promote mutual understanding. This can be done in a variety of ways: by acquiring shared experiences, by developing shared language, by surfacing background information, and by making efforts to put oneself in the other person's shoes. In all cases the purpose is to enable people to think from each other's point of view. The essence of this type of activity is *understanding*.

Type 2: Strengthening Relationships

Strengthening Relationships refers to activities that support people to get to know each other. It is easier to listen to a person's thinking when one has experienced that person's humanity. The essence of this type of activity is *interpersonal communication*.

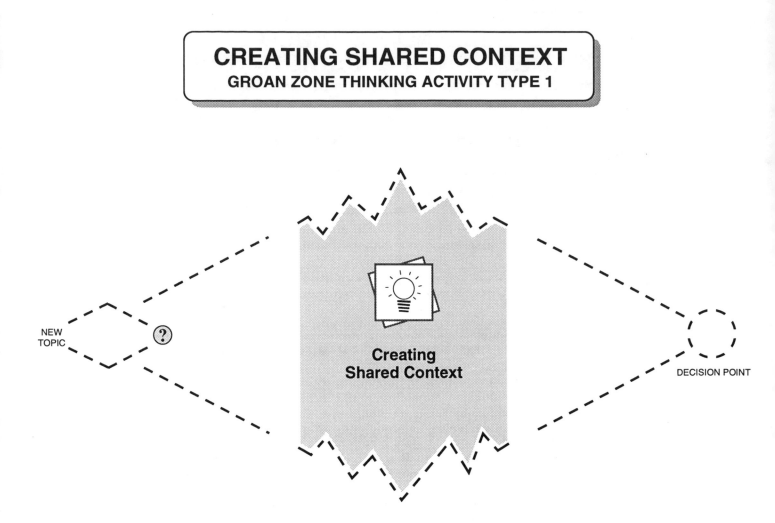

CREATING SHARED CONTEXT
GROAN ZONE THINKING ACTIVITY TYPE 1

NEW
TOPIC

?

**Creating
Shared Context**

DECISION POINT

In order for a group to develop sustainable agreements that take everyone's interests into account, the participants must be able to think from one another's points of view. They do not have to *agree* with someone else's perspective, but they do have to *understand* it.

The simplest way to help group members gain a deeper understanding of one another's perspectives is to encourage them to put themselves in each other's shoes. This can sometimes be accomplished straightforwardly, by encouraging them to ask direct questions and to listen carefully to the answers. But some participants fear that asking questions might appear confrontational or rude. Thus many groups require structured thinking activities to help them learn more about each other's frames of reference.

CREATING SHARED CONTEXT

LEARNING MORE ABOUT EACH OTHER'S PERSPECTIVES

WHY

The most basic method for promoting mutual understanding is to ask questions. Sometimes, however, people hesitate to ask questions about each other's perspectives because questioning is so often perceived as criticism. By providing structure, this activity helps people understand that the questions are not intended as attacks.

Facilitators often hesitate to use a tool like this one because it eats up precious meeting time. But the alternative – trying to proceed in the absence of understanding – ends up consuming much more time, with much worse results. Using this tool builds trust and patience, and it significantly improves mutual understanding.

HOW

1. Ask for a volunteer to be the "focus person." S/he begins by saying, "Here's the point I want to make." Give him/her three minutes to talk.

2. When s/he is done, have someone ask the focus person, "Can you explain why . . . ?" or "What do you mean by . . . ?" or something similar.

3. The focus person then answers the question.

4. Turn to the questioner and ask, "Is this clear to you now?" If so, continue to Step 5. If not, ask the questioner to state, first, what s/he believes the focus person has said, and then what she still finds unclear. For example, someone might say, "I hear the focus person saying we should all share the cleanup chores equally. But I'm still not sure why he feels so strongly about it."

5. When both the questioner and the focus person feel understood, ask for another questioner to take a turn.

6. After three or four people have had a chance to ask questions, ask for another person to volunteer to be the new focus-person.

   Note: *the goal of this activity is to promote understanding, not to resolve differences.* This should be emphasized beforehand and, if necessary, throughout the activity.

CREATING SHARED CONTEXT

IF I WERE YOU

WHY

Another straightforward way to promote mutual understanding is to have people look at the world through each other's eyes.

Exploring someone else's perspective helps people to suspend their own points of view. This activity thus provides some participants with insights that they may not have acquired through conventional discussion.

Furthermore, the process supports participants to feel understood and "seen" – and, if necessary, it allows them the opportunity to correct any misperceptions.

HOW

1. Have the group choose a statement to work with. The statement should begin with the words, "If I were you . . ." For example, two common choices are, "If I were you, a main concern of mine would be . . ." or "If I were you, one of my goals would be . . ."

2. Write each member's name on two separate slips of paper and put them into a hat.

3. Have each person draw out two slips, so that each person has the names of two different people. (If a person pulls his/her own name, s/he puts it back or trades with someone.)

4. Give everyone a turn being the "focus person." When someone is the focus person, the two people who have that person's name say to him or her, "If I were you . . ."

5. After listening to both people, the focus person may respond.

6. When everyone has had a turn, ask the group members to reflect on the activity and share any new insights they have gained.

BACKING UP
FROM SOLUTIONS TO NEEDS

WHY

When an argument seems to be going around in circles, it can be *extremely helpful* for everyone to stop arguing over proposed "solutions" and start talking about their individual needs instead.

For example, consider a dispute between three administrators over whether to schedule an important meeting in New York or Boston. The problem (where to meet) had two solutions (New York or Boston). But beneath the superficial solutions were everyone's individual needs. One person needed to stay near his office as much as possible because his assistant was on vacation. A second needed to keep her commitment to attend three other meetings that had long been planned. A third was expecting a drop-in visit from the regional director, and needed to be available "just in case." Once everyone understood each other's needs more clearly, they stopped imagining that the disagreement was due to "power struggles" and "turf battles." They realized that meeting on a Saturday would work for everyone no matter *where* they met.

As the example shows, it becomes easier to develop proposals that meet a *broader range of needs* when those needs have been made explicit – and, therefore, understandable to everyone.

HOW

1. Make sure everyone understands the difference between "their proposed solution" and "what they need." (For example, "holding the meeting in Boston" is a proposed solution; "honoring prior commitments to attend three other meetings" is a need.) Take time, if necessary, to teach this distinction to group members.

2. Ask everyone to answer these questions: "What are my needs in this situation?" and "What do I think *your* needs are?"

3. Continue until everyone feels satisfied that their own needs have been stated clearly, then ask the group to generate new proposals which seek to incorporate a broader range of people's needs.

CREATING SHARED CONTEXT
MEANINGFUL THEMES

WHY

Each participant comes to a meeting with his/her own unique set of interests and concerns. And in many cases, the participant wants to find out where others stand on the area of his/her special concern. For example, one person may need to know whether other members are committed to remaining in the group. Someone else may need to hear how people feel about the group's track record on diversity issues. Another member may want to know people's attitudes toward retaining a consultant.

Often, however, it is not clear how or when to raise those issues for discussion. Any of these themes might be very meaningful to a few people yet not very meaningful at all, to others. This creates a dilemma. How can a group devote sufficient time to such concerns – enough to prevent individual participants from becoming impatient or distracted and withdrawn – yet not so much that the agenda becomes derailed by focusing on topics that seem tangential or low-priority to other members. The activity described below offers a method for balancing the two sets of concerns, by providing members with a chance to make a *preliminary assessment* of the attitudes and biases pertaining to their area of interest.

HOW

1. Begin by having each group member identify one or two questions which, if everyone's answer were known, would enable that group member to participate more effectively. For example, "Do others think we should be prepared to spend a lot of money on this project?"

2. Ask each person to write their question on a sheet of paper. Collect everyone's questions and put them in a hat.

3. Draw out one sheet of paper, read that question, and ask the person who wrote that question to spend up to two minutes explaining why s/he wants to understand everyone's position on that question.

4. Ask for brief responses from everyone. "I feel such-a-way because . . ." When everyone has spoken, draw another question. If time is scarce, the remaining questions can be carried over till the next meeting.

CREATING SHARED CONTEXT

HOW WILL THIS PROPOSAL IMPACT OUR JOBS?

WHY

Sometimes a participant is clearly unhappy with a proposal but s/he cannot seem to communicate his/her concerns effectively. The difficulty may be rooted in the fact that most proposals affect different roles in different ways. When participants do not understand the nuances of one another's roles – a common state of affairs – they may have trouble understanding one another's concerns about a given proposal.

This activity helps the group focus their whole attention on how a proposal will impact each participant. As a result, many confusions and misunderstandings clear up as people gain insight into the subtle realities of each other's situations.

HOW

1. Identify which members are likely to be affected by the proposal on the floor. Ask for a volunteer to become the "focus person."

2. For five minutes, have the group brainstorm answers to the question: "If we implement our proposal, how will it affect this person's role?" While the brainstorm is in effect, no disagreements are allowed.

3. When five minutes are up, ask the focus person to come to the front of the room. S/he educates the group by elaborating on the items s/he thinks are important for everyone to understand. Encourage participants to ask questions.

4. Have the group choose a second focus person. Repeat steps 2 and 3.

CREATING SHARED CONTEXT

THINKING IN MULTIPLE TIME FRAMES

WHY

Thinking into the future is one of the hardest challenges for any group. Typically, when groups try to do this thinking, they become confused, because they don't distinguish between a goal (such as rebuilding an impoverished neighborhood) and a milestone (such as attracting new business to the area) and a step toward achieving a milestone (such as creating a task force of local politicians and community members). As a result, groups start several discussions simultaneously, and are often unable to focus on one level at a time.

This activity helps everyone focus on the same time frame. They can more easily discover where they agree and disagree, and they will emerge from the activity much closer to a shared framework of understanding.

HOW

1. Hang a long sheet of paper across the front of the room. At the far right-hand end of the paper, write the group's goal. For example, "Goal: Open a new office in Denver."

2. Ask the group to generate 3–5 milestones that must be completed in order to reach the goal. For example, "Complete our financial projections."

3. Write the milestones from left to right across the long sheet of paper. Leave as much space as possible between milestones.

4. Break into small groups and assign one milestone to each group. Each group now identifies and lists each step it would take to complete that milestone. Write each step on a sticky-note.

5. Have everyone come up to the front and put his/her sticky-notes up on the wall, each step in sequence, leading up to their milestone. At the same time, people can review each other's work and add any steps that may be missing.

STRENGTHENING RELATIONSHIPS
GROAN ZONE THINKING ACTIVITY TYPE 2

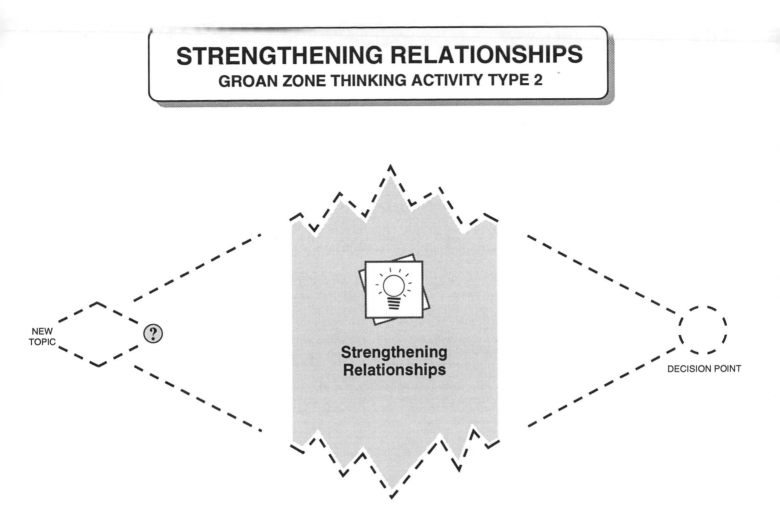

NEW TOPIC

?

Strengthening Relationships

DECISION POINT

People who know one another are more likely to overcome their differences and find common ground than people who remain personally isolated from one another. This principle is noticeable in business and in politics, where leaders often make a practice of building friendly relationships with their colleagues and the families of their colleagues. It holds true for grassroots movements, where activists – progressives and conservatives alike – intentionally design events to provide participants with a mixture of community building and social action. Yet this principle is undervalued in the realm of group decision-making. Bringing photographs of one's family members to a meeting, for example, or taking time to tell each other a little about the neighborhood where one grew up – these activities are hard for some people to imagine in the context of group decision-making.

The facilitator's task is to seek opportunities to strengthen relationships, in order to counterbalance the struggles that make the Groan Zone so painful. Participants need relief, even if temporary, from long, frustrating meetings. More importantly, broadening the context of working relationships allows people to see one another as real people, not just as "opponents" or "allies." Relationship-building strengthens the foundation of mutual understanding.

GETTING TO KNOW EACH OTHER

ANECDOTES & MEMENTOS

1. Ask everyone to come to the next meeting prepared to share something personal – a memento, a photograph or an anecdote.

2. At the next meeting, ask for volunteers to present their personal stories.

3. Before starting, establish an order for the presentations. Also, clarify what will happen if the group runs out of time. (For example, "We only have thirty minutes for this today. If we don't finish, we'll do the remaining people next time.")

4. Give each presenter five minutes to speak. Allow time for two or three questions.

TWO TRUTHS AND A LIE

1. Describe the activity.* Explain that each person will tell the group three things about him/herself – two truths and a lie. The lie must be a bald-faced lie, not a half-truth. For example, someone who has one brother may not say "I have two brothers." S/he *could* say "I have twelve brothers."

2. After each person tells their tale, have all group members quickly raise hands to indicate which "fact" they think was the lie. Ask, "How many people think the lie was such-and-such?"

3. Have the person reveal the lie. Then call on the next person to take a turn.

4. After everyone has gone, applaud those who did the best job of fooling the group.

THE SUPPORT SEAT

1. Arrange the chairs in a semi-circle and put one chair in front, facing the rest.

2. Describe the activity. Explain that each person will sit in the support seat for twenty minutes, while everyone else asks that person about his/her life away from work. Members may ask whatever they wish. The person in the center can always say, "I prefer not to answer that question."

3. Ask for someone to sit in the support seat.

4. Anyone can ask the first question. S/he may ask one follow-up question, but must then pass until everyone has had a turn.

Note: This activity is often spread over several meetings.

* This activity is a variation of "Two Truths and a Lie" presented by Bill Schmidt, instructor in Organizational Psychology at the Wright Institute, Berkeley, California, 1993.

GIVING AND RECEIVING FEEDBACK

OBSERVATIONS AND INTERPRETATIONS

1. Ask everyone to find a partner.

2. Allow each person five minutes to give his/her partner feedback as follows:
First: "Something I *observe* about you is..."
Then: "What I make up in my head about this observation is..."

3. When five minutes have passed, remind each pair to switch roles. The speaker becomes the listener, and vice versa. After ten minutes, ask everyone to find a different partner. Repeat Steps 2 and 3.

4. After a few rounds, bring everyone back to the large group and debrief.

APPRECIATIONS

1. Count the number of group members and subtract one, then distribute that many sheets of blank pages to each participant. For example, each person in an eight-person group would receive seven pages.

2. Ask everyone to write one thing they appreciate about each group member. This can be something simple, or something more personal and thoughtful.

3. When everyone has written one message to each member, ask everyone to fold their messages, stand up, and put each note on its proper chair.

4. When all messages have been delivered, have people return to their seats and read.

5. Debrief, allowing at least fifteen minutes.*

* Source: Nancy Feinstein, Ph.D. organization development specialist, as told to Sam Kaner, May 1995.

HOW DO I COME ACROSS?

1. Describe the activity. Explain that one person will ask the group, "How do I come across in our meetings? What are my strengths and weaknesses?" People will respond with statements like "I see you protecting Jim when he misses a deadline." Or, "You're the only person who really listens to everyone's opinions."

2. Ask for a volunteer. Set a firm time limit for this person to hear how s/he comes across. Allow at least fifteen minutes.

3. While people state their perceptions, make sure the recipient listens without speaking. When time is up, give him/her at least five minutes to respond.

4. Move to another volunteer. Note: if members prefer to continue interacting with the first person, set another limit.

BUILDING A SHARED FRAMEWORK OF UNDERSTANDING

SUMMARY

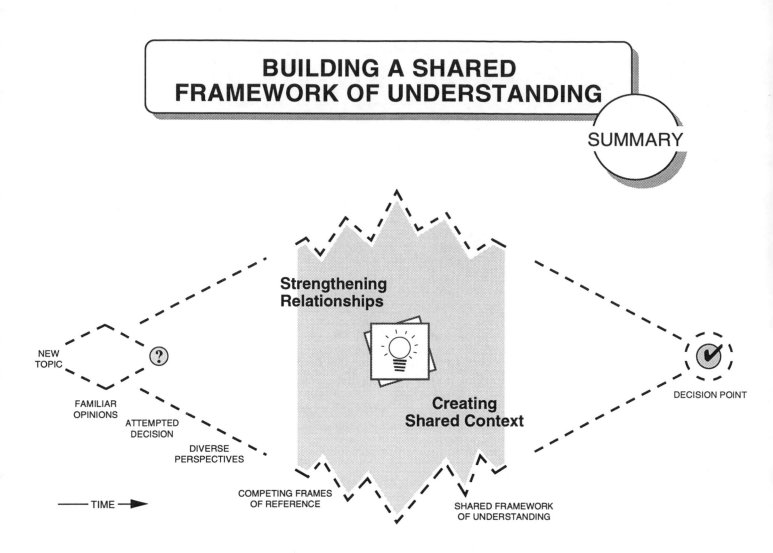

Strengthening
Relationships

Creating
Shared Context

NEW
TOPIC

?

FAMILIAR
OPINIONS

ATTEMPTED
DECISION

DIVERSE
PERSPECTIVES

COMPETING FRAMES
OF REFERENCE

SHARED FRAMEWORK
OF UNDERSTANDING

DECISION POINT

TIME

Structured activities like those presented in this chapter are very helpful during periods of misunderstanding. They help people focus on the same thing at the same time. But it's not easy for a facilitator to obtain a group's agreement to *do* a structured activity. People oppose facilitators regularly – and this is particularly true in the Groan Zone, when the trust-levels are low and the tension-levels are high. Thus, someone may oppose a suggestion because s/he imagines it was proposed as a direct, personal response to something s/he said. Someone else may interpret a facilitator's suggestion as a power play. Others may feel that the proposed activity would slow down the pace of discussion, or move the group in the wrong direction. For all these reasons and more, facilitators must expect the group to challenge, and probably reject, a high percentage of such suggestions.

When this happens, remember to *honor objections and ask for suggestions.* In the Groan Zone, everyone's ideas are frequently misunderstood – and yours will be too. Keep in mind that your role is to help, not to be "right." Be patient, be tolerant, be flexible; don't be attached to what you suggest. Here's the general rule: in the Groan Zone people are under pressure – *they need the facilitator's support.*

15

DEVELOPING INCLUSIVE SOLUTIONS

PRINCIPLES AND TOOLS FOR FINDING
SOLUTIONS THAT TAKE EVERYONE'S
INTERESTS INTO ACCOUNT

- **Introduction to the Convergent Zone**

- **Principles for Achieving Both/And Solutions**

- **Six Case Studies for Exploring Inclusive Principles**

- **Seven Tools for Creative Reframing**

- **Five Tools for Strengthening Good Ideas**

- **Summary**

DEVELOPING INCLUSIVE SOLUTIONS

INTRODUCTION

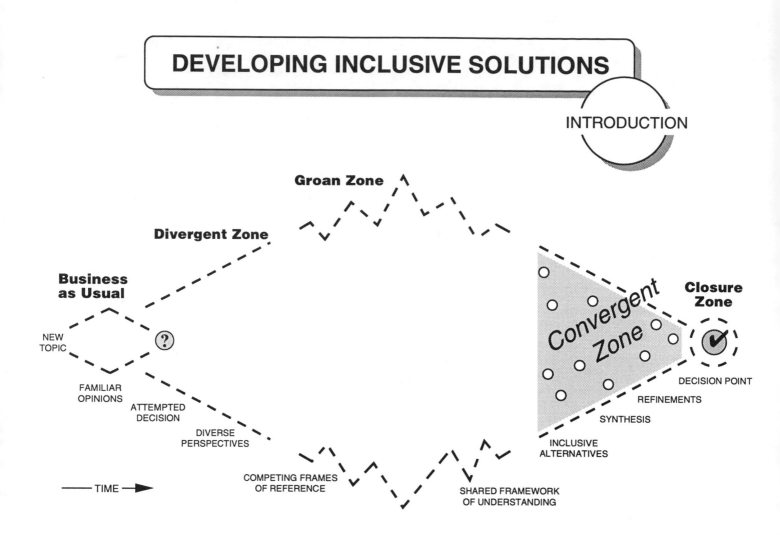

In the Convergent Zone, the facilitator's main task is to help the group explore alternatives and synthesize them into a solution that will work for everyone. This is often easier than it sounds. Once a group has managed to build a shared framework of understanding, the discussion can move pretty quickly, and quite comfortably, with little intervention.

There are many exceptions, however. Some groups have trouble thinking creatively – they need help breaking out of their habitual mental categories. To spur their imagination, a facilitator may wish to provide them with case studies of inclusive solutions. S/he can present real-life examples, and then ask people for insights that may apply to their current situation.

There are other groups who become almost intoxicated with the excitement of fast-paced thinking – they are prone to make hasty decisions that are destined to become underfunded and overcommitted. Those groups need a facilitator's help to be rigorous, not impulsive, as they fine-tune their thinking and strengthen the logic and the quality of their ideas.

DEVELOPING INCLUSIVE SOLUTIONS

THREE TYPES OF THINKING IN THE CONVERGENT ZONE

A group enters the Convergent Zone when it has developed a shared framework of understanding. Its discussion then becomes much easier. Here's a sample of what happens: First someone offers an interesting idea and others try it on for size. Someone else adds to it or blends it with a completely different idea. People are able to say to themselves, "I know why so-and-so would not like that idea; I wonder if I can think of a solution to that difficulty." The whole group is operating within a shared context of meaning. When this happens – when the members of a group can realistically include one another's perspectives in their thinking – they are on their way to finding a solution that will incorporate everyone's needs and goals. This is the work of the Convergent Zone.

Three types of convergent thinking will be discussed in this chapter: *Exploring Inclusive Principles; Creative Reframing;* and *Strengthening Good Ideas.*

Type 1: Exploring Inclusive Principles

Exploring Inclusive Principles entails identifying and discussing principles that promote creative problem solving. A group can use these principles to develop a solution that works for everyone. A fine way to explore inclusive principles is to study case examples and discuss their relevance to the situation at hand. The essence of this type of thinking is *application.*

Type 2: Creative Reframing

Creative Reframing involves altering one's beliefs about the nature of the problem at hand. Members identify core assumptions and deliberately replace or reverse them in order to gain an alternative perspective. The goal is to acquire a "breakthrough experience," a significant change in outlook. The essence of this type of thinking is *paradigm-shifting.*

Type 3: Strengthening Good Ideas

Strengthening Good Ideas refers to the group's efforts to evaluate and refine the logic and quality of their thinking. The process is iterative – every new insight causes the basic idea to strengthen and grow. The essence of this type of thinking is *critical reasoning.*

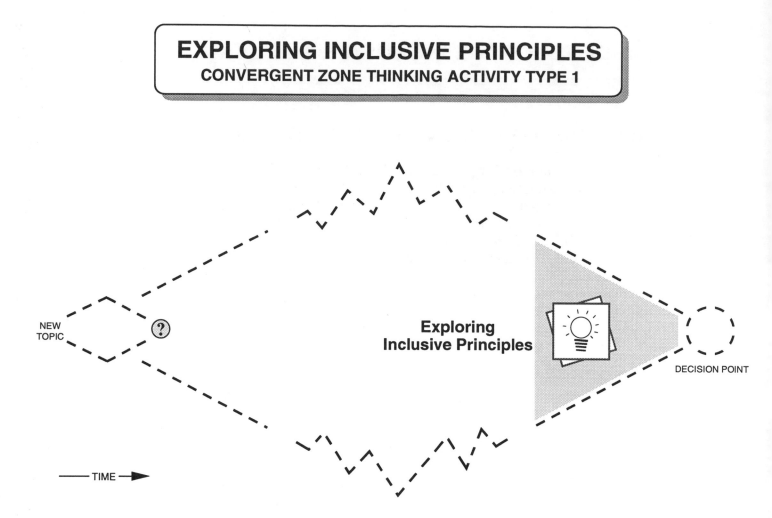

EXPLORING INCLUSIVE PRINCIPLES
CONVERGENT ZONE THINKING ACTIVITY TYPE 1

Inclusive, nonadversarial, problem solving principles – like those listed on the next page – are often at the heart of sustainable agreements. For example, consider the case of the Mendocino County timber tax committee (see Chapter 12). After years of disagreement over the rate of logging, they found an inclusive solution when they realized that a change in the tax code would benefit everyone. Thus they switched from taxing *standing trees* – a method they had used for forty years – to taxing *cut trees*. Underlying this change was a creative problem solving principle: *challenge fixed assumptions – just because something has always been done one way doesn't mean it has to be done that way in the future.*

A facilitator can encourage group members to identify and discuss inclusive principles that might apply to their current situation. This will foster creative thinking. For example, you might show a group the Mendocino case, discuss it and then ask, "What are *our* group's fixed assumptions? Are there any *we* can challenge?" As this example shows, real-life cases are an excellent vehicle for helping groups explore inclusive principles. Several more case studies are presented in the following pages.

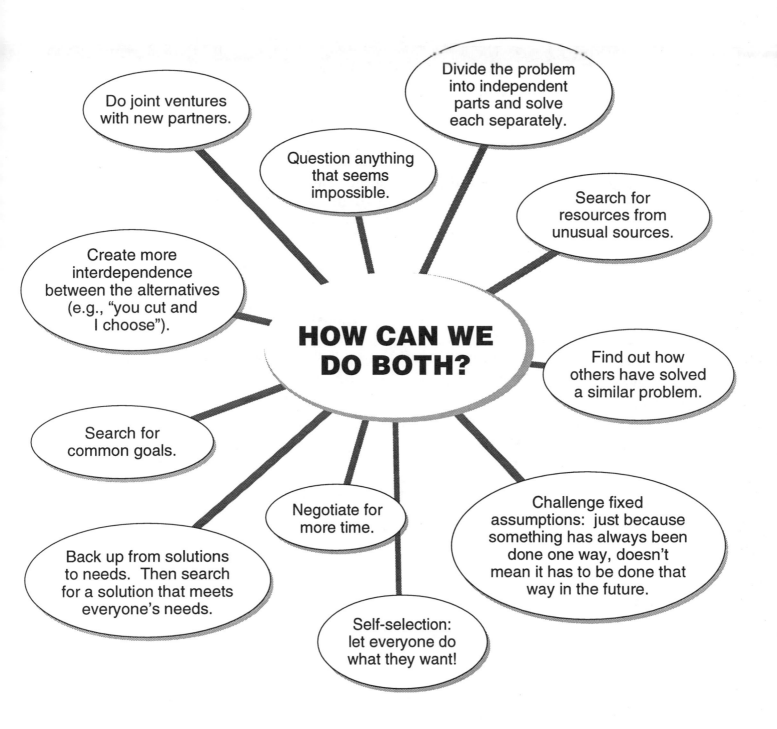

These problem-solving principles help people synthesize seemingly opposing alternatives into an integrated solution. Note that none of these require group members to use adversarial methods to resolve their differences; *they all lead to solutions that work for everyone.*

USING CASE STUDIES

WHY

The next six pages present capsule summaries of inclusive solutions to difficult real-life problems. Each case demonstrates the use of an *inclusive principle* – that is, a problem solving principle that enables participants to develop a creative solution that takes everyone's interests into account.

Left to their own inclinations, few groups make the effort to keep looking for fresh ideas. Thus the facilitator has a key role in motivating people to search for inclusive solutions. But this creates a challenge. Some facilitators offer their groups potential solutions, but many groups don't respond well to facilitators who attempt to "join the group." There is a surprisingly high likelihood that a group will reject a facilitator's solution without even considering its merits.

Fortunately, there are alternatives. One particularly useful method is to present real-life examples of inclusive solutions to difficult problems, and encourage discussion. For many people, discussing a case study is more effective than listening to a lecture. This approach preserves the facilitator's neutrality even as it inspires group members to keep working toward sustainable agreements. Accordingly, the following examples have been designed to be used as tools that can stimulate discussion.

HOW

1. Photocopy and distribute some or all of the following case studies.

2. Ask everyone to read one or two cases.

3. Have everyone find a partner and discuss their case studies. Ask, "What reactions are you having to what you just read?"

4. After five minutes, reconvene the large group and ask, "Has anyone found a principle that might shed new light on *our* situation?" Allow ample time for discussion.

EXPLORING INCLUSIVE PRINCIPLES

CASE STUDY: BREAKING WITH TRADITION

PROBLEM

At San Jose National Bank, many of the employees were women. One year, ten percent of the staff became pregnant. A high rate of maternity leave would clearly have caused a serious drop in productivity. Management pondered the options. Should maternity leave be limited? Should some of the employees be laid off? The expectant mothers recognized that the bank could suffer, but they also felt it was important to be with their babies during their first months of life. Each group understood the other's point of view, but no one felt able to change positions.

SOLUTION

Mothers were allowed to bring their infants to the office and keep them by their desks. They stayed at work the whole day and tended to their infants' needs as necessary. Their pay was slightly reduced to reflect the actual hours they worked. When the infants became toddlers, they were placed at a nearby day care center sponsored by the bank.

APPLICATION

The solution to this problem was to break with the tradition that parents must choose between working and being with their children. Here, the bank's needs (getting the work done) and the mothers' needs (staying with their infants) were combined. In your situation, is there a tradition that locks you into an either/or position? What are the needs of each "side"? Is there a solution that incorporates all those needs?

Source: *West Magazine*, San Jose Mercury News, March 6, 1994.

EXPLORING INCLUSIVE PRINCIPLES

CASE STUDY: YOU CUT AND I CHOOSE

PROBLEM

Representatives from many nations met to develop international policies regarding the mining of oceanic resources. One problem they addressed was how to best allocate underwater mining sites. The Enterprise, a U.N. organization representing poorer countries, charged that rich countries had an unfair advantage. They feared that private companies from wealthy countries could identify the superior mining sites because they had better radar and mining equipment and superior expertise. With this knowledge, the rich countries could propose an unequal allocation of mining resources, and the poorer countries would have no way to evaluate the fairness of the allocation.

SOLUTION

The representatives decided to ask a private company to identify two mining sites of equal value, using its sophisticated equipment and expertise. The Enterprise would then choose one of the sites for the poorer countries to mine. The private company would get the other one. In this way, the private companies would have an incentive to identify two sites of equal value, thus giving poorer nations the benefit of their expertise.

APPLICATION

Does your situation involve competition for a fixed resource? If so, how might you create more interdependence among the competitors? In other words, what could be done to tie the success of the more powerful party to the success of the less powerful party? What incentives might induce the more powerful party to participate?

Source: *Getting to Yes*, R. Fisher and W. Ury, New York: Penguin Books, 1983. p. 58.

CASE STUDY:
DISCOVERING COMMON GROUND

PROBLEM

A suburb of a large city was becoming more and more racially diverse. Residents formed a community council to preserve the neighborhood's character while simultaneously promoting racial integration. The council suspected that financial institutions were cutting back on their investment in the neighborhood because of the demographic changes. After investigating several local lending institutions, the council found evidence that lenders were indeed using discriminatory tactics. The council demanded more investment in its neighborhood, and it threatened to boycott the lenders. The lenders denied the charges and refused to cooperate with further monitoring.

SOLUTION

At first the two sides locked horns and argued over who was to blame for the disinvestment. Their breakthrough came when they realized they all shared a common concern: preserving the neighborhood. Together they founded a local development corporation that promoted commercial revitalization, and they created a foreclosure rehabilitation program for which the lenders raised funds.

APPLICATION

Focusing on shared concerns and developing a shared vision helped these groups move from blaming each other for the current situation to taking effective action.

In your situation, are you affixing blame rather than recognizing mutual interest? Perhaps you can identify a shared problem, a shared goal or another source of common ground.

Source: *Collaborating*, B. Gray, San Francisco: Jossey-Bass, 1989. p. 95.

CASE STUDY: INCLUDING THE "TROUBLEMAKERS" IN THE SOLUTION

PROBLEM

A community had a problem with its high school youth, whose public behavior was becoming increasingly unruly, especially at night. The city administration decided to increase police patrols and impose a curfew upon the youth in the neighborhood. Community members rejected this decision. They felt that the curfew would restrict everyone's freedom, and the increased police presence would probably *increase* violence in the neighborhood.

SOLUTION

Neighborhood residents met and discussed ideas for solving this problem. They decided that a midnight basketball program would provide the youths with an alternative to hanging out and getting in trouble. The community members saw this as a way to improve neighborhood safety without requiring outside intervention. The city administrators were pleased because the program would help keep youth off the streets at night.

APPLICATION

The neighborhood residents' solution supported the youthful tendency to release energy instead of repressing it. In your situation, is there a specific group of "trouble makers" who appear to be causing the problem? Suppose that you disqualify all repressive solutions. What supportive possibilities arise?

Source: Marshall Rosenberg's workshop on *Compassionate Communication*, February 1995, as related by Liz Dittrich to Sam Kaner's *Group Facilitation Skills* class, June 1995.

CASE STUDY: UNUSUAL PARTNERSHIP

PROBLEM

A small Western city had a multi-million dollar budget surplus. Two groups immediately began vying for the funds. On one side a coalition of women's groups wished to use the money to expand the city's inadequate day-care facilities. On the other side homeowners and the city's fire fighters wanted to upgrade their antiquated fire fighting equipment to protect homes and lower insurance costs.

SOLUTION

A small portion of the money was used to convert the city's old fire stations into day care centers. The new centers were used to attract state and federal matching funds to operate them. The majority of the money was then used to build three new fire stations. The new stations raised the city's "fire rating" from AA to AAA, thus lowering insurance rates and raising property values.

APPLICATION

Initially the two groups were competing for limited resources. When they worked together as partners they were able to identify additional resources.

In your current situation, can your group partner with its competitors? Are there other unusual alliances you could imagine making?

Source: *How to Make Meetings Work*, M. Doyle and D. Straus, New York: Jove Press, 1982, p. 56.

CASE STUDY: LOCATING RESOURCES TO SUPPORT LONG-TERM STABILITY

PROBLEM

In a rainforest in New Guinea, the indigenous people were approached by a large lumber corporation. The company offered to pay a lump sum for the right to clear-cut the forest and extract the hardwood trees. The deal sounded fantastic to many members of the impoverished forest tribe; they wanted to sell their only marketable commodity in exchange for money, which they could use to buy things they could not produce themselves. Local environmentalists, however, were alarmed; the forests would be completely and irreplaceably destroyed.

SOLUTION

Environmentalists helped the indigenous people start their own lumber company with a small portable saw mill that could process trees one at a time. The cut lumber was worth significantly more than the company had offered for the trees, so the people did not feel pressured to log more than was appropriate for the health of the forest. The logging company purchased the lumber, which it then resold at a profit overseas.

APPLICATION

Once the indigenous people acquired a mill, they were able to look out for their long-term interests. In your situation are you attempting to solve a problem with a one-shot-deal solution? If so, what additional resources might allow you to find a solution that takes into account your needs over time? Where might you obtain those resources?

Source: Told to Sarah Fisk by John Seed, environmentalist and author.

CREATIVE REFRAMING
CONVERGENT ZONE THINKING ACTIVITY TYPE 2

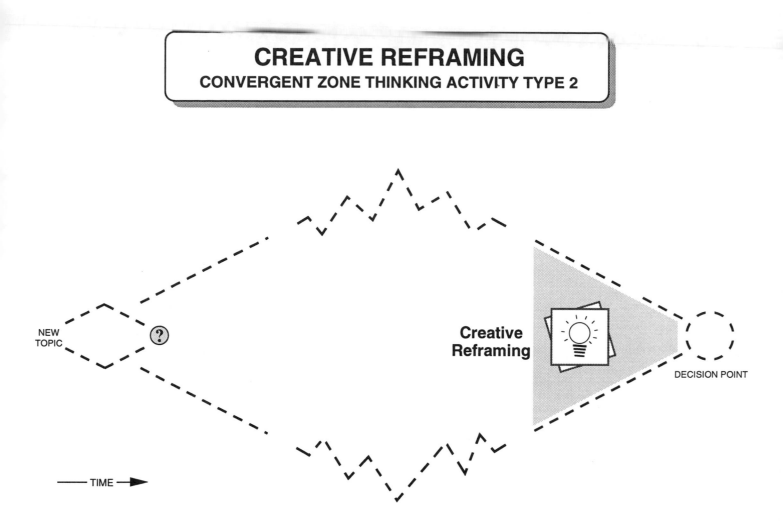

Creative Reframing activities – like those presented on the pages ahead – invite group members to break out of their normal categories of analysis and re-examine their beliefs and assumptions. These activities require participants to make deliberate mental shifts in order to look at a problem from a completely different angle. Making these shifts can lead group members to see choices to which they were blind, just moments before.

Because it is counterintuitive and "unnatural," creative reframing is a type of thinking that rarely happens spontaneously. Nonetheless a facilitator can also use informal techniques to help participants shift their thinking. For example, you could ask questions like, "Is that the only way to do such-and-such?" or "Suppose such-and-such had never happened; would that change your choice of action?" These are simple questions that can be proposed with relatively little forethought. By comparison the structured thinking activities that follow are more elaborate. Either method works.

TWO WAYS OF LOOKING AT THE SAME PROBLEM

PRESENTING PROBLEM	REFRAMED PROBLEM
It's them.	It's all of us.
It's a problem.	It's an opportunity.
Our goal is unachievable.	We don't have our goal broken into realistic steps.
Our product won't sell.	We're trying to sell our product to the wrong people.
We don't have enough resources.	We are wasting the resources we do have.
We need to gather more input.	We need to pay more attention to the input we're already getting.
Our employees are incompetent.	Our employees don't have enough time to do a quality job.
We don't have enough money.	We haven't figured out how to find new sources of money.
We can't get along with each other.	We haven't made the commitment to work through our feelings toward one another.
We don't have any power in this system.	We haven't found our leverage points in this system.
We don't have enough time to do all of these things.	We have to decide what to do now, and what to do later.

CREATIVE REFRAMING

INTRODUCING REFRAMING TO A GROUP

WHY

Once someone perceives a problem in a particular way s/he may find it difficult to see that problem in any other way. Our minds tend to lock into a pattern of thought. For example, many job recruiters routinely decline to hire a talented applicant because of the applicant's dress or appearance; yet this habit persists even when recruiting for technical positions, when appearance would have no impact on performance.

When tackling difficult problems, most people reach conclusions quickly. They believe they have explored every option for a solution and that it would be pointless to waste more time. The idea that it might be possible to reframe a problem – that is, to dramatically alter their understanding of the nature of the problem – is, for most people, a paradigm shift.

Thus, when a facilitator decides to encourage a group to undertake a creative reframing process, s/he often finds that the main challenge is to motivate people to invest the time. This tool is designed to help facilitators overcome that initial wall of resistance.

HOW

1. Hand out copies of the facing page, *Two Ways Of Looking At A Problem.*

2. Ask people to discuss the differences between a presenting problem and a reframed problem. Remember that many people will be thinking about this concept for the first time ever; as part of digesting a new idea they may say things that sound rigid or naive. Expect remarks like, "As far as I'm concerned, this whole idea is ridiculous." Remember to honor all points of view and remain supportive throughout the discussion.

3. After several minutes say, "Now let's apply this theory to our own situation. Could someone please state *our* presenting problem?" Write the presenting problem on a flipchart. Then ask the group to brainstorm a list of *reframes* of the problem. Record all answers on flipcharts.

4. After the brainstorm, encourage members to discuss the implications of their new ideas. Say, "As you look over the list, what are your reactions?"

WHAT'S UNCHANGEABLE ABOUT THIS PROBLEM?

WHY

Habits of thought are as hard to break as habits of any other kind. Suppose, for example, that someone thinks his/her boss is afraid of confrontation. That person may find it very difficult to change his/her opinion – even if the boss has actually changed.

Entire groups fall into these habits of thought, too. For example, a management team had to refill a specific staff position five times in less than a year. Yet every time they lost another person, the managers simply recruited someone else for the job and crossed their fingers. Not till the end of the year did they consider re-organizing the department and doing away with that job altogether.

"What's Unchangeable About This Problem" allows a group to explore hidden assumptions and biases in the way they have defined a problem. Once a group has identified a self-limiting assumption, they often discover a new line of thought that leads to a creative, innovative solution to their problem.

HOW

1. At the top of a flipchart, write "What's unchangeable about our problem?"

2. List everyone's answers.

3. Ask the group to look over the list and identify any hidden assumptions and biases. Encourage open discussion.

4. Based on these insights, list any aspects of the problem that may be changeable after all.

CREATIVE REFRAMING

KEY WORDS

WHY

Everyone makes assumptions. People often take it for granted that everyone else is making the same assumptions about such things as the meanings of words, the likelihood that an event will occur, and the motives behind a person's actions – to name just a few. When members are unaware of differences in their assumptions, they may find it very difficult to understand each other's thinking and behavior.

For example, the director of a city agency asked her staff for input on a proposed reorganization. A few people took her request seriously, but many others treated it lightly. This caused turmoil at staff meetings until the explanation was found. Several people had heard a rumor that the director was leaving; they doubted the reorganization would ever occur. The few who worked hard to give input were those who had not heard the rumor. These differences in assumptions were never mentioned, but they influenced everyone's commitment to the task.

Key Words helps people explore the meaning of the statements they make to one another. By discussing the meanings of key words, people can identify unspoken assumptions that are causing miscommunication.

HOW

1. Have the group compose a problem statement. For example, "New computers are too expensive to purchase." Write it on a flipchart.

2. Ask group members to identify the key words in the statement. Underline all key words. For example "<u>New computers</u> are too <u>expensive</u> to <u>purchase</u>."

3. Have the group identify which word to focus on first. Then ask, "What questions does this word raise?" Record all responses. Then ask, "Does this word suggest any assumptions that can be challenged? For example, is 'purchase' the only way to obtain new computers?"

4. Repeat Step 3 for each key word. Note: Encourage open discussions throughout this activity.

This tool was inspired by an exercise called "Lasso" in *How To Make Meetings Work*, M. Doyle and D. Straus, New York: Jove Books, 1982.

TWO REFRAMING ACTIVITIES

REVERSING ASSUMPTIONS

1. Hang a sheet of chart paper titled, "Assumptions About This Problem."

2. Have the group list its beliefs about
   • the causes of the problem
   • the connections between different aspects of the problem.

3. Ask someone to select an item from the list, and reverse it. For example, consider an item like "We are losing our best employees." Reverse this to "We're *keeping* our best employees."

4. Ask, "How could we bring about this new, opposite state of affairs?" Encourage a brainstorm of answers.

5. Choose another assumption and repeat steps 3 and 4. When done, discuss ideas that seem promising.

A version of this activity appears in *ThinkerToys*, M. Michalko, Berkeley, CA: Ten Speed Press, 1992, p. 45.

REMOVING CONSTRAINTS

1. Have the group generate constraints by asking, "What is keeping us from developing the best solution to this problem?"

2. Upon completing the list, consider each item one at a time, asking, "What if *this* were not a problem? For example, "What if we had plenty of funds available? How would we solve our problem in *that* case?"

3. Treat all answers as a brainstorm. Suspend judgment and discourage discussion at this point.

4. When finished with all items on the list, encourage the group to identify ideas that seem worthy of further discussion.

CREATIVE REFRAMING

TWO MORE REFRAMING ACTIVITIES

RECENTERING THE CAUSE

1. Ask the group to break the problem into its major components. For example, consider the problem of keeping public libraries open. This might divide into such components as "funding," "usage," "staffing," "civic priorities" etc.

2. Ask a volunteer to select any component. For example, suppose someone picks "staffing".

3. Treat that selection as the central cause of the problem. Ask, "How might this affect our view of the problem?" For example, suppose "staffing" is viewed as the central cause of the problem. Someone might now suggest a new approach to the problem: perhaps volunteers could help staff the library during busy hours, enabling the library to remain open with less funding.

CATASTROPHIZING
(WE'RE DOOMED NO MATTER WHAT WE DO.)

1. Ask everyone to think about the problem from their own perspective, imagining anything and everything that could go wrong.

2. Have each person in turn state his/her worst-case scenario.

3. Encourage each new speaker to build on the previous ideas, until the situation seems doomed. Note that complaining and whining are perfectly acceptable now.

4. When the humor has subsided, have the group identify obstacles that merit further discussion.

5. Go down the list of obstacles one at a time, asking "Is *this* one capable of producing a catastrophe?" If so, ask, "What could be done to reduce its potential impact?"

STRENGTHENING GOOD IDEAS
CONVERGENT ZONE THINKING ACTIVITY TYPE 3

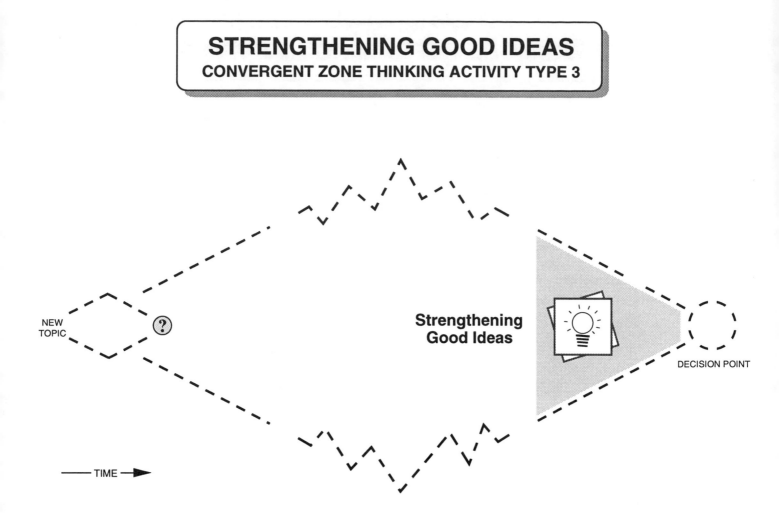

**Strengthening
Good Ideas**

NEW
TOPIC

DECISION POINT

— TIME →

Strengthening Good Ideas is a type of thinking that encompasses such questions as, "What resources will we need to make this work? Do we have them?" and "Who else should take a look at this idea? What would *they* say?" and "If we actually decide to move forward, who will do what by when?" During this period of critical thinking, the facilitator's job is to help group members analyze potential problems with their game plan. Are there flaws in the reasoning? Are there other options that have not been adequately explored? Does the idea really meet the group's stated criteria for success? The more questions like these a group can discuss, the better will be the quality of the group's eventual decisions. And that translates into sustainability.

But bringing these questions to the group's awareness is quite a challenge for most facilitators. The role of facilitator, after all, is neutral and non-judgmental. As a rule, groups who have built a shared framework of understanding can evaluate and refine their ideas without formal structure – and without much facilitation, either. But occasionally – especially when the stakes are high – a group may want to ensure the caliber of its work by using structured thinking activities.

STRENGTHENING GOOD IDEAS

CLARIFYING EVALUATION CRITERIA

WHY

How should a group choose one proposal over another? One way is to agree on the criteria to use in evaluating each proposal. For example, suppose a group agreed that its most important criteria were "easy to do" and "inexpensive." These criteria could help them reject a proposal that would be expensive or difficult, even if the project seemed interesting.

This activity helps group members to discuss and reach agreement on a list of five or fewer criteria, by defining criteria *before* specific proposals are brought up for consideration.

HOW

1. Have the group brainstorm a list of answers to this question: "By doing this project (or, solving this problem, developing this plan, etc.), what are we trying to accomplish?"

2. Start a new chart titled "selection criteria." Facilitate the group to reword the items on the first list so that each item is now a statement of a possible selection criterion. For example, if an item from the brainstorm list is "We're trying to get two opposing factions to work together," the rewording might be, "It allows both factions to work together." Another rewording might be, "It appeals to both factions."

3. Explain that the list will soon be reduced to no more than five items. To prepare members to make that final judgment, have people break into small groups and discuss which criteria seem most important, and why.

4. Reconvene the large group. Have people select items from the list of criteria and ask them to advocate for retaining those items on a final list of five or fewer criteria.

5. Give everyone five votes. Tally the results and eliminate all but the top five vote-getters.

STRENGTHENING GOOD IDEAS
PAYOFFS AND RISKS

WHY

This activity improves the viability of a proposal by reducing the costs and risks that are associated with it.

For example, the mayor of a large city recently received several million dollars to improve public transportation. The public favored a proposal to spend the money on new bus routes. But the mayor was *also* committed to upholding a hiring freeze. No new city employees were to be hired until the budget was balanced. On one hand, without new bus drivers, no more routes could be added. On the other hand, if new bus drivers were hired the other government agencies would lobby for exemptions for *their* programs.

Payoffs and Risks helped the mayor's planning staff explore in detail the risks they would face if they went ahead with a route expansion. Through the analysis, they discovered a way to reduce their risk. They enlisted the local newspapers in an editorial campaign to build political support for this exception to the hiring freeze. It was successful and they were able to add three new bus routes without opposition.

HOW

1. Hang three sheets of flipchart paper. Title the first page, "Payoffs" and the second page, "Risks." Leave the third page untitled.

2. On page one, list the payoffs associated with the proposal.

3. On page two, list the risks associated with the same proposal.

4. Now title page three, "Ways to reduce risk." For each risk listed on the "Risks" page, discuss options for reducing the costs and/or the extent of the risk. Record the discussion on page three.

5. After the costs are more fully understood, ask for new proposals that preserve the payoffs while incorporating some of the risk-reducing options.

STRENGTHENING GOOD IDEAS

RESOURCE ANALYSIS: CAN WE REALLY MAKE THIS WORK?

WHY

Sometimes groups agree to proposals that sound wonderful, but have not been thought through very well. This is usually not a problem, because most such agreements pertain to matters of small importance. But occasionally, a group will agree to a huge undertaking with absolutely no sense of what they're in for.

For example, a group of eight nurses once agreed to organize a large conference that would bring together representatives from hundreds of agencies in Los Angeles. The purpose of the conference was to build a coalition that could influence state and county funding policies. The organizers did not have the slightest grasp of the effort it would take them – yet they publicized the conference and kept taking on new responsibilities as they came up. Eventually one person lost her job and another got very sick. The conference itself was disorganized, poorly attended and, ultimately, insignificant. In retrospect the nurses said, "We should have been more realistic to begin with."

HOW

1. Ask the group to list the major tasks which must be achieved if the proposal under consideration is to be implemented.

2. Assign two or three people to think about each task. Have them choose a record-keeper and a spokesperson.

3. Give the small groups the following instruction. "For the next ten minutes, think about the steps necessary to complete your assigned task. Break the task into small, do-able action steps."

4. When time is up, reconvene the large group and ask the spokesperson from each group to report on his/her group's work.

5. After all committees have reported, ask everyone to discuss whether the overall proposal is adequate or whether it requires modification.

STRENGTHENING GOOD IDEAS

WHO ELSE NEEDS TO EVALUATE THIS PROPOSAL?

WHY

Most decisions do not just affect the people who make them. Obviously, not everyone who will be affected can participate in making a decision and planning its implementation. Nonetheless, it can be very, very costly to overlook the perspectives of those who did not participate in developing the reasoning that led to the decison.

This activity helps a group to think proactively about the question, "Who else needs to be consulted?" *It usually takes a group two or three hours – sometimes longer – to go through all the steps.* Obviously this is a significant investment of group time. To decide whether or not to do this activity, ask, "How much time will we lose if we don't do this thinking?"

HOW

1. Have group members generate lists of people who:

   - will be directly affected by this decision;
   - have final sign-off authority;
   - have to implement the decision;
   - could sabotage the process.

2. Take a few moments to examine the list. Discuss the following questions: "What's the likelihood that any of these stakeholders would disagree with our ultimate decision? Would their disagreement impact our ability to implement this decision?"

3. Next, consider in turn each person or group on the list: who should be consulted before the final decision is made?

4. For each person or group who should be consulted, decide on the best method for doing so. Some methods for including other stakeholders are interviews, focus groups, questionnaires and an invitation to a core group meeting.

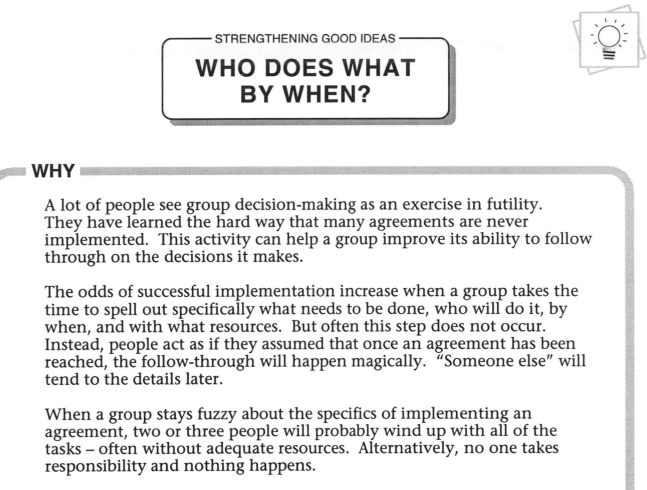

STRENGTHENING GOOD IDEAS

WHO DOES WHAT BY WHEN?

WHY

A lot of people see group decision-making as an exercise in futility. They have learned the hard way that many agreements are never implemented. This activity can help a group improve its ability to follow through on the decisions it makes.

The odds of successful implementation increase when a group takes the time to spell out specifically what needs to be done, who will do it, by when, and with what resources. But often this step does not occur. Instead, people act as if they assumed that once an agreement has been reached, the follow-through will happen magically. "Someone else" will tend to the details later.

When a group stays fuzzy about the specifics of implementing an agreement, two or three people will probably wind up with all of the tasks – often without adequate resources. Alternatively, no one takes responsibility and nothing happens.

This activity supports group members to consider, in advance, the resources needed to undertake these efforts and to commit to well defined tasks by specific times. Moreover, the responsibilities often are distributed more evenly, because the issues are discussed openly when everyone is listening.

HOW

1. Draw a matrix with four vertical columns. Title the columns: "Task"; "Who"; "By When"; "Resources Needed."

2. Under the first heading, "Tasks," list all tasks that need to be done. If additional tasks are identified later, add them to the list.

3. For each task on the list, answer these three questions: *"Who will do this? By when? What resources are needed?"* Often this thinking is done in an open discussion format, in which group members flip back and forth from one question to another.

4. As specific agreements are made, write them on the chart.

DEVELOPING INCLUSIVE SOLUTIONS

SUMMARY

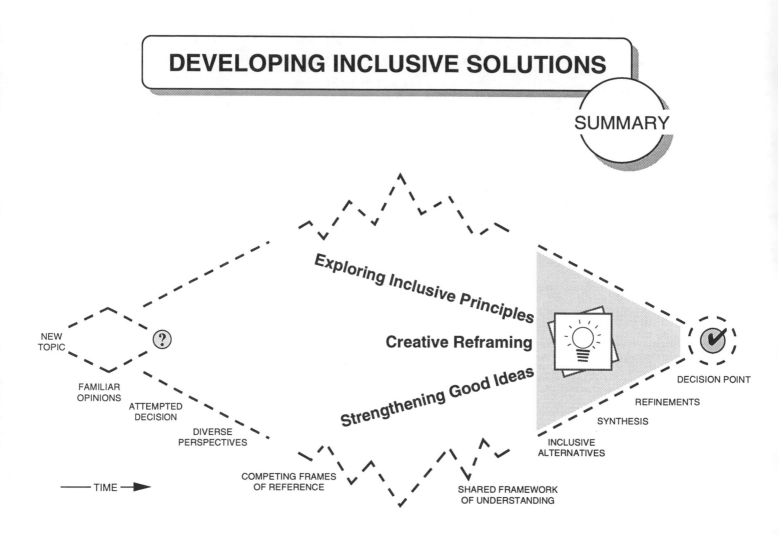

Three common types of convergent thinking are shown above. Each type can be supported by activities like those presented in this chapter. Some activities help a group gain insight into the principles underlying inclusive solutions. Others enable a group to manipulate their assumptions, in order to break out of fixed positions. Still others support participants to evaluate and refine the quality and the logic of their thinking.

Structured thinking activities are useful when a group appears to be trapped in an *Either/Or* mentality. Groups in this condition need inspiration and stimulation. Structured activities also support groups to do the nitty-gritty work of making sure their ideas can be implemented. But it would be misleading to suggest that groups in the Convergent Zone spend much time engaged in structured thinking. The truth is the opposite. Convergent Zone discussions are largely self-managing. For many facilitators, the hardest part is learning to sit down and get out of the group's way!

Sustainable agreements require well-thought-out ideas that incorporate everyone's needs and goals. If the struggle of the Groan Zone is the heart of a sustainable agreement, the ingenuity of the Convergent Zone is the brain.

16

STRIVING FOR UNANIMITY

WORKING WITH
GRADIENTS OF AGREEMENT

▶ Unanimity and Consensus
  Decision-Making

▶ Gradients of Agreement:
  Yes, No, and Shades in Between

▶ The Continuum of Unanimity:
  Enthusiastic Support
  Lukewarm Support
  Ambivalent Support
  Meager Support

▶ Tools for Using
  a Gradients of Agreement Scale

▶ Summary

STRIVING FOR UNANIMITY
INTRODUCTION

THE POWER OF UNANIMOUS AGREEMENT

The word "unanimous" comes from two Latin words: *unus*, meaning "one;" and *animus*, meaning "spirit." A group that reaches unanimous agreement is a group that acts from one spirit. By this understanding a unanimous agreement can be expected to contain wisdom and soundness of judgment, because it expresses an idea that is felt by each person to be true. As the Quakers say, the decision speaks for everyone.

To reach unanimity, everyone must agree. This means that everyone has an individual veto. Thus, anyone who perceives that his/her interests are *not* being taken into account can keep the discussion alive for as many hours or weeks or months as it takes, to find a solution that works for everyone. This veto-capacity is the crux of the power of unanimous agreement. When a group is committed to reaching unanimous agreement, they are in effect making a commitment to remain in discussion until they develop a solution that takes everyone's needs into account.

UNANIMITY AND CONSENSUS

"Consensus" also has Latin origins. Its root word is *consentire,* which is a combination of two Latin words: *con,* meaning "with" or "together with" and *sentire,* meaning "to think and feel." *Consentire* thus translates as "to think and feel together."

Consensus is *the process* – a participatory process by which a group thinks and feels together en route to their decision. Unanimity, by contrast, is the point at which the group *reaches closure*. Many groups that practice consensus decision-making use unanimity as their decision rule for reaching closure – but many groups *do not*. For example, the Seva Foundation uses "unanimity minus one." So does the renowned collective, the Hog Farm. Some chapters of the Green Party use 80% as their acceptable level of agreement. Yet all such groups consider themselves to be sincere adherents of a consensus decision-making process.

In these cases, no single member has personal veto power. Nonetheless, individual voices wield significant influence – enough to ensure that the group will engage in a genuine process of thinking and feeling together.

STRIVING FOR UNANIMITY

Unanimous agreement may seem like a wonderful idea – but is it realistic? Most people answer this question with certainty: "No way!" And this includes many of those who have participated in groups that made an effort to strive for unanimity.

It has become increasingly common in recent years to hear a manager say to his or her staff, "I'd like everyone to agree on this issue." Or, "I want to get everyone's buy-in today." Both of these statements mean, "I want us to reach a unanimous agreement." Yet – as anyone knows who has attended one of those meetings – the ensuing discussion can produce some pretty mediocre results. All too often, a meeting ends with an agreement that never gets implemented. Just because someone declares that s/he wants everyone to agree, that doesn't mean people *will* agree.

Suppose someone asks the members of a group, "Can everyone agree to this proposal?" Now suppose that everyone answers, "Yes." At this point, the group has made a decision that, presumably, satisfies everyone. Since the agreement is unanimous, one would expect commitment from everyone to implement the decision, even under pressure. Yet it doesn't always work this way. Why not? Why is it that so many groups' attempts at seeking unanimous agreement produce such disappointing results?

One major reason is that "yes" and "no" can have many different meanings. Someone who says "yes" might mean, "This is one of the best decisions we've ever made." But they might also mean, "I'll go along with this idea but it doesn't thrill me." Similarly, "no" can mean anything from "Hold on, I don't understand this proposal yet," to "This offends my deepest values."

Using unanimity means that every person has veto over every decision. Thus, every time someone says "no" they are saying, "I require the group to spend more time on this discussion." This causes some group members to be very hesitant to say "no." They do not want to feel responsible for dragging out a discussion. In such cases, "yes" does not really mean "I agree." It means, "I don't really like this, but I don't want to hold us back."

On the other hand, many groups have members who will not say "yes" until every concern, big or small, has been thoroughly digested. They might say "No, I won't agree," when what they *mean* is "Wait, I have a question. There's something I don't understand."

GRADIENTS OF AGREEMENT

BETTER VOCABULARY

Endorsement	Endorsement with a Minor Point of Contention	Agreement with Reservations	Abstain	Stand Aside	Formal Disagreement, but Willing to Go with Majority	Formal Disagreement, With Request to Be Absolved of Responsibility for Implementation	Block
"I like it."	"Basically I like it."	"I can live with it."	"I have no opinion."	"I don't like this, but I don't want to hold up the group."	"I want my disagreement noted in writing, but I'll support the decision."	"I don't want to stop anyone else, but I don't want to be involved in implementing it."	"I veto this proposal."

This is the Community At Work *GRADIENTS OF AGREEMENT SCALE.*

The scale makes it easier for participants to be honest. Using it, members can register less-than-whole-hearted support without fearing that their statement will be interpreted as a veto.

COMMUNITY AT WORK ©1996

GRADIENTS OF AGREEMENT

ENTHUSIASTIC SUPPORT

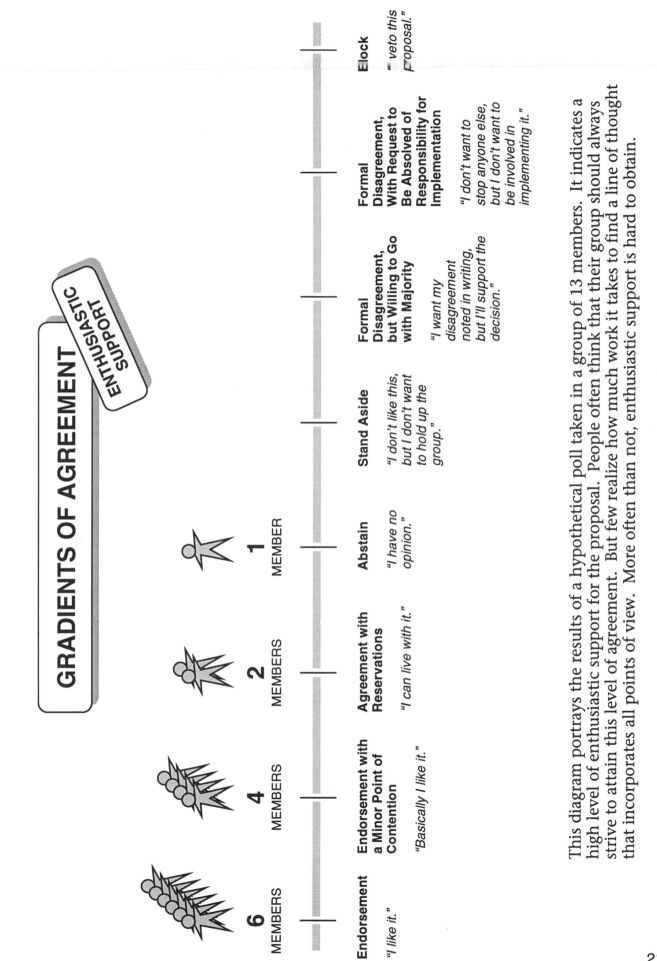

6 MEMBERS	4 MEMBERS	2 MEMBERS	1 MEMBER				
Endorsement	**Endorsement with a Minor Point of Contention**	**Agreement with Reservations**	**Abstain**	**Stand Aside**	**Formal Disagreement, but Willing to Go with Majority**	**Formal Disagreement, With Request to Be Absolved of Responsibility for Implementation**	**Block**
"I like it."	*"Basically I like it."*	*"I can live with it."*	*"I have no opinion."*	*"I don't like this, but I don't want to hold up the group."*	*"I want my disagreement noted in writing, but I'll support the decision."*	*"I don't want to stop anyone else, but I don't want to be involved in implementing it."*	*"I veto this proposal."*

This diagram portrays the results of a hypothetical poll taken in a group of 13 members. It indicates a high level of enthusiastic support for the proposal. People often think that their group should always strive to attain this level of agreement. But few realize how much work it takes to find a line of thought that incorporates all points of view. More often than not, enthusiastic support is hard to obtain.

COMMUNITY AT WORK ©1996

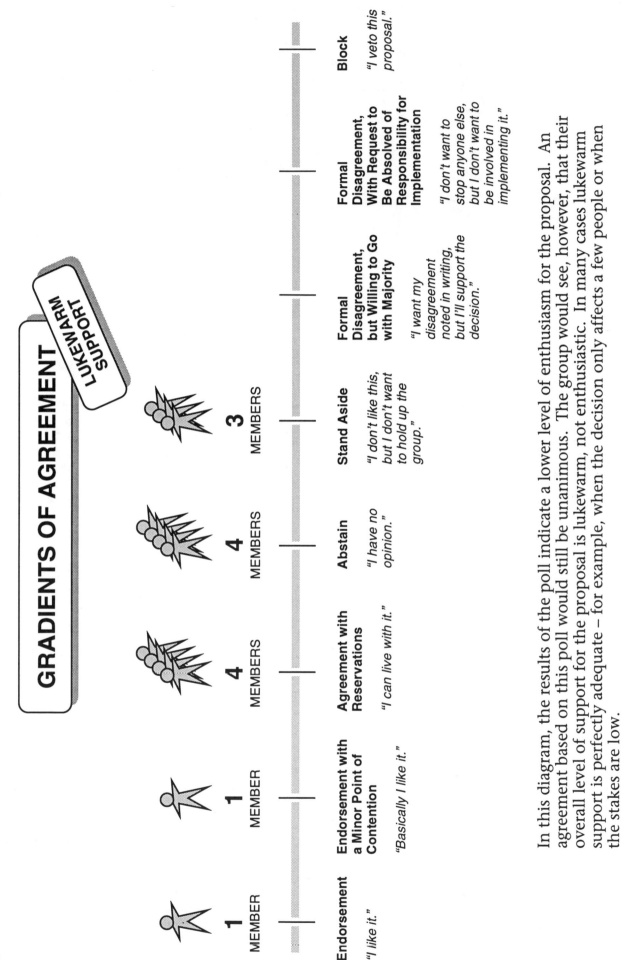

GRADIENTS OF AGREEMENT

LUKEWARM SUPPORT

Endorsement	Endorsement with a Minor Point of Contention	Agreement with Reservations	Abstain	Stand Aside	Formal Disagreement, but Willing to Go with Majority	Formal Disagreement, With Request to Be Absolved of Responsibility for Implementation	Block
"I like it."	"Basically I like it."	"I can live with it."	"I have no opinion."	"I don't like this, but I don't want to hold up the group."	"I want my disagreement noted in writing, but I'll support the decision."	"I don't want to stop anyone else, but I don't want to be involved in implementing it."	"I veto this proposal."
1 MEMBER	1 MEMBER	4 MEMBERS	4 MEMBERS	3 MEMBERS			

In this diagram, the results of the poll indicate a lower level of enthusiasm for the proposal. An agreement based on this poll would still be unanimous. The group would see, however, that their overall level of support for the proposal is lukewarm, not enthusiastic. In many cases lukewarm support is perfectly adequate – for example, when the decision only affects a few people or when the stakes are low.

COMMUNITY AT WORK © 1996

GRADIENTS OF AGREEMENT

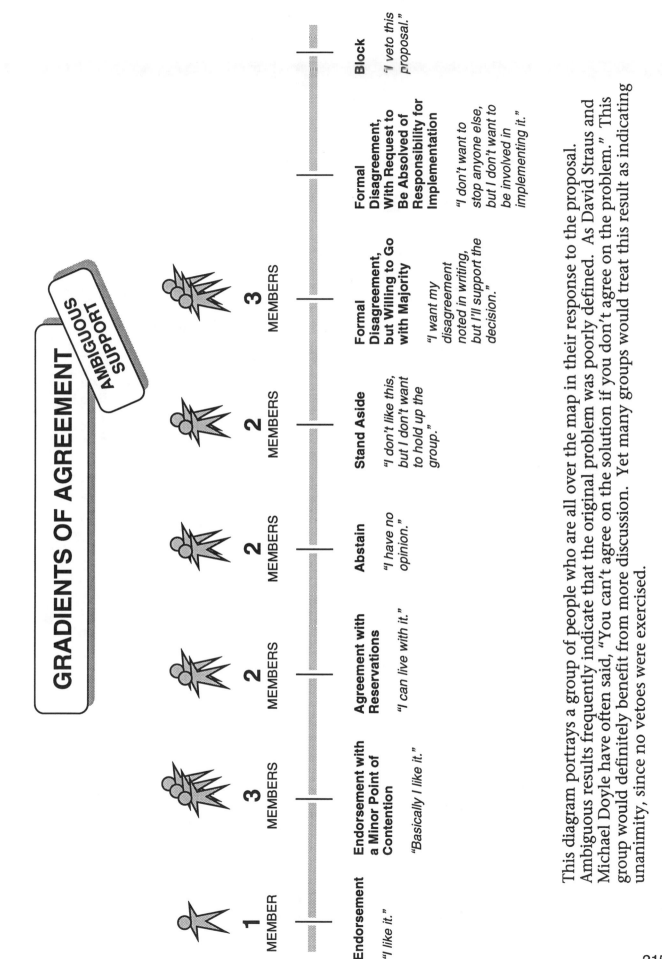

AMBIGUOUS SUPPORT

1 MEMBER	3 MEMBERS	2 MEMBERS	2 MEMBERS	2 MEMBERS	3 MEMBERS

Endorsement

"I like it."

Endorsement with a Minor Point of Contention

"Basically I like it."

Agreement with Reservations

"I can live with it."

Abstain

"I have no opinion."

Stand Aside

"I don't like this, but I don't want to hold up the group."

Formal Disagreement, but Willing to Go with Majority

"I want my disagreement noted in writing, but I'll support the decision."

Formal Disagreement, With Request to Be Absolved of Responsibility for Implementation

"I don't want to stop anyone else, but I don't want to be involved in implementing it."

Block

"I veto this proposal."

This diagram portrays a group of people who are all over the map in their response to the proposal. Ambiguous results frequently indicate that the original problem was poorly defined. As David Straus and Michael Doyle have often said, "You can't agree on the solution if you don't agree on the problem." This group would definitely benefit from more discussion. Yet many groups would treat this result as indicating unanimity, since no vetoes were exercised.

COMMUNITY AT WORK © 1996

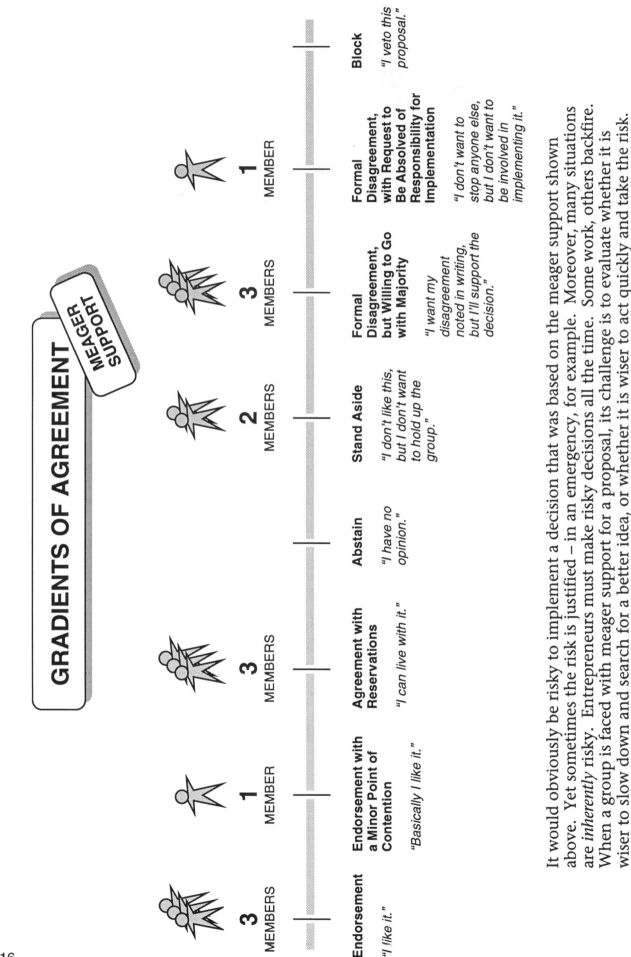

GRADIENTS OF AGREEMENT

MEAGER SUPPORT

Endorsement

"*I like it.*"

3 MEMBERS

Endorsement with a Minor Point of Contention

"*Basically I like it.*"

1 MEMBER

Agreement with Reservations

"*I can live with it.*"

3 MEMBERS

Abstain

"*I have no opinion.*"

Stand Aside

"*I don't like this, but I don't want to hold up the group.*"

2 MEMBERS

Formal Disagreement, but Willing to Go with Majority

"*I want my disagreement noted in writing, but I'll support the decision.*"

3 MEMBERS

Formal Disagreement, with Request to Be Absolved of Responsibility for Implementation

"*I don't want to stop anyone else, but I don't want to be involved in implementing it.*"

1 MEMBER

Block

"*I veto this proposal.*"

It would obviously be risky to implement a decision that was based on the meager support shown above. Yet sometimes the risk is justified – in an emergency, for example. Moreover, many situations are *inherently* risky. Entrepreneurs must make risky decisions all the time. Some work, others backfire. When a group is faced with meager support for a proposal, its challenge is to evaluate whether it is wiser to slow down and search for a better idea, or whether it is wiser to act quickly and take the risk.

COMMUNITY AT WORK © 1996

WHEN TO SEEK ENTHUSIASTIC SUPPORT

When does a group need to seek enthusiastic support? And when is lukewarm or even ambivalent support sufficient? Here are some variables that help to answer this question:

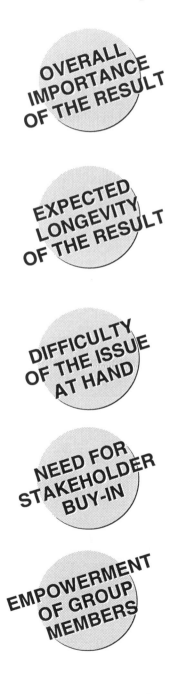

OVERALL IMPORTANCE OF THE RESULT

Enthusiastic support is desirable whenever the stakes are so high that the consequences of failure would be severe. By contrast, when the stakes are lower, a group may not wish to invest the time and energy it takes to develop enthusiastic support.

EXPECTED LONGEVITY OF THE RESULT

Some decisions are not easily reversible – for example, the decision to relocate headquarters to a new city. Decisions like these are worth spending whatever time it takes to get them right. But others decisions – such as the question of how to staff a project during an employee's two-week vacation – have a short lifespan. To get such a decision perfectly right might take longer than the entire lifetime of the decision.

DIFFICULTY OF THE ISSUE AT HAND

The chief factors that make problems hard to solve are complexity, ambiguity and the severity of conflict.* The tougher the problem is, the more time and effort a group should expect to expend. Routine problems, by contrast, don't require long drawn-out discussions.

NEED FOR STAKEHOLDER BUY-IN

When many people have a stake in the outcome of the decision, it is more likely to be worth the effort to include everyone's thinking in the development of that decision. When the decision affects only a few people, the process need not be as inclusive.

EMPOWERMENT OF GROUP MEMBERS

The more likely it is that members will be expected to use their own judgment and creativity to implement a decision, the more they will need to understand the reasoning behind that decision. The process of seeking enthusiastic support pushes people to think through the logic of the issues at hand.

*Source: *Solving Tough Problems*, Paul C. Nutt, San Francisco: Jossey-Bass, 1989

HOW TO USE
THE GRADIENTS OF AGREEMENT SCALE

▷ ## Let each group create their own set of gradients

Show the group the handouts on gradients of agreement. Ask them to select which gradients *they* want to use. Many groups invent brand new gradients; for example, a typical adaptation is shown at right.

Write the group's gradients on a flipchart and hang it where everyone can see it.

After a group has used their gradients a few times, they can use numbers to represent the different gradients. For example, a group might use numbers 1 through 5 instead of "Endorse" through "Veto."

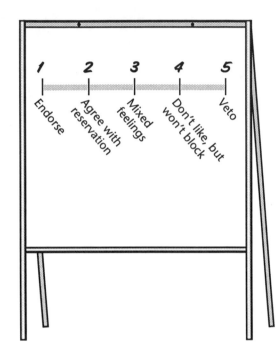

▷ ## Record the results of the poll on a flipchart

Draw a scorecard like the one shown at right. Use it to capture everyone's positions and tally the results.

The diagram at right shows the results of a poll of 12 participants using the gradients shown in the upper diagram. Four people said they endorsed the proposal. Five said they agreed with reservations. Two said they had mixed feelings. One said they didn't like it, but wouldn't block it. This type of graphic presentation gives everyone a quick, clear picture of the degree of collective support or nonsupport for any given proposal.

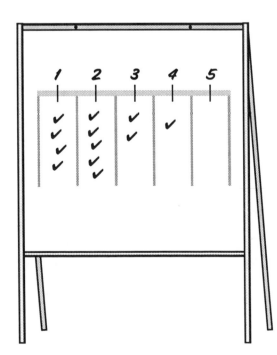

HOW TO USE
THE GRADIENTS OF AGREEMENT SCALE

▶ **Five ways to find out where people stand**

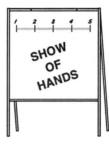

Say, "Please raise your hands if you endorse this proposal." Count the raised hands. Record the data on a flipchart. Now say, "Please raise your hands if you agree with minor reservations." Count hands and record. Repeat for all gradients.

Go around the room, one person at a time, and ask each person to state which gradient s/he prefers and why. No discussion is allowed. As everyone declares his/her preference, record the data.

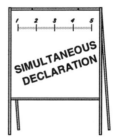

Have each person write the gradient (word or number) of his/her preference in block letters on a large piece of paper. On cue, have everyone hold up his/her card. Record the data on the scorecard.

Have each person write his/her preference on a slip of paper. When everyone has finished, collect the ballots and tally the results.

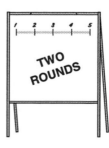

Before beginning the poll, let people know that the first poll is a preliminary round and that it will be followed by a brief discussion and then a final poll. Next, gather the data in any of the ways listed above. After a brief, time-limited discussion, poll again. This method lets a person see where others stand before s/he registers a final preference.

17

REACHING CLOSURE

CLARIFYING THE SINGLE MOST
IMPORTANT STRUCTURAL ELEMENT
OF GROUP DECISION-MAKING

▶ **The Significance of Having
a Clear Decision Rule**

▶ **Common Decision Rules**

▶ **Decision-Making
Without Decision Rules**

▶ **Uses and Implications of Major
Decision Rules**

▶ **A Basic Dilemma:
Clarity vs. Flexibility**

▶ **Meta-Decisions and
How to Use Them**

▶ **Six Real-life Case Examples**

▶ **Summary**

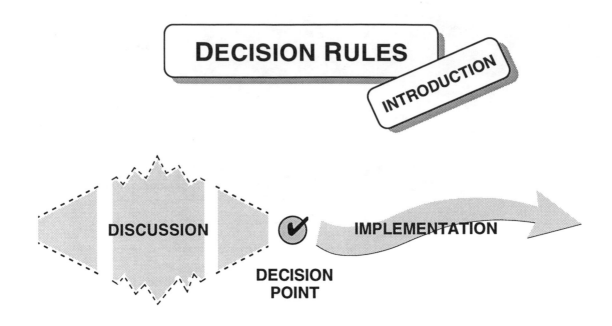

DECISION RULES

INTRODUCTION

DISCUSSION

DECISION POINT

IMPLEMENTATION

This diagram depicts two entirely different domains of group behavior. During a discussion, the group is operating in *the world of ideas;* after the decision the group is operating in *the world of actions.* For example, in a discussion people *figure out the budget* for a project; in the implementation of that project, people *spend the money.*

In the world of ideas, people explore possibilities; they develop models and try them on in their imagination. They hypothesize. They extrapolate. They evaluate alternatives and develop plans. In the world of actions, the group has made a commitment to take an idea and make it come true. Contracts are signed. People are hired. Departments are restructured, and offices are relocated.

The point-of-decision is the point that separates thinking from action. It is the point of authorization for the actions that follow. The discussion occurs *before* a decision has been made; the implementation happens *after* the decision has been made. Actions taken prior to the point-of-decision are treated by other group members as renegade actions; inaction after the point-of-decision is treated as recalcitrance.

The point-of-decision is also the formal marker that says, "From this moment onward, the view of reality to which we have agreed, will be treated as the officially authorized reality. Disagreements will no longer be treated as alternative points of view; from now on objections are officially out of line."

DECISION RULES

THE CLASSIC PROBLEM

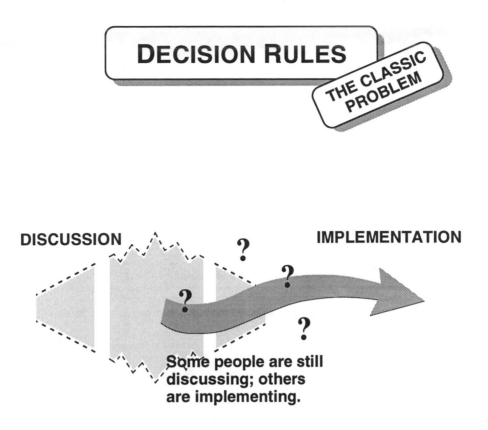

DISCUSSION   IMPLEMENTATION

Some people are still discussing; others are implementing.

In practice, however, group members are often not sure whether a decision has actually been made. After being blamed for not following through on a task, it's common to hear people defend themselves by saying, "I don't recall us making an actual decision about that," or "Hey, I never agreed to this!" And the reverse scenario is equally common: a group member accused of acting prematurely and inappropriately, will justify his/her action by saying, "I was sure we decided to go ahead with that plan."

These examples remind us that people need a clear, explicit indicator that a decision has been made. Some groups *can* clearly tell when a decision has or has not been made. For instance, groups that make decisions by majority rule know they are still in the discussion phase until they vote and tally the results. But most groups are fuzzy about how they make decisions. Members are therefore confused about whether a decision has been made or not.

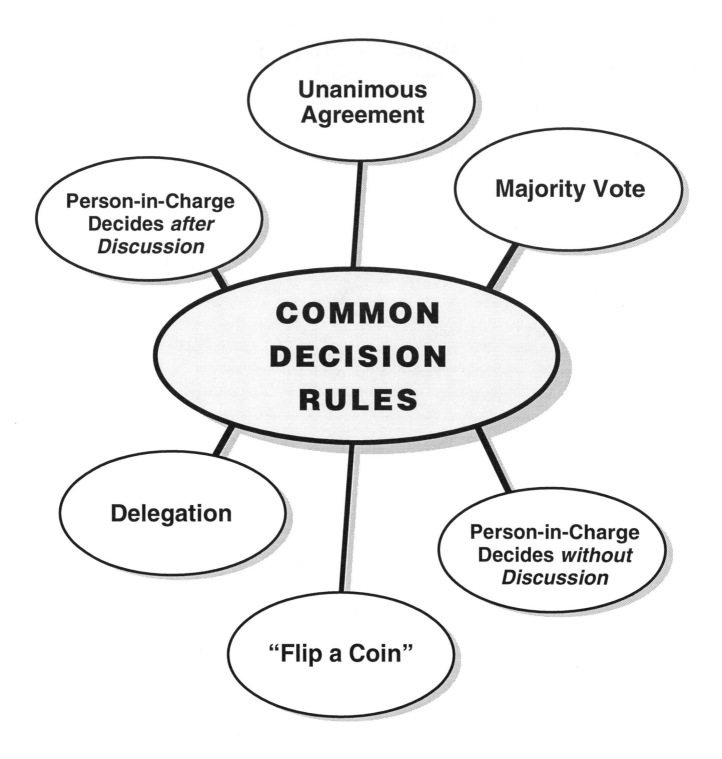

A decision rule is a mechanism that answers the question, "How do we know when we've made a decision?" Each of the six rules shown above performs this basic function.

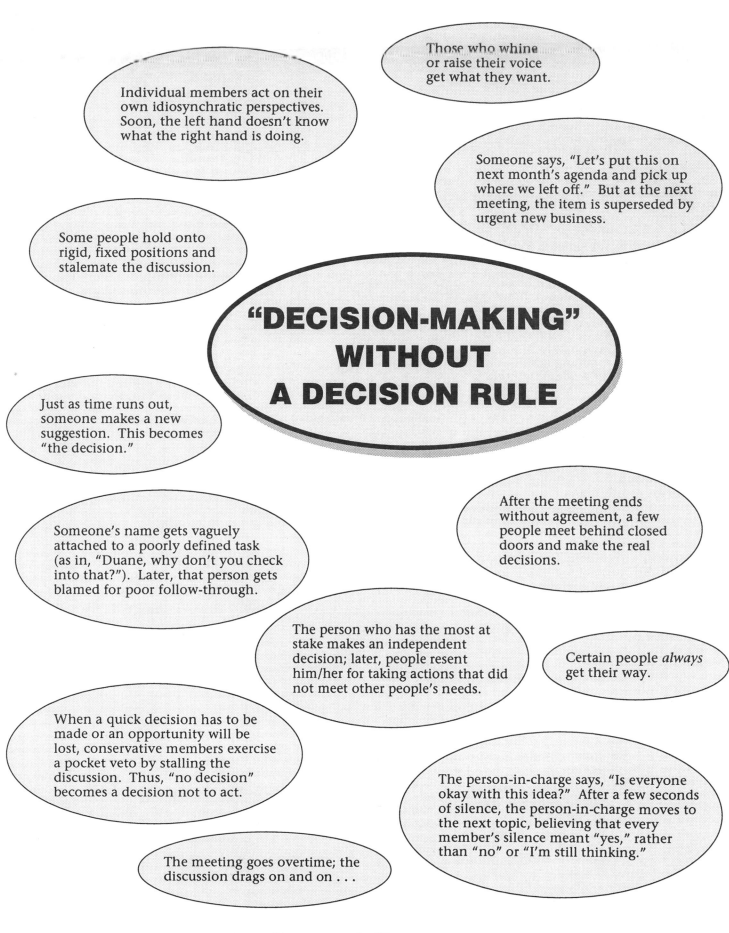

Individual members act on their own idiosyncratic perspectives. Soon, the left hand doesn't know what the right hand is doing.

Those who whine or raise their voice get what they want.

Someone says, "Let's put this on next month's agenda and pick up where we left off." But at the next meeting, the item is superseded by urgent new business.

Some people hold onto rigid, fixed positions and stalemate the discussion.

"DECISION-MAKING" WITHOUT A DECISION RULE

Just as time runs out, someone makes a new suggestion. This becomes "the decision."

After the meeting ends without agreement, a few people meet behind closed doors and make the real decisions.

Someone's name gets vaguely attached to a poorly defined task (as in, "Duane, why don't you check into that?"). Later, that person gets blamed for poor follow-through.

The person who has the most at stake makes an independent decision; later, people resent him/her for taking actions that did not meet other people's needs.

Certain people *always* get their way.

When a quick decision has to be made or an opportunity will be lost, conservative members exercise a pocket veto by stalling the discussion. Thus, "no decision" becomes a decision not to act.

The person-in-charge says, "Is everyone okay with this idea?" After a few seconds of silence, the person-in-charge moves to the next topic, believing that every member's silence meant "yes," rather than "no" or "I'm still thinking."

The meeting goes overtime; the discussion drags on and on . . .

MAJOR DECISION RULES: USES AND IMPLICATIONS

» UNANIMOUS AGREEMENT

High-Stakes Decisions

In groups that decide by *unanimous agreement,* members must keep working to understand one another's perspectives until they integrate those perspectives into a shared framework of understanding. Once people are sufficiently familiar with each other's views, they become capable of advancing innovative proposals that are acceptable to everyone. It takes a lot of effort, but this is precisely why the unanimous agreement decision rule has the best chance of producing sustainable agreements when the stakes are high.

The difficulty with using unanimous agreement as the decision rule is that most people don't know how to search for Both/And solutions. Instead, people pressure each other to live with decisions that they don't truly support. And the group often ends up with a watered-down compromise.

This problem is a function of the general tendency of groups to push for a fast decision: "We need unanimous agreement because we want everyone's buy-in, but we also want to reach a decision as quickly as possible." This mentality undermines the whole point of using unanimous agreement. Its purpose is to utilize the tension of diversity for creative purposes – to invent brand new ideas that really do work for everyone. This takes time. In order to realize the potentials of unanimous agreement, members should be encouraged to keep working toward mutual understanding until they develop a proposal that will receive enthusiastic support from a broad base of participants.

Low-Stakes Decisions

With low-stakes issues, unanimous agreements are usually comparable in quality to decisions reached by other decision rules. Participants learn to go along with proposals they can tolerate, rather than hold out for an innovative solution that would take a lot of time and effort to develop.

One benefit of using the unanimous agreement rule to make low-stakes decisions is that it prevents a group from making a decision that is abhorrent to a small minority. Other decision rules can lead to outcomes that are intolerable to one or two members, but are adopted because they are popular with a majority. By definition, such a decision will not be made by unanimous agreement.

MAJOR DECISION RULES: USES AND IMPLICATIONS

» MAJORITY VOTE

High-Stakes Decisions

Majority vote produces a win/lose solution through an adversarial process. The traditional justification for using this rule when stakes are high is that the competition of ideas creates pressure. Thus, the quality of everyone's reasoning theoretically gets better and better as the debate ensues.

The problem with this rationale is that people don't always vote based on the logic of the arguments. People often "horse trade" their votes or vote against opponents for political reasons. To increase the odds that people will vote on the merits of a high-stakes proposal, the use of secret ballots is worth considering.

Low-Stakes Decisions

When expedience is more important than quality, majority vote strikes a useful balance between the lengthy discussion that is a characteristic of unanimous agreement, and the lack of deliberation that is a danger of the other extreme. Group members can be encouraged to call for a quick round of pros and cons, and then to get on with the vote.

» FLIP A COIN

High-Stakes Decisions

Flip a coin refers to any arbitrary, random method of making a decision, including common practices like drawing straws, picking numbers from a hat or "eeny-meeny-miney-moe." Who in their right mind would consider using this decision rule to make a high-stakes decision?

Low-Stakes Decisions

Knowing a decision will be made arbitrarily, most members stop participating – their comments won't have any impact on the actual result. However, this is not necessarily bad. For example, how much discussion is needed to decide whether lunch should be forty-five minutes or one hour?

MAJOR DECISION RULES: USES AND IMPLICATIONS

>> PERSON-IN-CHARGE DECIDES *AFTER DISCUSSION*

High-Stakes Decisions

There is strong justification for using this decision rule when the stakes are high. The person-in-charge, after all, is the one with the access, resources, authority and credibility to act on the decision. Seeking counsel from group members, rather than deciding without discussion, allows the person-in-charge to expand his/her understanding of the issues, and form a wiser opinion about the best course of action.

Unfortunately, some group members give false advice and say what they think their boss wants to hear, rather than express their true opinions. *

To overcome this problem, group members can design a formal procedure to ensure/include "devil's advocate" thinking, thus allowing people to debate the merits of an idea without the pressure of worrying whether they're blocking the group's momentum. Or, group members can schedule a formal discussion without the person-in-charge. They can then bring their best thinking back to a meeting with him/her to discuss it further.

Low-Stakes Decisions

There are three decision rules that encourage group discussion: unanimous agreement, majority rule, and person-in-charge decides after discussion. With low-stakes issues, all three decision rules produce results that are roughly equivalent in quality.

Low-stakes issues provide a group with the opportunity to practice honest, direct advice to the person-in-charge. When the stakes are low, the person-in-charge is less likely to feel pressured to "get it right," and is therefore less defensive, and more open-minded. Similarly, group members are less afraid of being punished for taking risks.

---

* Irving Janus, in his ground-breaking classic on the group dynamics of conformity, *Victims of GroupThink* (Boston: Houghton Mifflin, 1972), describes many case studies demonstrating this problem. For more suggestions on ways to overcome this problem, see pages 207-224.

MAJOR DECISION RULES: USES AND IMPLICATIONS

» PERSON-IN-CHARGE DECIDES *WITHOUT DISCUSSION*

High-Stakes Decisions

When a person-in-charge makes a decision without discussion, s/he assumes full responsibility for analyzing the situation and coming up with a course of action. Proponents argue that this decision rule firmly clarifies the link between authority, responsibility and accountability. Detractors argue that this decision rule creates a high potential for blind spots and irrationality.

The most appropriate time for a person-in-charge to make high-stakes decisions without discussion is in the midst of a crisis, when the absence of a clear decision would be catastrophic. In general, though, the higher the stakes, the more risky it is for anyone to make decisions without group discussion.

How will group members behave in the face of this decision rule? The answer depends on one's values. Some people believe that good team players are loyal, disciplined subordinates who have the duty to play their roles and carry out orders. Other people argue that group members who must contend with this decision rule should develop a formal mechanism, like a union, for making sure their points of view are taken into account.

The fundamental point is that whenever one person is solely responsible for analyzing a problem and solving it, the decision-maker may lack essential information. Or those responsible for implementation might sabotage the decision because they disagree with it or because they don't understand it. The more the person-in-charge understands the dangers of deciding without group discussion, the more capable s/he is of evaluating in each situation whether the stakes are too high to take the risks.

Low-Stakes Decisions

Not all decisions made this way turn out badly. In fact, many turn out just fine. And when the stakes are low, even bad decisions can usually be undone, or compensated for.

Low-stakes decisions are often implemented by someone other than the person-in-charge. The person-in-charge may want to delegate decision-making authority to those most responsible for implementation.

DECISION RULES: A BASIC DILEMMA

Many work-groups have difficulty establishing a clear *decision rule*. This is especially common in groups that are run by a person-in-charge. Frequently, the problem is that the person-in-charge does not feel obligated to use a single decision rule. "Sometimes," said a division manager, "I want everyone in my group to agree to a plan before we act on it. At other times I don't want to waste time, so I make the decision myself."

From the point of view of the person-in-charge, it does not make sense to be tied down to a particular rule. But from the perspective of the group members, the inconsistency can be enormously confusing.

For example, a software publishing company held monthly meetings that were chaired by the chief operating officer and attended by all department managers. The managers complained that the meetings were very frustrating. "Sometimes the boss cuts off discussion after five minutes," they grumbled. "At other times he lets it run on and on. Sometimes it seems like he wants us to buy into a decision he's already made; other times he couldn't care less what we think; and then there are times when he wants us to figure out every little detail. It's driving us crazy!"

This is an intriguing example. From the perspective of the person-in-charge, his behavior was perfectly logical! He knew what the decision rule was – *person-in-charge makes the decision after group discussion*. But in each particular case he made a judgment call to determine how much discussion the issue warranted. At times – when the stakes were low or when a solution seemed obvious – he decided it was fine to make a quick decision with very little discussion. At other times, when he wanted everyone to take ownership of the outcome, he kept the discussion going in search of better ideas.

The problem was that he did not share this reasoning with the group. He made all his judgments in his head. The group members had no idea that there was a method to his madness. To explain his apparent inconsistency, they made up all kinds of stories: He was manipulating them. He was fearful of corporate politics. He was incompetent as a leader.

This group provides a classic illustration of the tension between flexibility and clarity. The person-in-charge felt that clarifying his decision rule would handcuff him. He needed the flexibility to allocate time wisely. But leaving the decision rule vague didn't work, either. It prevented the group members from knowing whether and when their manager valued their participation.

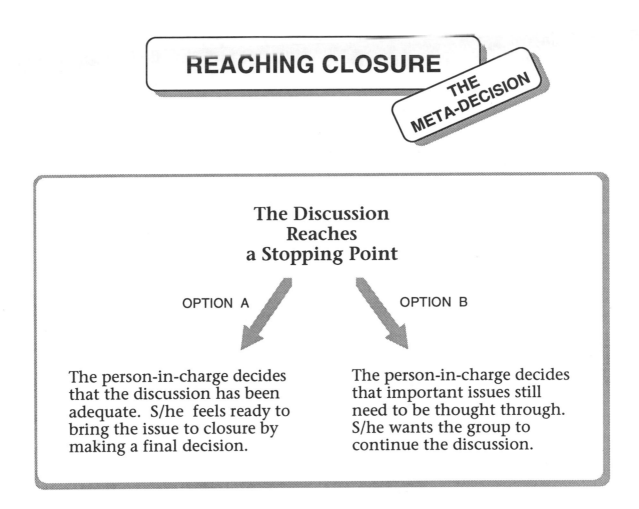

REACHING CLOSURE

THE META-DECISION

The Discussion Reaches a Stopping Point

OPTION A

The person-in-charge decides that the discussion has been adequate. S/he feels ready to bring the issue to closure by making a final decision.

OPTION B

The person-in-charge decides that important issues still need to be thought through. S/he wants the group to continue the discussion.

This diagram portrays a situation that comes up all the time in groups: at a certain point in practically every discussion, the person-in-charge has to decide whether or not to end the discussion and make a decision.

To most people who play the role of person-in-charge, this fact is intuitively obvious. They recognize the situation because they deal with it every day. But it is *not* so obvious to the other participants at a meeting. They often don't know *how* to interpret what's going on. As a result of such confusion, people can become frustrated, angry and passive – exactly as happened in the example on the previous page.

Fortunately, it is easy to reduce the disparity between the perspective of the person-in-charge and the perspective of the other members. *The solution is to show everyone what the person-in-charge is doing.* When the choice point is made explicit, the confusion is removed.

Deciding whether or not to make a decision is called *making a meta-decision.**

* The word *meta* is Greek and means "above" or "about."

REACHING CLOSURE

THREE META-DECISIONS

THE DOYLE AND STRAUS *FALLBACK*

One of the most well-known meta-decision procedures is the Doyle and Straus *fallback*. Here's how it works.

Whenever a new topic is introduced, the person-in-charge sets a time limit. During that period of time, the group will strive to reach a unanimous agreement. If time runs out, the person-in-charge makes the meta-decision: either s/he will now bring the discussion to closure and make a final decision, or s/he will set a new time limit and reopen the discussion.

CAROLINE ESTES' *VOTE TO VOTE*

Meta-decisions also occur in groups that have no person-in-charge. For example, the U.S. Green Party, which uses unanimous agreement as its decision rule, has a meta-decision that allows it to switch from unanimity to majority vote. This meta-decision, called *vote to vote,* was popularized by Caroline Estes, one of the nation's leading experts in the field of large-group consensus decision-making.

The Greens have adapted this procedure: any group member can call for a vote to close discussion and switch from unanimity to majority. Immediately following this call, the vote is taken. If 80% of the voters favor switching, the discussion ends and the group uses majority rule to reach a decision on the proposal at hand; if fewer than 80% want to switch, the unanimity rule remains in effect and the discussion continues.

SAM KANER'S *META-DECISION*

This procedure is shown on the next page. Its central premise is that *polling helps a group obtain maximum benefit from the use of a meta-decision.*

In groups with a person-in-charge, it is highly advantageous for that person to use a *Gradients of Agreement scale* to take a poll before s/he makes a decision. If s/he sees adequate support from the group, s/he can make a decision with confidence that it will be implemented. However, if s/he sees that a proposal lacks sufficient support, s/he can reopen the discussion rather than make a decision that would be difficult to implement.

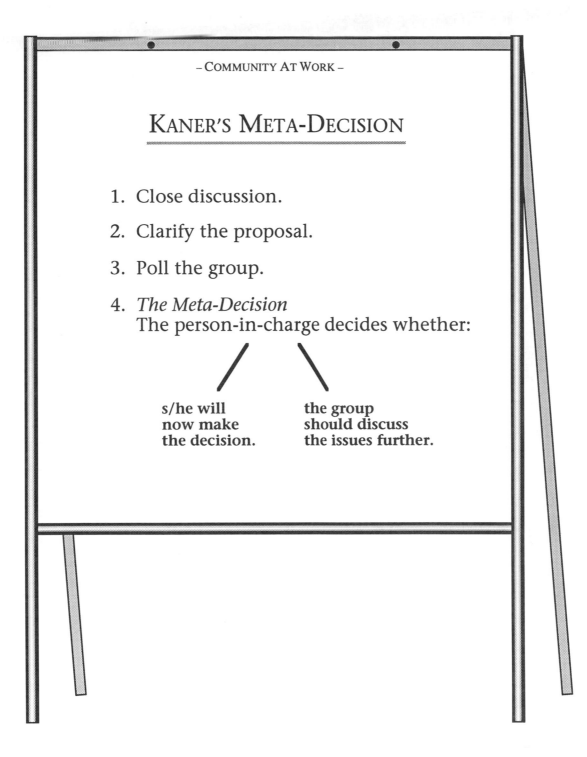

Kaner's meta-decision is designed to combine the benefits of participatory decision-making with the realities of hierarchical decision-making.

KANER'S META-DECISION
REAL-LIFE EXAMPLES

The Spectrem Group Consulting Services

1. Anyone may call for closure.

2. Someone seconds.

3. The proposal is summarized.

4. Poll, using gradients of agreement.

5. If no one vetoes the proposal, the person-in-charge decides:

she will now make the decision.	the group should continue to discuss the issues.

Used with permission from Amy J. Errett, Chairman.

Hospitality Valuation Financial Services

1. Identify issues as *group issues* or *person-in-charge decisions*. For group issues, proceed as follows:

2. Clarify the proposal.

3. Poll the group.

4. The person-in-charge decides:

s/he will now make the decision.	the group should continue to discuss the issues.

5. Proceed as specified in step 4.

6. After the person-in-charge has made the decision, feedback is welcome.

Used with permission from Harvey Christensen, Vice Pres.

Santa Cruz County Office of Education

1. Call for closure to end discussion. If anyone is not ready to close, ask why. Then set a brief time-limit to decide whether to:
   a) complete the discussion now;
   b) re-assign to another agenda; or
   c) drop it.

2. Collect proposals.

3. Poll for preferences.

4. The person-in-charge decides whether:

she will now make the decision.	the group should continue to discuss the issues.

Used with permission from Nancy Giberson, Ph.D. Assistant Superintendent of Educational Services.

The steps in Kaner's Meta-Decision are deliberately designed to be generic. All groups that use this procedure are encouraged to tailor it to fit their own needs.

KANER'S META-DECISION
MORE REAL-LIFE EXAMPLES

Urban Strategies Council
Leadership Technical Team

1. *Call for closure,* to end discussion.

2. Clarify the proposal.

3. Check for consensus by polling.

4. The *meta-decision-maker,* a role that rotates each meeting, decides:

   there is enough agreement to formalize the decision. / there is not enough agreement to make a decision. Reopen the discussion.

Used with permission from Maria Campbell Casey, President.

Youth Advocates
Of Marin County

1. Close discussion by unanimity.

2. Collect proposals.

3. Poll for preferences among options.

4. The person-in-charge decides:

   s/he will now make the decision. / the *Procedure Person, a rotating role,* will now make the decision.

   the group should continue discussing the issues.

5. Proceed as specified in step 4.

Used with permission from David Barkan, Program Director.

Larkin Street
Youth Services

1. Collect proposals.

2. Poll for preferences among alternatives.

3. Time-limited attempt to reach unanimity:
   • set time limit,
   • proceed until time expires.

4. The person-in-charge decides:

   she will now make the final decision. / the group should continue to discuss the issues.

Used with permission from Diane Flannery, Executive Director.

In hierarchical groups, the person-in-charge is usually the meta-decision-maker. In non-hierarchical groups, the role of meta-decision-maker can rotate among group members.

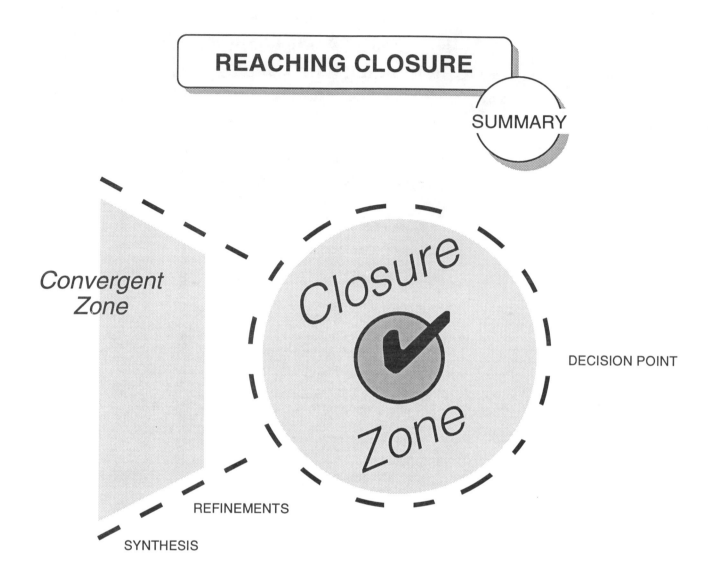

REACHING CLOSURE

SUMMARY

Convergent Zone

Closure Zone

DECISION POINT

REFINEMENTS

SYNTHESIS

The Closure Zone can be viewed as the final phase of decision-making. As such, it consists of four distinct steps:

1. Ending discussion;
2. Clarifying the proposal;
3. Polling the group members;
4. Using the group's decision rule to reach a final decision.

Sometimes these steps can be navigated quickly and informally, without the help of explicit procedures – for example, when someone proposes a clear, compelling solution to the problem at hand and everyone gladly accepts it. But in the long run, for all the reasons discussed in this chapter, groups will benefit from establishing an explicit, formal decision rule – even if they only use it now and then. Facilitators are advised to study carefully the principles covered in this chapter. Understanding the mechanics of reaching closure is essential for anyone who wants to help a group build sustainable agreements.

18

FACILITATING SUSTAINABLE AGREEMENTS

A SUMMARY AND INTEGRATION OF THE MAIN POINTS OF THIS BOOK

- ▶ Overview

- ▶ The Divergent Zone

- ▶ The Groan Zone

- ▶ The Convergent Zone

- ▶ The Closure Zone

- ▶ One Last Look at the Role of Facilitator

FACILITATING SUSTAINABLE AGREEMENTS

INTRODUCTION

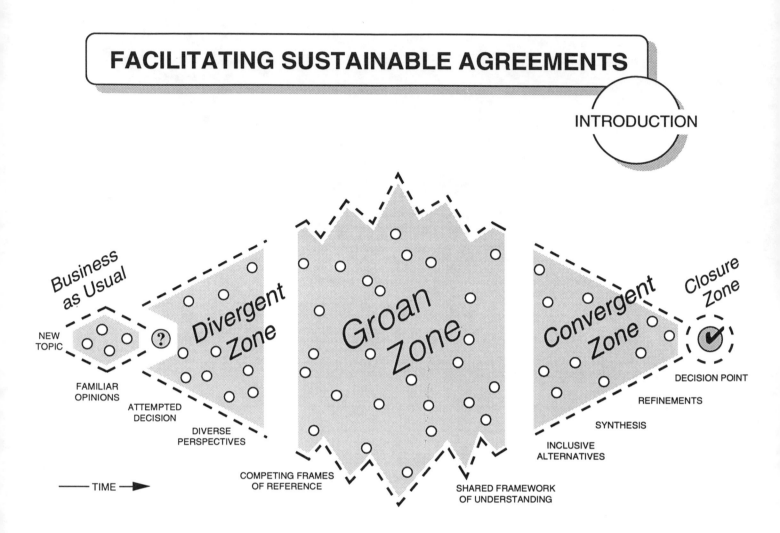

Sustainable agreements don't happen in a burst of inspiration; they develop slowly. It takes time and effort for people to build a shared framework of understanding, and groups need different types of support at different points in the process. Facilitators who understand this will vary their technique accordingly, to match the group's current dynamics. The first two parts of this book presented concepts, skills and tools that are useful in *every* zone. The third part presented material that is helpful primarily in a *specific* zone.

The following pages review the Diamond of Participatory Decision-Making. Each page summarizes the significance of one zone of the Diamond, with emphasis on issues that hold particular interest for facilitators.

FACILITATING SUSTAINABLE AGREEMENTS

BUSINESS AS USUAL

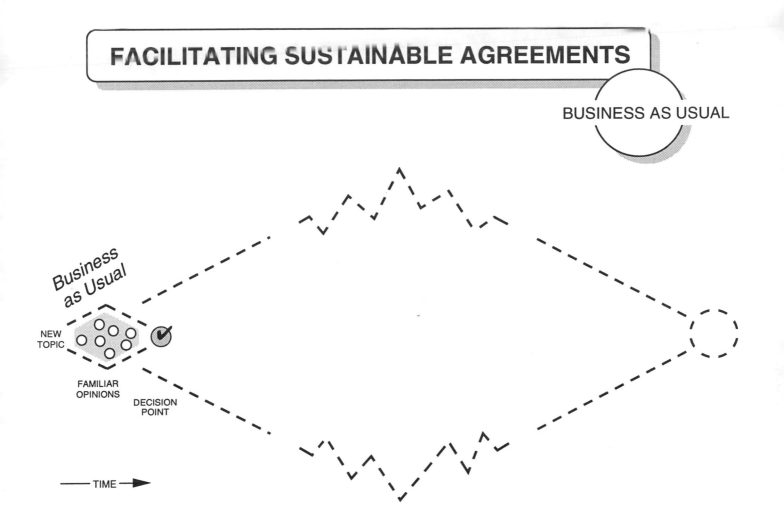

Business as Usual

NEW
TOPIC

FAMILIAR
OPINIONS

DECISION
POINT

→ TIME →

When a new topic comes up for discussion in a group, people normally begin the conversation by proposing obvious solutions to obvious problems. The emotional atmosphere is usually congenial but superficial. People refrain from taking risks that would put them in vulnerable positions. If an idea seems workable, it usually leads to quick agreement. "Sounds good to me," people say. The facilitator's main task during this phase is to pay attention to the quality and quantity of each person's participation. Is everyone engaged? Does everyone seem comfortable with the discussion? If so, great! The facilitator then summarizes the proposals under consideration, and helps the group reach agreement quickly.

But suppose the facilitator notices that some people do not support the proposal – as indicated by statements like "I don't think this will work, but I don't want to stand in the group's way." The facilitator should then start looking for ways to encourage the group to break out of the narrow band of familiar opinions and move their discussion into the Divergent Zone.

FACILITATING SUSTAINABLE AGREEMENTS

THE DIVERGENT ZONE

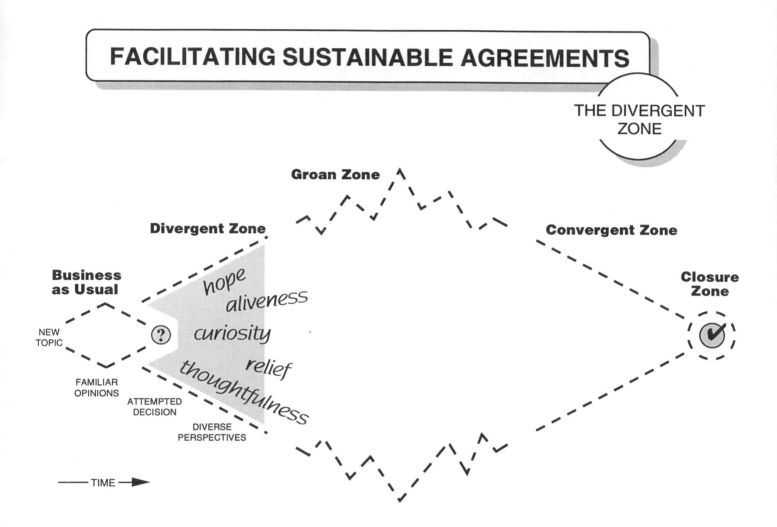

When a facilitator helps a group move from Business As Usual to the Divergent Zone, the mood changes dramatically. Business-as-usual discussions are tedious and stiff; people censor themselves rather than risk being embarrassed by criticism. In contrast, laughter and playfulness are common in the Divergent Zone. So are feelings of curiosity and discovery. ("Whoa," said one group member to another, "you mean *that's* your point of view? I had no idea!")

What creates such a difference between the two zones? To a large extent, the answer is simple: *the attitude of suspended judgment.*

Suspended judgment is one of the most important *thinking skills* facilitators can teach their groups. Facilitators can provide their groups with opportunities to *experience* suspended judgment, through formats like idea-listing and go-arounds. By teaching suspended judgment, and by modeling it whenever possible, a respectful, supportive facilitator can create a relaxed, open atmosphere that gives people permission to speak freely.

FACILITATING SUSTAINABLE AGREEMENTS

THE AGONY OF
THE GROAN ZONE

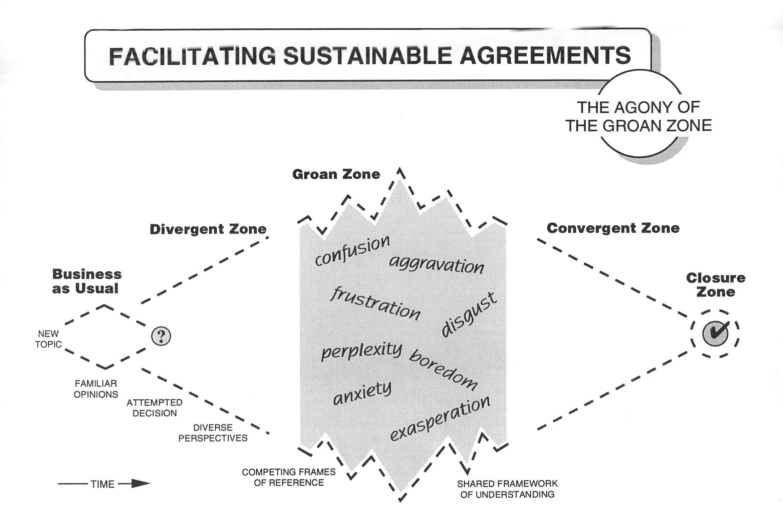

Once a group has expressed several diverging points of view, the members face a quandary. They often don't understand each other's perspectives very well, yet they may not be able to resolve the issue at hand until they do understand each other. This is one of the fundamental problems of working in groups.

Even in groups whose members get along reasonably well, the Groan Zone is agonizing. People have to wrestle with foreign concepts and unfamiliar biases. They have to try to understand other people's reasoning – even when that reasoning leads to a conclusion they don't agree with.

The difficulties are compounded by the fact that many people respond awkwardly to this kind of stress. Under pressure, some people lose their focus and start rambling. Others become short-tempered and rude. Some people feel misunderstood and repeat themselves endlessly. Others get so impatient they'll agree to anything: "Let's just get this over with! Now!"

FACILITATING SUSTAINABLE AGREEMENTS

THE COMMITMENT
TO STRUGGLE

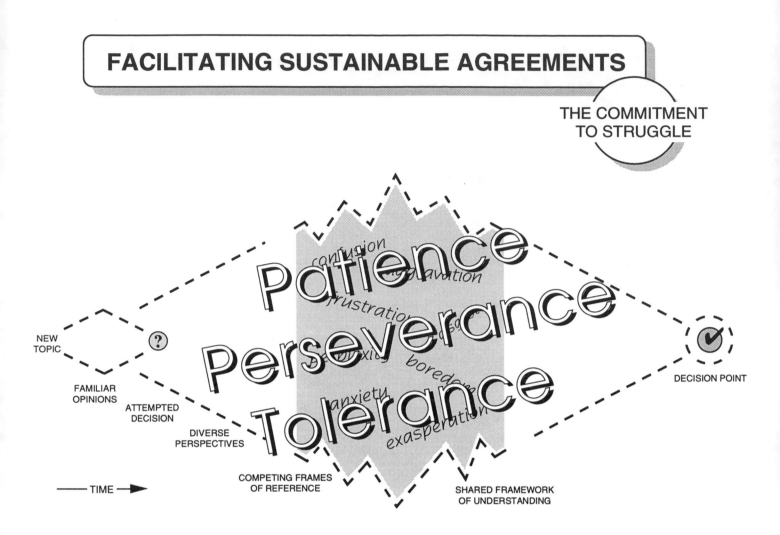

NEW
TOPIC

FAMILIAR
OPINIONS

ATTEMPTED
DECISION

DIVERSE
PERSPECTIVES

COMPETING FRAMES
OF REFERENCE

SHARED FRAMEWORK
OF UNDERSTANDING

DECISION POINT

TIME

Patience Perseverance Tolerance

confusion
frustration
anxiety
boredom
exasperation

Many facilitators, especially beginners, think their task is to prevent people
from experiencing the pain and frustration groups face in the Groan Zone.
This is a mistake. The only way to insulate a group from the Groan Zone is
to block them from doing the hard work necessary to build a shared
framework of understanding.

What, then, *is* the facilitator's task in the Groan Zone? Essentially, the job
is to hang in there – hang in and support people while they struggle to
understand each other.

The facilitator's tenacity is grounded in a *client-centered attitude* – a faith that
the wisdom to solve the problems at hand *will emerge* from the group, as
long as people don't give up trying. It is this attitude that allows a
facilitator to tolerate the labor pains of authentic collaboration.

FACILITATING SUSTAINABLE AGREEMENTS

THE CONVERGENT ZONE

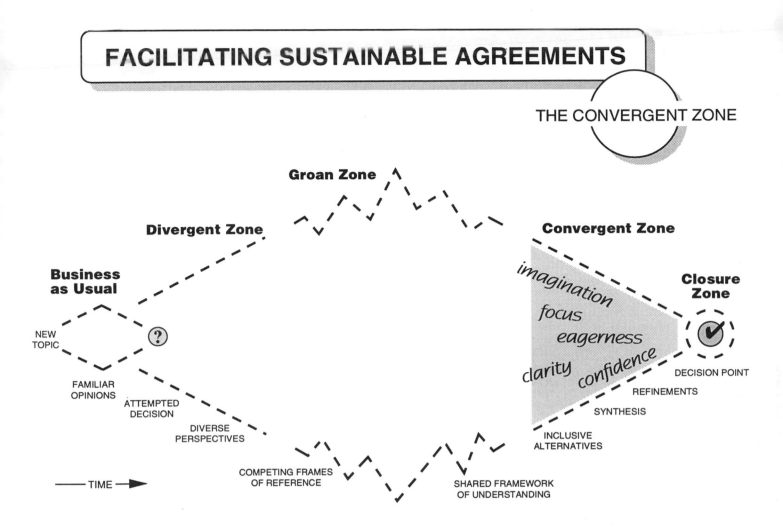

Once a group has a developed a shared framework of understanding, everything feels faster, smoother, easier. The pace of discussion accelerates. People say, "Finally, we're getting something done!" Confidence runs high during this period. People show up on time, and stay until the end of the meeting. Between sessions, work that needs to be done, gets done.

The experience of searching for an inclusive solution is stimulating and invigorating. People are surprised to discover how well they seem to understand one another. Members now perceive the group as a team. Years later, many people can still remember the *joyful intensity* of this phase.

Facilitators play a double role during this period of a group's work: sometimes teaching and sometimes getting out of the way. It may be crucial for a facilitator to teach participants how to turn an Either/Or problem into a Both/And solution – often the facilitator is the only one who recognizes that Both/And thinking is even possible. But for much of the time, a facilitator might be reduced to chartwriting and keeping track of time. When this happens, be happy! It means the facilitation is succeeding.

FACILITATING SUSTAINABLE AGREEMENTS

THE EXPERIENCE OF
REACHING CLOSURE

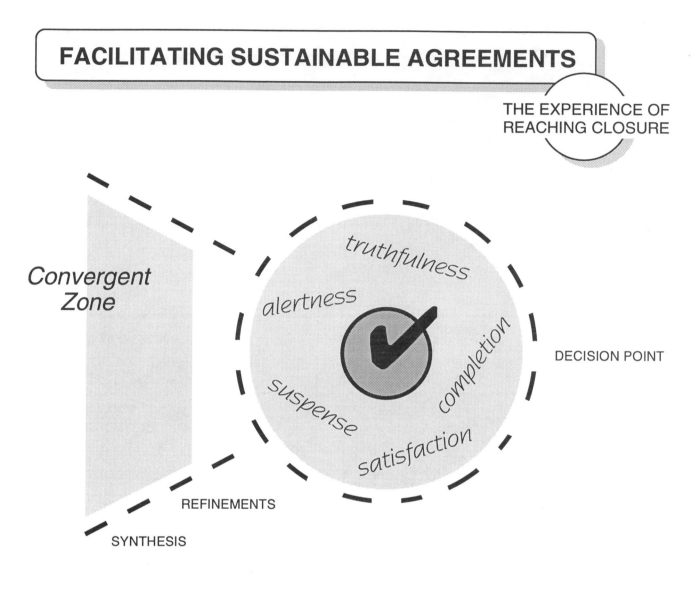

*Convergent
Zone*

truthfulness

alertness

suspense

completion

satisfaction

DECISION POINT

REFINEMENTS

SYNTHESIS

In the Closure Zone most people are *focused*. They pay attention to nearly every comment – and most comments are brief and to the point.

These experiences occur, of course, only when the group knows *how the decision will be made*. When a group *does not* have a clear understanding of how they are going to reach closure, the facilitator must look for the earliest opportunity to help the members clarify their decision rules.

The tools for reaching closure might be the single most important set of thinking skills a facilitator can teach a group. The *Gradients of Agreement Scale* helps members discern the *actual* degree of support for a proposal. Furthermore, a meta-decision procedure allows a group to use different decision rules for different circumstances.

Overall, when members grasp the principles and mechanics of reaching closure, it will strengthen their capacity dramatically.

FACILITATING SUSTAINABLE AGREEMENTS

FACILITATOR'S
FOUR FUNCTIONS

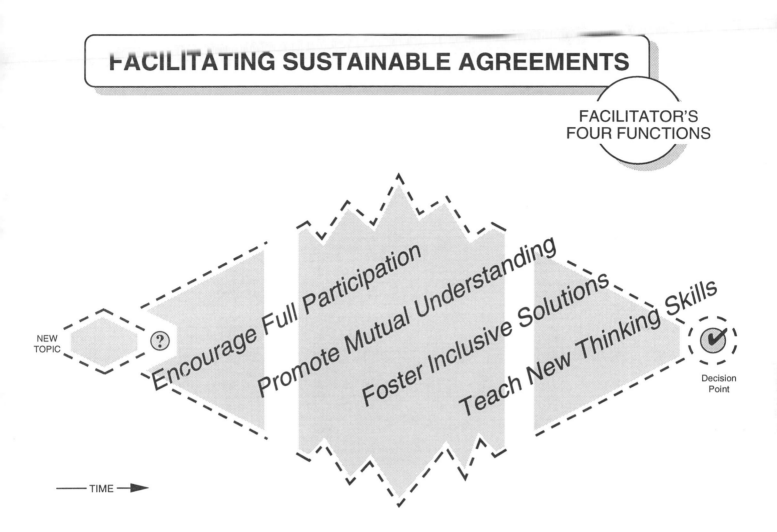

NEW
TOPIC

Encourage Full Participation

Promote Mutual Understanding

Foster Inclusive Solutions

Teach New Thinking Skills

Decision
Point

TIME ➡

The diagram on this page expresses a set of principles that, fundamentally, are more important than anything that has appeared on the preceding pages of this chapter.

There are many models that describe group dynamics. Each has its own set of strengths. But no matter what models a faciliator draws from, s/he can benefit from remembering why groups need facilitation.

The facilitator's mission is to support a group to do its best thinking. To accomplish this, the facilitator encourages full participation, promotes mutual understanding, fosters inclusive solutions and teaches the group new thinking skills. When facilitators do the job well, they produce several highly-prized outcomes. They advance the personal learnings of the members of their groups. They improve the capacity and the effectiveness of the groups they work with. And by enabling groups to tap the deep collective wisdom of their membership, facilitators are midwives to the emergence of sound, intelligent, sustainable agreements.

PHOTOCOPYING POLICY

YES: Photocopying portions of this book is encouraged for the purpose of supporting a group you are facilitating.

If a group has retained you as a facilitator to help them solve problems and make decisions, and you feel that your group needs to use one or more of the tools presented in this book, feel free to photocopy and distribute the relevant page(s). We want you to be able to use this book to become as effective as possible at facilitating group decision-making.

NO: Photocopying portions of this book to conduct fee-for-service training requires our written permission.

If a group has retained you specifically to train them in the process of group facilitation, group decision-making, or a related topic, and your primary role is to teach them skills, you may not photocopy these pages without express written permission from *COMMUNITY AT WORK*. Our policies are fair and supportive, but please ask first. If you are making money from our work, we will ask you to make a reasonable contribution.

BIBLIOGRAPHY

Adams, James. *Conceptual Blockbusting.* New York: W.W. Norton and Company, 1974.

Auvine, Brian et al. *A Manual For Group Facilitators.* Madison, Wis.: The Center for Conflict Resolution, 1978.

Avery, Michel et al. *Building United Judgment.* Madison, Wis.: The Center for Conflict Resolution, 1981.

Butler, C.T. Lawrence and Amy Rothstein. *On Conflict and Consensus.* Cambridge, Mass.: Food Not Bombs Publishing, 1991.

DeBono, Edward. *Lateral Thinking.* New York: Harper and Row, 1970.

DeBono, Edward. *Serious Creativity.* New York: Harper Collins, 1992.

Child Development Project. *Ways We Want Our Class To Be.* Oakland: Developmental Study Center, 1996.

Doyle, Michael and David Straus. *How To Make Meetings Work.* New York: Berkley Books, 1993.

Estes, Caroline. "Consensus." *In Context.* Autumn 1984, 19-22.

Fisk, Sarah. *Psychological Effects of Involvement in Ecological Restoration.* Ann Arbor, Mich.: University Microfilms International, 1995.

Fisher, Roger and William Ury. *Getting To Yes.* New York: Penguin Books, 1981.

Gastil, John. *Democracy In Small Groups.* Philadelphia and Gabriola Island, B.C.: New Society Publishers, 1993.

Gray, Barbara. *Collaborating.* San Francisco: Jossey-Bass, 1989.

Howard, V.A. and J.H. Barton. *Thinking Together.* New York: William Morrow and Company, 1992.

Howell, Johnna L. *Tools For Facilitating Team Meetings.* Seattle: Integrity Publishing, 1995.

Janis, Irving. *Victims Of Groupthink.* Boston: Houghton-Mifflin, 1972.

Janis, Irving and Leon Mann. *Decision Making.* New York: The Free Press, 1977.

Johnson, David W. and Frank P. Johnson. *Joining Together.* Englewood Cliffs, N.J.: Prentice-Hall, 1975.

Kaner, Sam, Duane Berger and Jim MacQueen. *Participatory Decision Making: Uses and Implications of Different Decision Rules.* Proceedings of the 1995 National Conference of the Organization Development Network. South Orange, N.J.: Organization Development Network, 1995.

Kaner, Sam and Eileen Palmer. "What Can O.D. Professionals Learn From Grassroots Peace Activists?" *Vision/Action*, September 1989, Vol. 9, #1, page 8-12.

Kearny, Lynn. *The Facilitator's Toolkit*. Amherst, Mass.: HRD Press, 1995.

Kepner, C.H. and Tregoe, B.B. *The Rational Manager*. New York: MacGraw-Hill, 1965.

Lakey, George and Berit Lakey, Rod Napier and Janice M. Robinson. *Grassroots and Nonprofit Leadership: A Guide for Organizations in Changing Times*. Philadelphia and Gabriola Island, B.C.: New Society Pubishers, 1996.

Lawler, Edward E. *The Ultimate Advantage*. San Francisco: Jossey-Bass, 1992.

Michalko, Michael. *Thinkertoys*. Berkeley: Ten Speed Press, 1991.

Nutt, Paul C. *Making Tough Decisions*. San Francisco: Jossey-Bass, 1989.

Osborne, Alex. *Applied Imagination*. New York: Charles Scribner's Sons, 1953.

Parker, Marjorie. *Creating Shared Vision*. Clarendon Hills, Ill.: Dialog International, Ltd., 1990.

Phillips, Gerald M. and Julia T. Wood. *Emergent Issues in Human Decision Making*. Carbondale, Ill.: Southern Illinois University Press, 1984.

Rogers, Carl R. *The Carl Rogers Reader*. Edited by Howard Kirschenbaum and Valerie Land Henderson. Boston: Houghton Mifflin, 1989.

Russo, J. Edward and Paul J.H. Shoemaker. *Decision Traps*. New York: Simon and Schuster, 1989.

Schrage, Michael. *Shared Minds: The New Technologies of Collaboration*. New York: Random House, 1990.

Sheeran, Michael J. *Beyond Majority Rule*. Philadelphia: Philadelphia Yearly Meeting of the Religious Society of Friends, Book Services Committee, 1983.

Shields, Katrina. *In The Tiger's Mouth: An Empowerment Guide For Social Action*. Philadelphia and Gabriola Island, B.C.: New Society Publishers, 1994.

Sibbet, David. *I See What You Mean*. San Francisco: Sibbet and Associates, 1981.

Spencer, Laura J. *Winning through Participation*. Dubuque, Iowa: Kendall/Hunt Publishing Co., 1989.

Toldi, Catherine. *Collaborative Thinking: Becoming a Community That Learns*. Ann Arbor, Mich.: University Microfilms International, 1993.

Troxel, James P. *Participation Works: Business Cases from Around the World*. Alexandra, Va.: Miles River Press, 1993.

VanGundy, Jr., Arthur B. *Techniques of Structured Problem-Solving*, 2nd edition. New York: Van Nostrand Reinhold Company, 1988.

Weisbord, Marvin. *Productive Workplaces: Organizing and Managing For Dignity, Meaning and Community*. San Francisco: Jossey-Bass, 1987.

Williams, R. Bruce. *More Than Fifty Ways to Build Team Consensus*. Palatine, Ill.: IRI/Skylight Publishing, 1993.

ABOUT THE AUTHORS

SAM KANER, Ph.D.

Sam Kaner is the executive director of *Community At Work*. He has devoted his professional career to helping groups make saner, wiser decisions. He is an expert in consensus decision-making, and his models and methods are used in many businesses and community organizations.

LENNY LIND

Lenny Lind is president of the organization development firm, CoVision, Inc. He is a pioneer in the field of computer-assisted meetings and he is a co-developer of Council™ – a groupware system designed for facilitators. Lenny is the creative force who crafted the design and layout of every page of this book.

CATHERINE TOLDI, M.A.

Catherine Toldi is a collaboration specialist who supports people to bring both structure and heart to their planning and problem-solving efforts. Three key influences on her work are: her 18 years as a public school teacher; her graduate studies in organization development; and her practice of Zen Buddhism.

SARAH FISK, Ph.D.

Sarah Fisk is a clinical psychologist, a seasoned facilitator and a designer of participatory processes. She has conducted formal research on the beneficial effects of community involvement. As a senior trainer for Playfair Inc., she has led community-building workshops attended by more than 10,000 people.

DUANE BERGER, M.A.

Duane Berger is co-founder of the Resource Center for Consensus Decision-Making. He has been examining the underlying principles of participatory decision-making since 1979. As a consultant he specializes in helping individuals and groups clarify their mission, vision and values.

NEW SOCIETY PUBLISHERS

New Society Publishers is a socially and environmentally responsible company whose mission is to publish books for fundamental social change through nonviolent action. We focus especially on sustainable living, progressive leadership and educational and parenting resources.

Other books in NSP's progressive leadership series include:

The Mediator's Handbook (Revised and Expanded 3rd Edition), by Jennifer E. Beer with Eileen Stief, Developed by Friends Conflict Resolution Programs. The classic "how-to" mediation manual continuously in print for 15 years and now thoroughly revised and updated.
8.5" × 11" 176 pages Paperback
US$19.95/CAN$24.95 ISBN 0-86571-359-6

Grassroots and Nonprofit Leadership: A Guide for Organizations in Changing Times, by Berit Lakey, George Lakey, Rod Napier, and Janice Robinson.
Full of concrete suggestions, this is an indispensable sourcebook for all leaders and active members of change organizations.
6" × 9" 224 pages Paperback
US$16.95 ISBN 0-86571-328-6
CAN$18.95 ISBN 1-55092-275-0

Democracy in Small Groups: Participation, Decision-making and Communication, by John Gastil.
A thorough examination of the problems facing small, democratic groups—with an emphasis on solutions—this book includes a survey of the full range of democratic processes.
6" × 9" 224 pages Paperback
US$14.95 ISBN 0-86571-274-3
CAN$17.95 ISBN 1-55092-217-3

Our full list of books to build a new society can be browsed on the World Wide Web at: www.newsociety.com

 NEW SOCIETY PUBLISHERS

PO Box 189, Gabriola Island,
BC V0R 1X0, Canada

CoVision is an organization development firm that supports a growing national network of facilitators and consultants with the use of Council™ groupware.

Council supports and enhances dialogue in tough meetings by quickly gathering participants' ideas and concerns at strategic moments. Themes emerge clearly, for all to see, thus allowing groups much more time for rich, fully-informed dialogue.

CoVision makes Council available where and when it's needed most – in certain client meetings which, for many reasons, are predicted to be the *toughest.* Council works most effectively in:

LARGE GROUP MEETINGS (30-300 People)

Council allows for mass participation in large meetings. Each participant can have a "voice" by responding to questions put to the whole group through Council's screens. For example, "What improvements can you think of re the xyz system?" or "What responses do you have to the last speaker?"

VISIONING and STRATEGY MEETINGS (8-25 People)

When the stakes are high and the time is short, Council is most effective. A timely Council brainstorm will reveal the deep issues quickly – saving hours of meandering discussion. Using Council's polling tools, groups can express preferences safely – maximizing time for dialogue in areas of misunderstanding.

VOICE OF THE CUSTOMER, SUPPLIER, etc. (8-25 People)

The Voice of the Customer is a focused process for problem identification and analysis. It can be used with any group of stakeholders. It takes four hours and results in a ranked list of critical issues, backed-up by hundreds of specific improvements.

For further information, contact Lenny Lind at 1-800-318-3521.

COMMUNITY AT WORK

Community At Work is both a think tank and a consulting firm.

AS A THINK TANK   Our purpose is to study the actual dynamics of group decision-making and develop more accurate models in order to support people to solve the world's toughest problems. This book, for example, was written in "think tank mode." For five years the co-authors met for three days a month to develop, test and refine the ideas presented in this book. We intend our models to combine the insights of the social sciences with the practical ingenuity of the American business world and the wisdom of nonviolent social activism.

AS A CONSULTING FIRM   We specialize in group decision-making. Our clients usually need help solving complex problems that cannot be solved by traditional hierarchical structures. For example, a number of our cases involve the delivery of community services (education, health care, transportation, housing, etc.) A common goal in such a case is to improve the working relationships among, on the one hand, the state and local government entities that fund and regulate the services and, on the other hand, the community-based organizations that provide and deliver the services. This requires meaningful participation from diverse stakeholders. As consultants, we help the principals create a *collaborative process design*. Then we facilitate the involved parties to think together in search of innovative, inclusive solutions that will lead to sustainable agreements. Our clients also include large businesses that retain us to assist in planning-and-design projects that require broad participation. From the perspective of group decision-making, the principles that allow a marketing department to collaborate with a research and development department are the same principles that help government and community agencies to work together. Thus we consult to diverse organizations, whenever our specialization can be helpful to their goals.

TRAINING   A distinctive feature of all our work is our tendency to provide clients with training in the concepts and skills of group decision-making. Sometimes the training is conducted as a formal workshop; often it is done informally, as part of the agenda of each meeting. Information about the formal workshops is presented on the following page.

TRAINING FROM COMMUNITY AT WORK

Community At Work provides training in every aspect of group decision-making. Our workshops are designed in the same spirit that underlies this book: we are *committed* to helping people *learn skills* for putting participatory values into practice.

GROUP FACILITATION SKILLS

This series of workshops offers basic, intermediate and advanced training in the mechanics of effective facilitation. Workshops include: Group Facilitation Theory and Practice; Process Management Skills; Facilitating Difficult Discussions; Facilitating Creative Thinking in Groups and many more.

BUILDING SUSTAINABLE AGREEMENTS

This series of workshops teaches principles and methods for helping groups reach agreements that work for everyone. Workshops include: Goal-Setting in Multiple Time Frames; Group Problem-Solving Models and Methods; Developing Inclusive Solutions; Tools for Reaching Closure and many more.

CONSULTING SKILLS FOR CHANGE AGENTS

This series provides grounding in the theory and practice of organization development. Workshops in this series include: Assessment and Diagnosis of Organizations; Psychological Dynamics of Groups; Mission, Vision and Values; Designing Whole-System Collaborations and many more.

For more information

Community At Work
1 Tubbs Street
San Francisco, CA 94107

Phone: (415) 641-4840
Fax: (415) 282-9878
E-mail: skaner@aol.com

255